Alpha
the unofficial guide

Essential Truths
on the Alpha Course

Elizabeth McDonald
and Dusty Peterson

Alpha – The Unofficial Guide: Church
First published in Great Britain in August 2005
by St Matthew Publishing Ltd
Copyright © Elizabeth McDonald & Dusty Peterson 2005.
All rights reserved.
Printed in the U.K. by Cambridge Printers Ltd.

Use of a given publisher must not be construed as any type of endorsement
of other items produced by that publisher.

For details of how to obtain further copies of this book, please see the page
immediately preceding the Cross-Reference at the very end.

$\mathscr{C}$ONTENTS

With love to our precious
brothers and sisters in the
Lord who have readily
contributed excellent advice,
inspired material, lots of
prayer – and endless patience.

"…the LORD thy God shall
bless thee…"
(Deuteronomy 16:15)

Most of all, though, we want to
dedicate this book to our
Heavenly Father who has
faithfully supplied everything
we have needed to produce it
and has graciously directed
our steps.

"Because Thou hast been my
help, therefore in the shadow
of Thy wings will I rejoice."
(Psalm 63:7)

$\mathcal{I}$MPORTANT INTRODUCTION!

"[A] masterful work" *(Glenn Chatfield., U.S.A.)*

St Matthew Publishing is delighted to be able to offer this crucial volume to the Church. The reader should find it one of the most helpful and vital books available today.

The authors have both invested a great deal of time and care into producing this volume, and their commitment has resulted in a profoundly useful work. For instance, the material has been structured and written to provide an exceptionally clear and logical flow. (As such, it is particularly effective when read from the *start*.)

St Matthew Publishing also commends the book's *Preface* to the reader, as this provides information which should significantly enhance your appreciation of this very fine work.

**"[The] research is thorough
and well documented throughout"** *(G.C., U.S.A)*

**St Matthew Publishing
Cambridge, England**

$\mathscr{P}$REFACE

What is Alpha? The Alpha Course is normally described as "a practical introduction to the Christian faith". Originating in England, it usually comprises a series of fifteen talks plus some ministry times, and typically takes place over ten weeks – including a day or weekend retreat. Each talk is generally preceded by a meal and is followed by a 'small group' session where questions raised by the talks can be freely discussed. It has been used in almost every nation on earth.

Please forgive the huge delay in the release of this book. All we can say is that this is the Lord's timing - and His timing is always perfect.

As explained in the adverts, this is a pre-publication draft and is thus being offered at a reduced price. There are quite a few reasons for taking this route, four of which are given below:

1) *A lot of people have become aware of the topics covered in this volume, and a number have taken the trouble to ask us about progress and to request early copies.*
2) *We consider the material in this volume to be really vital and we therefore don't want to delay its release a moment longer than we have to.*

3) *Researching and writing this particular volume has been a major undertaking and indeed is ongoing. We felt it right to release the work in stages so as to avoid too daunting a single climb without any intermediate 'camps'.*

4) *We are eager to ensure that the final draft is as helpful as possible, and hence we are keen to receive feedback from any kind souls who spot ways in which our material could be improved.*

This volume is designed to stand alone, but it is actually the <u>second half</u> of our main study on Alpha. The first half is called the 'World' volume (outlets for which are listed towards the back of this book). It is not always necessary to have read the first volume before tackling the book you are now holding, but the reader will need to be open to correction if they have not taken that route.

Finally, please be aware that this draft has focused on getting our teaching right rather than on injecting lots of quotes from Alpha resources. Although this book does contain a reasonable number of such quotations, especially in Part Five, nevertheless there are a lot more quotes to come in future editions.

This book is multi-purpose and should be a considerable asset to all believers, especially those concerned with Alpha in any way. (That includes Course helpers and participants.) Among its aims, the book has been designed to furnish readers with just about everything they need in order to gain, and bring others to, a significantly deeper knowledge of the truth.

Regardless of the reader's links with Alpha, from onlooker to veteran leader, all should find the material seriously informative and interesting. The commentary should also enable past attendees to fully grasp what they have been through. If the reader is thinking of attending their first Alpha Course, we encourage them to explore this volume beforehand.

We have sought to make the book's content as readable and accessible as possible (please forgive the UK spellings if they are unfamiliar though). For example, we have been able to quote many high-quality sources, and even the most advanced material normally starts from first principles. Another feature of the book reflects the fact that people both inside and outside the Church want to know and understand the Bible better. This volume has been constructed to be a real aid in every way and therefore includes a sensible quantity of Scripture reference in the text, remembering that God's written Word says we should receive

> "...**knowledge** rather than choice **gold**. For **wisdom** is **better** than **rubies**; and **all** the things that may be desired are **not to be compared to it**." *(Proverbs 8:10-11)*

Each of the chapters comprising the body of this book covers a different area of Alpha and is quite self-contained. Thus, if any readers find they are having problems with a given chapter, they can move on to the next. They will be able to do so without difficulty. Each chapter looks at topics of crucial importance, so the book should greatly bless readers even if they decide to skip a portion. (Note that it is ordered by subject rather than by Alpha talk. This has enabled us to create a vastly more useful work which can also cater for the various Alpha-related books and post-Alpha resources, as well as for local adaptations and other variants of the Course.)

Although this volume has been written to answer questions raised as it goes along, this has not *always* been appropriate. The reader is therefore urged to continue with subsequent sections even if a matter does not seem to be totally dealt with *in situ*. They should find, by the end, that outstanding queries have been handled and that the fabric of the book holds together very cohesively.

A number of people have worked on this volume, or have diligently reviewed it and agree with it. However, readers must be discerning *for themselves* and check what they read against Scripture. After all, we are commanded to test "**all** things" (1 Thess. 5:21). If any errors are identified, *please* write to us so that they can be corrected for a subsequent printing.

Finally, the reader should be advised that this manual is committed to the truth and, as such, may seem a little unsentimental in places. Alpha deals with life-and-death issues, so we feel it is important that believers do not allow anything to cloud their judgment. (This is one reason why we have decided not to accept any royalties from the project.)

Our earnest desire is to edify the Body of Christ, but please be prepared for thought-provoking material. This book should inspire, but we have also not hesitated to express concerns where necessary. We are convinced that anyone who is genuinely eager to search out the truth and is open to learning more about the Lord will find this book very rewarding. Those rigidly set in their ways will inevitably have a more difficult time! The Lord's advice to us is "Buy the truth and sell it not" (Proverbs 23:23). May God bless you.

Dusty Peterson and Elizabeth McDonald

PART FOUR
PURE UNITY

CHAPTER 17
𝒟IVERSITY

17:1 IS TEACHING IMPORTANT? Alpha Course leaders need *consistently* to attach the same value to teaching that Christ did. The Lord Jesus clearly felt that teaching was of enormous importance. After all, He spent the lion's share of His ministry doing just this. There are more than 50 separate references in the Gospels to Him teaching. In fact, so closely was He associated with it that He was referred to as "Master" or "Rabbi" (both meaning "teacher") over 70 times in the four Gospels. Not only did He obviously consider this aspect of His ministry to be absolutely vital, but He also showed that there are a *lot* of things that His People need to be taught, for "...He taught them **many** things..." (Mark 4:2a. See also Mark 6:34 and Luke 19:47).

The Lord also demonstrated the crucial importance of sound teaching (and the *quantity* of teaching that comprises the full gospel) by the way in which He nurtured His disciples. He was the greatest teacher ever, yet He still felt He needed to spend *years* teaching His disciples *full-time* before they were adequately equipped to be sent out to preach on His behalf - and these were people who already had an awareness of three quarters of our present Bible.

1

The term 'doctrine' is regularly thought of as a dirty word in modern Christian circles, yet it essentially just means 'teaching'. Indeed the word is used in place of 'teaching' dozens of times throughout the King James Bible, not least in reference to the Lord - e.g. in Mark 4:2, Luke 4:32, and John 18:19-20 (as well as in Matthew 7:28-29, where the Lord told His disciples to teach men *everything* He had ever taught them.)

Note that a similar misconception frequently exists over the word "law". The Hebrew equivalent 'torah' means 'direction' or 'instruction' rather than just a set of obsolete, legalistic, regulations.[1] Perhaps the passage which most clearly reveals the importance of teaching is to be found in 1 Timothy 4:

> "Till I come, **give attendance** to **reading**, to exhortation, to **doctrine** ... **Meditate upon** these things; **give** thyself **wholly** to them ... **Take heed** unto thyself, and **unto the doctrine**; **continue** in them: for **in doing this** thou shalt both **save** thyself, **and them that hear thee**" vv13-16).

With regard to Alpha, the question is whether the course needs any improvement in this regard. This is one of the important questions we shall be looking at in the next two chapters.

This volume has not been easy to write, and some elements of it may surprise, but for the sake of truth we entreat folks to continue reading. We encourage everyone to weigh fully the evidence we give before reaching their conclusions. We believe that we supply solid scriptural backing, but if any definite errors are found then we would be very grateful for the details. We only ask that any reproof be accompanied by the relevant Scriptures and done in accordance with 2 Tim. 4:2:

> "Reprove ... with all **longsuffering** and **doctrine**." See also Rom. 15:4-5; Col. 1:9-11; 1 Thess. 5:15; 2 Tim. 2:24-25 etc.

17:2 HOW MANY TEACHINGS ARE THERE?   God is *not* the author of confusion (1 Cor. 14:33). It is the *enemy* who introduces confusion - so as to disarm and undermine the People of God. There can thus be only ONE correct set of teachings about Christ and His Kingdom. This statement not only makes sense, but is also biblical. For example, Paul besought Timothy to "Take heed unto ... **the** doctrine [singular]"; Paul also told him to "charge

---

[1] This is why the Psalmist was able to say, in Psalm 119:97, "O how **love** I Thy law! it is my meditation **all** the day" and, in verse 165, "Great peace have they which **love** Thy law".

some that they teach **no other** doctrine" (1 Tim. 1:3). Paul recognised that there was only *one* true doctrine.

While there are many areas of teaching which are not essential to *salvation*, nevertheless these areas *are* apparently needed for a fully (and properly) functioning church which wants to bring its members up safely in the Lord. If they are *not* needed, why else are these areas taught in the Word that the Lord has given us? We must remember, "Thy Word is true **from** the **beginning**: and **every one** of Thy righteous judgments endureth **for ever**" (Psalm 119:160). See also Matt. 4:4; Luke 11:28 and others verses. What we are saying here is that a full, trusted, member of the church needs a great deal more knowledge (and *correct* understanding) of the Bible than does a new believer.

(Obviously until an individual has been thoroughly *taught* about a particular matter then they may understandably hold an erroneous view on it, but no-one should be allowed to *teach* on a matter until they know what the Word says about that matter. Note: We will shortly look at those personal beliefs that are a private matter between each Christian and God – and which may thus legitimately vary across the Church.)

In a sense, the essence of the "gospel" is that the Bible is the truth, the whole truth, and nothing but the truth. Sure enough, as dictionaries like Webster's or the Oxford English tell us, the word "gospel" is an Anglo-Saxon compound meaning "God's Word" rather than simply "good news" as Nicky states. This fuller definition is borne out by Scriptures like Acts 8:25; Col. 1:5; 1 Thess. 1:5-6; Rom. 10:16-17; 2 Cor. 4:2-3; and 2 Tim. 2:8-9. So the actual gospel comprises much more than just the contents of Matthew, Mark, Luke and John (each of which point us to the rest of the scriptures anyway).

> "Ye heard the **Word of truth**, the gospel of your salvation" (Eph. 1:13).

> "But the Word of the Lord endureth for ever. And this is the Word which by **the** gospel is preached unto you" (1 Pet. 1:25).

Now, according to the Word of God, a matter is established by "two or three witnesses", i.e. two or three unambiguous testimonies which agree. Thus, let us look at some more, similarly unmistakable, scriptural witnesses testifying that there *is* only ONE true gospel:

"Though we, or an angel from Heaven, preach **any other** gospel unto you than **that** [not "those"] which we have preached unto you, **let him be accursed**. As we said before, so say I now again, If any man preach **any** other gospel unto you than **that** ye have received, **let him be accursed**" (Gal. 1:8-9).

This matter was clearly of the utmost importance to Paul, and yet how often do we hear this message given today? Later on we will consider the implications of permitting false doctrines to persist – implications so serious that they led Paul to write these grave words.

A position taken up by some folks is that accurate teaching about Christ Jesus is not crucial. This view stems from the fact that, whether "in pretence" or in sincerity, Paul rejoiced that "Christ is preached" (Php. 1:18). Surely this is the important thing? The problem is that Paul only rejoiced when the *real* Christ was preached. To give erroneous details about a person is to describe *another* person. The following text shows how Paul felt about any divergence from what he preached:

"But **I fear**, lest by any means, as the serpent beguiled [i.e. charmed and deceived] Eve through his **subtlety**, so your minds should be **corrupted** from the simplicity that is in Christ. For if he that cometh preacheth **another** Jesus ... or **another** gospel ... ye might well bear with him" (2 Cor. 11:3-4).

We are uncovering the enormous importance that God attaches to thorough and accurate teaching in the Church. It comes as a shock in these 'enlightened' days to realise that the Lord is never quoted as having said "OK, this bit I'm about to teach isn't actually important". Amazingly, none of His apostles were recorded as suggesting that any portion of their teaching wasn't essential for a strong and healthy Church. Although the Lord did say that some areas of doctrine are "**weightier**" than others, this does not mean that others are disposable (Matt. 23:23).

If a part of a Fellowship's teaching is wrong then that Fellowship ceases to have a totally consistent and cohesive view of the Lord. This makes the remaining teachings less solidly supported, less sure, and thus less convincing to others. If we liken holy Scripture to the (now old-fashioned) blueprints for a building then we can see that we need *all* the blueprints, *and* we need to involve the Architect - especially for any parts that may be less easy to interpret. We need to stay committed and faithful to the blueprints otherwise the building is going to be misshapen, unsafe and even unusable – not to mention unattractive to outsiders.

17:3 DISPUTABLE MATTERS   Of course, Scripture also makes plain (in Romans 14 and Colossians 2:16ff) that there are areas which church members are permitted to approach differently, but consider the following extraordinary facts:

(a) These areas are extremely few in number. In fact in both passages only the same *two* areas are mentioned - i.e. eating habits and the observance of special days. In neither passage is there any suggestion that these are only *examples* or that there are all sorts of other matters which are also arguable. (See below for more details.)

(b) These areas are insignificant compared to the rest of the teachings given in Scripture. (And the very length of the Bible indicates the importance God attaches to accurate teaching about Himself.)

(c) These areas have to do with personal practices, *not* with teaching about the Lord or His Church. That is why Paul says that these two areas are merely "a shadow of things to come" (Col. 2:17) rather than being required for sound doctrine.

We realise this is a radical and very startling suggestion, at odds with the prevailing attitude in much of the Church today. But let the reader examine the evidence we provide below, and the scriptural answers we give to the arguments that people use, and let them consider if we do not offer ample proof of our assertion. We believe that this is much too important a question not to discuss fully and openly.

The first point to make is that the Western church today has easy, inexpensive, access to accurate translations, good concordances, and many other aids to knowing and following God's Word. Unlike some previous generations, we have the *complete* Bible available (and in audio form too), plus many commentaries, lexicons and other resources. We even have a variety of powerful Bible computer programs. We also have the lessons of Church history to help us. As churches, we have *no* excuse for ignorance or wrong teaching of God's Word. We need to remember Christ's statement in Luke 12:48…

"unto whomsoever much is **given**, of him shall be **much required**"

In view of this, Western churches have no reason not to operate in accordance with God's holy scriptures. This includes the teachings churches give. We must all be true to "the truth". So what does "the truth" say about disputable matters? We know of five ways in which this was revealed in the New Testament, and the identical pattern is displayed in each:

1) The Pharisees were continually looking out for any unbiblical acts on Christ's part, in order that they could prove He was not the Messiah. Unfortunately for them, He was totally committed to God's Word (as we demonstrated at the start of chapter 1). Despite their careful testing of His words, and all their efforts to trip Him up, there was nothing for them to fault. Apart from Jesus' claim to Messiahship, the only two matters that the Pharisees challenged as unbiblical were His views on **eating habits** (e.g. in Matthew 15:1-2 and Mark 7:2-5) and on the **observance of special days** (e.g. in Luke 14:1-6 and John 9:14-16). Since Christ Jesus never sinned, we can safely conclude that these two areas are the only ones He discussed which are personal to each believer rather than doctrinal ones which are crucial to godly church operation.

2) At the start of Matthew 12, the Pharisees condemned Christ's disciples for the manner of their Sabbath observance. Our Lord's defence (vv3-8) was to give two examples from the Hebrew scriptures where believers justifiably 'broke' the law. The first example centred on David's **eating habits** (in using the showbread). The second looked at **observance of special days** (i.e. temple priests doing work on the Sabbath). Nowhere did Christ Jesus permit His followers to 'pick and choose' which of His teachings they accepted, nor do any of the Epistles suggest that church members are allowed to harbour conflicting views about the Bible once the correct view has been determined and the members taught it.

3) Once again, although He spent most of His time on Earth *tightening up* their obedience to the complete Word, the two doctrines Christ reproved people for being *too* rigid over, were **eating habits** (e.g. in Matt. 15:10-20) and **observance of special days** (e.g. in John 7:22-23 and Matt. 12:10-12). Note the total contrast. As if to hammer home the point, the Lord even combined the two issues in Luke 6:1-10.

4) Romans 14 does say there are "doubtful", "disputable" areas. However, it then goes on to tell us what they are. The only things mentioned are **eating habits** (vv2-3, 6, 14-15, 17, 20-21 and 23) and the **observance of special days** (see vv5-6). Note that a brother is still not permitted to hold 'any old' position regarding his own behaviour in these areas – he must always act *in faith*. Furthermore, Paul's teaching is very clearly

delineated and he does not invite us to extend this concept to doctrine…
e.g. as to the way in which a church is to conduct itself.[2]

5) There is one remaining passage which unambiguously talks about this
subject. It is Colossians 2:16-23. Once again, the only areas in view are
eating habits (e.g. in v21) and the **observance of special days** (e.g. in
v16). When Paul had an opportunity to move on to other examples of
teachings which people today think don't really matter for a church, he
strangely neglected to take it. Could the idea that there are all sorts of
teachings in Scripture which are perfectly disputable be an invention of
man rather than a truth from the Lord?

The very early Church (which already enjoyed a knowledge of, and
much respect for, the "Old Testament" - which was, of course, what Christ
taught from) was not given free rein over its 'non-essential' beliefs. For it
"**continued steadfastly** in the apostles' doctrine [i.e. what is now called the
'New Testament']" (Acts 2:42). Note the way in which they followed "the
apostles' **doctrine** [singular]". This combination gave the early Church a
sure foundation for the doctrinal attacks that were later to come upon it from
the enemy.

Note again that the apostles spent most of their time *teaching*. This
is hardly surprising given that the Lord had sent them out to "teach all
nations … to observe **all** things **whatsoever** I have commanded you" (Matt.
28:19-20). For example, Paul spent three *years* at the church in Ephesus,
teaching them "night and day" (Acts 20:27,31). If the only doctrines needed
by a church could be communicated in a few days or weeks then why did he
bother staying for three *years*?[3] (We will see Alpha's take on this matter in a
moment.)

17:4 WHAT ABOUT INTERPRETATION? It is argued that Bible
passages can have several possible interpretations attached to them. This is
true, but there are crucial provisos to this:

---

[2] Some people would try to claim that 1 Cor. 10:31-32 extends this concept beyond eating
habits and observance of special days but this is to base a view on **very** ambiguous ground.
Consider too that this passage, alongside 1 Cor. 8:4-13, focuses again on *eating habits*.

[3] It is true that no-one can know absolutely everything there is to know about every doctrine of
the Bible, but: (a) this doesn't mean we cannot know a great deal, (b) we must all be willing to
seek as much truth as possible, and (c) if we are able to prove something biblically which a
person subsequently rejects, then we need to question that person's commitment to the truth,
and hence our degree of our attachment to them.

(a) We do not see Christ or His apostles teaching *divergent* interpretations of Scripture from each other;

(b) *Only* interpretations which fit with the *whole* of the rest of Scripture can be true, even if the wording of a particular passage may suggest other interpretations when taken *on its own*. The Bible will provide the full picture regarding the subject discussed in any individual passage; and

(c) It is very true that Scripture has depth, and that a given passage may have more than one 'level', but correct interpretations will *never* be in conflict with each other. (For example, a prophecy may have many partial fulfilments before the complete, final one. After all, the Word of God has to apply in every age. This is why antichrist-like figures have arisen throughout history as per 1 John 2:18.)

Accurate Bible interpretation requires honesty and consistency and prayer - and a good knowledge of the Word - but accuracy is *vital* for those who seek to teach. If someone teaches an interpretation which is not compatible with the rest of Scripture then they are misleading, rather than feeding, the flock, and are therefore dangerously out of God's will (as per James 3:1 and Ezekiel 34:8-10). To continue our architectural analogy, we must be sure not to get the blueprints for each floor confused. When studied carefully they should all fit together perfectly without leaving loose ends (or 'problem passages' in terms of the Bible).

*Important Note: Despite the claims of some people, the Bible never genuinely contradicts itself. However, to test our love for the truth, God has created the Word in such a way that a small, but noticeable, amount of the evidence for any given doctrine would seem to point away from the truth when the scriptures are read **superficially**. It is absolutely vital to interpret this minority ambiguous evidence in the light of the majority unambigous evidence rather than the other way around. (Please see the transcripts of the 'Beware False Balances' talks, available from our web site, for proof of this whole matter.)*

*The Lord has arranged that, for those who want to find reasons to reject the Bible, or want to reject any given doctrine, discrepancies seem to exist when the scriptures are read out of the context of the rest of the Bible. This observation is itself entirely biblical, for, if someone does not want to believe the truth, God promises them a "**strong** delusion" (2 Thess. 2:11-12).*

Every supposed 'contradiction' in the Holy Scriptures is perfectly reconcilable when it is properly investigated. For example, the apparent disharmony between the gospels over certain events can often be the result of each Gospel recording a similar, but *separate*, occurrence. However, if the *same* event *is* in view, differences are explained thus:

The Gospels each have a specific purpose. They serve to illustrate Christ's Kingship, Servanthood, Humanity, and Divinity respectively. The Gospels therefore describe a given event from different (but never mutually exclusive) viewpoints. Thus, for instance, the 'differing' inscriptions over the cross of Christ simply reflect different perspectives on the *same* wording. They do not preclude each other. See Matt. 27:37; Mark 15:26; Luke 23:38; and John 19:19...[4]

```
FULL:  THIS IS JESUS OF NAZARETH THE KING OF THE JEWS
MATT:  THIS IS JESUS              THE KING OF THE JEWS
MARK:                             THE KING OF THE JEWS
LUKE:  THIS IS                    THE KING OF THE JEWS
JOHN:          JESUS OF NAZARETH  THE KING OF THE JEWS
```

It is time to move on. We have looked at the *biblical* meaning of the words "truth" and "gospel" - indeed, the word "gospel" is often used today to *mean* "truth". It is now time to look at the phrase "the faith". In Scripture, "the faith" often refers to the gospel - i.e. the teaching, or doctrine, that Christ and His apostles taught, hence: "Stand fast ... together for **the faith** of the gospel" (Php. 1:27b), and "Continue in **the faith** grounded and settled, and be **not moved away** from the hope of the gospel" (Col. 1:23), and "Some shall depart from **the faith**, giving heed to ... **doctrines** of devils" (1 Tim. 4:1). As we can see, Scripture talks of "**the** faith", further proving that there is only *one* true faith, *one* true gospel, *one* true doctrine.

In this Part, then, we intend to look at Alpha's position regarding "other" doctrines (and the groups which hold and teach them), and compare this with what God's Word says. This will reveal if there are any significant ways in which the Alpha Course could do with modification in this regard.

17:5 GOD'S TRUTH   God plainly considers the truth to be of absolutely *paramount* importance, thus the Bible refers to the concept of truth several *hundred* times. In Part One we looked at some scriptures which declared that the Bible is *the* truth. Here are some more which reveal just how closely the Lord aligns Himself with His Word, the truth:

---

[4] This illustration was obtained from E.W. Bullinger, although we cannot endorse everything he taught.

> "For the **word** of the LORD is **right**; and **all** His works are done in **truth**. He **loveth** righteousness and **judgment**" (Psalm 33:4-5), "The **Word** was made flesh ... **full** of grace and **truth**" (John 1:14), "The works of His hands are verity [i.e. truth/reality] and judgment; **all** His **commandments** are **sure**. They **stand fast for ever and ever**, and are done in **truth** and uprightness." (Psa. 111:7-8)

To reiterate: the Bible is the truth, and anyone who undermines the Bible is attacking truth. Since everything stems from truth, dishonouring the Bible is an homicidal (not to mention suicidal) activity.

The authors of the Alpha Course recognise the importance of truth. They have laid down the rule that the Alpha Course should only ever be run 'as is' - i.e. with no material changes. This avoids the potential danger of some sect or cult taking advantage of the high profile gained by Alpha and attracting unsuspecting people to the cult's own version (i.e. *per*version) of the gospel which is not the whole truth - and thus cannot save people but, rather, will deceive them.

While this limitation imposed by HTB must inevitably restrict the freedom that the Holy Spirit has in tailoring the material to the attendees at a given talk, nevertheless the ruling does avoid the risks that more freedom would bring. We must take great care to protect the truth. But what does the Alpha Course *itself* say about "other gospels" and those who promote them? And how does this compare with what the Word says on the subject? We will answer these questions shortly.

17:6 WHAT DOES SCRIPTURE SAY ABOUT OTHER TEACH-INGS?

As we've seen, there is only one *true* gospel - the one which is completely true to God's Word and does not twist it in any way. All other gospels, no matter how right they sound or how close they are to the true, must, by definition, be *false*:

> "I marvel that ye are so soon **removed from Him** that called you into the grace of Christ unto **another gospel**: Which is **not** another [i.e. there is only one *true* gospel, only *one* which saves]; but there be some that trouble you, and would **pervert** the **gospel** of Christ" (Gal. 1:6-7).

Satan loves to confuse, so it should not be surprising that he has generated many other versions of the gospel, some of which are extremely difficult to spot - especially if we do not bother to check them thoroughly against Scripture. Apart from being false, these other teachings:

(a) Are *never* from God and are therefore from the other Kingdom - Satan has been injecting false teachings into churches since the beginning,
(b) Are *always* dangerous because they take us away from God's truth and thus away from God (see Prov. 3:1-4 and Col. 1:22-23),
(c) Are *inevitably* going to lead to, among other things, "envy, strife" and "**evil** surmisings" (1 Tim. 6:3-5, see also Jas. 3:14-16 and 2 Tim. 2:16), and
(d) Are like leaven which, if not quickly and properly purged, will spread ever more widely (1 Cor. 5:6-8; Gal. 5:7-9).

The Lord gives us many strong warnings in His Word regarding "other" doctrines. That is a measure of how dangerous they are. The enemy seeks to corrupt the truth and pass it off to the church as the real thing. We should not assist him in his strategies but instead be very wary; for this is exactly the reason Israel often fell. They usually coped with the *physical* onslaughts that Satan made through the Philistines and others, but they failed to keep purging out the corrupt *beliefs and practices* that the enemy artfully introduced into their midst.

For instance, when Balak realised, in Numbers 22, that brute force was not going to work against the People of God, he consulted Balaam who revealed that the way to destroy them was through encouraging them to *compromise*, thus subtly seducing them into false ways. Hence Peter says of some in the church that they are those: "[w]hich have **forsaken** the **right** way, and are **gone astray**, following the way of **Balaam**" (2 Pet. 2:15a).

It is interesting to recognise that this is the self-same method used by the enemy against that part of the early Church located in Rome. Satan's terrible persecutions, through various Roman Emperors, served to produce a very pure, and thus very *effective*, underground, church. So he changed tack and went after the Word instead of the people. He did this by publishing a corrupt version of the Bible (and then giving away copies of it), as well as by telling the remaining Roman pagans that they were all Christians. A flood of heresy was introduced as all these people were added, unsaved, to the visible church. Within a short time this leaven had spread throughout the church at Rome and, once the foundations had been destroyed, it was simply too late for recovery (Psa. 11:3).[5]

---

[5] This is yet another reason why it is pointless to try to change the Roman Church from within, rather than attempt to lead people out of it. If the reader does not agree with this, we would

False teaching, regardless of how trivial it appears to be, denotes a wrong "dividing" of God's Word. If such a bias is allowed to continue, it will corrupt other aspects of the faith and lead to a skewed, and hence false, view of God. This will seriously undermine our worship and prayer. If God should withdraw at all because of this, as per John 4:23-24, then we are even less well placed to put things right again and could end up in a vicious circle of error. This is why Scripture exhorts us to struggle constantly for the truth (Jude 1:3) and that, if unchecked, false teaching will lead to sin and thus ultimately to a destroyed witness and even to our *own* destruction (see 2 Tim. 2:16-18 and Titus 1:10-13). Obviously much of the error taught in the Church is the result of ignorance rather than malice, but the effect is just the same.

In view of all of the above, it seems extraordinary that Nicky should almost *encourage* multiple doctrines and divergent beliefs about God and His Word. He says, at the end of a speech about *doctrine*, that "**God creates variety**", and he claims, regarding groups with contradictory views: "We all belong to the body, but unity does **not** mean **uniformity**. There is diversity in the Body of Christ".[6] 'Unity in diversity' is a classic catchphrase within ecumenical circles, yet doctrinal diversity is actually *condemned* in the Bible (Heb. 13:9). In other words, Nicky communicates that it does not matter if Christians disagree about the truth, whereas God's Word says:

> "Stand fast in **one** spirit, with **one mind** striving together for **the** faith" (Php. 1:27b), "Now I **beseech** you, brethren, by the name of our Lord Jesus Christ, that ye **all** speak the **same** thing" (1 Cor. 1:10a).

> "There is ... **one** hope ... One Lord, **one** [true] faith" (Eph. 4:4-5), "Finally, brethren ... be of **one** mind" (2 Cor. 13:11). See also Php. 2:2.

We need clear, unambiguous, accurate teaching of the Bible. The world needs it too. Are non-Christians *really* impressed by the fact that churches aren't bothered if their views differ significantly from each other? Are those unbelievers who are searching for the truth not shocked by the way most Christians today have very scant knowledge of, and little devotion to, their Bibles? Compare this devotion with that seen in Islam!

---

urgently direct them to Parts 1-2 of the 'World' volume of this *Unofficial Guide*.
[6] Talk 14.

In closing this chapter, we need to make one other observation. Many in the Church today are convinced that they can never be deceived. Yet Paul spent *years*, in one church alone, warning believers that they *could* be. Scripture talks about people "not **abiding** in the doctrine of Christ", "**straying** concerning the faith", "**erring from** the faith" and ultimately "**departing** from the faith". The Bible also talks of "many" being deceived and of "whole houses" being subverted, and that there is a real danger of churches believing false spirits and false prophets (e.g. see Rev 2:20-24). Remember, even the most anointed men of God in Scripture were deceived at times, including Joshua, David, Solomon, Peter, Barnabus...

Earlier we mentioned the Ephesian church. Having quoted from Paul's epistle to them, it would be appropriate to hear what Paul had to say at his very last meeting at Ephesus. It will put into perspective whether Paul believed that his flock could be deceived - and whether "diversity" of belief, or commitment to *the Word,* is the most important thing for a healthy, safeguarded, church:

> "**Take heed** therefore unto yourselves ... For I **know** this, that after my departing shall **grievous wolves** enter in among you, not sparing the flock. Also **of your own selves** shall men arise, speaking perverse things, to **draw away disciples** after them. Therefore **watch**, and remember, that by the space of three **years** I ceased **not** to warn **every** one **night and day** with **tears**. And now, brethren, I commend you to God, and to the **Word** of His grace, **which is able to build you up, and** to give you an **inheritance** among all them which are sanctified" (Acts 20:27-32).

CHAPTER **18**

*T*EACHERS AND ALPHA

18:1 SHOULD WE QUESTION TEACHINGS?   Many teachers today demand that we never question what they say. Yet all of them are fallible men and we all make mistakes (James 3:2). Telling a congregation never to question one's teaching is itself an example of erroneous teaching because, as we have already seen, it is a *biblical* command that we: "Prove [i.e. test] **all** things" (1 Thess. 5:21a).

Why would a teacher ban people from checking what they say? What great harm can it do? Paul did not ban people from testing his words; indeed the Bereans were *applauded* for doing so (Acts 17:10-11). When writing to the Corinthians, Paul exhorted: "Judge ye what I say" (1 Cor. 10:15b, see also 11:13). Likewise to the Romans he wrote "Judge this". Similarly, the Lord praised the church in Ephesus for testing the teachings it received:

> "I know thy works, and thy labour, and thy patience, and how thou **canst not bear** them which are evil: and thou hast **tried** [i.e.

tested] them which **say** they are **apostles**, and are not, and hast **found them liars**" (Rev. 2:2).

These 'apostles' probably claimed that, along with their exceptional ministry, they had a uniquely divine anointing which meant they were above testing. They may well have tried to insist that their special knowledge was obtained directly from the throne-room of God and was therefore beyond question. Thankfully, the Ephesians were more committed to their scriptures than to men.

If we are not weighing and checking everyone's teaching, then how can we possibly obey the commandment in 1 Timothy 6:3 to "withdraw" ourselves from anyone who teaches "otherwise" to the things Paul taught? In fact, Scripture tells us that one of the ways we determine whether or not a person is "approved of God" is by the *biblical* nature of their doctrine (1 Cor. 11:19). In other words, the test that God commands us to use is *exactly the opposite* of the one that some teachers insist on. The truth of someone's teaching indicates that the person is sound, *not* "my teachings are true (and therefore not to be checked) because I appear to be sound".

When faced with the above scriptures, some people might try to deny them by quoting the verse in Phillipians which says "Do all things without murmurings and disputings". But, as is frequently the case today, it would be one indeterminate phrase wrenched out of context whose supposed meaning cannot stand up to scrutiny nor to the weight of clarifying passages. The surrounding text shows that *truth* needs to be present first:

> "Fulfil ye my joy, that ye be **likeminded**, ... being of **one** accord, of **one** mind ... That ye may be blameless and harmless ... Holding forth the **Word of life**; that I may rejoice in the day of Christ, that I have not run in vain, neither laboured in vain" (Php. 2:2-16).

God renews the minds of His sincere disciples so that they have the "mind of Christ". Are we really being told that someone with the mind of Christ cannot question teachings?! "Judge ye not what is **right**?" (Luke 12:57). If we are to prevent error from coming into our Fellowships then one important way to do this is by not assuming that what is said from the front is necessarily 'gospel'. And how can we obey the following command if we are not comparing what leaders say against God's Word?

> "Let the elders that rule **well** be counted worthy of double honour, **especially** they who labour in **the Word** and **doctrine**" (1 Tim. 5:17).

18:2 DO NOT JUDGE   We have seen that Paul *instructs* us to judge teachings so that we can distinguish between true and false. Similarly, "Let the prophets speak two or three, and let the other **judge**" (1 Cor. 14:29). But, in extreme cases, this will sometimes mean having to conclude that someone is actually a *false* teacher / prophet. A common retort to any such suggestion that we can know whether someone is a true or false brother / teacher / prophet / apostle is "Judge not, that ye be not judged" (Matt. 7:1). As always, we need to check if the apparent meaning of this is true to the *rest* of Scripture - or whether another lone verse has been interpreted without reference to its context. So let us look at the context here:

> "Judge not, that ye be not judged. For **with what** judgment **ye** Judge, ye shall be judged [i.e. this can't be referring to fair and reasonable judgment!]: and with **what** measure ye mete, it shall be measured to you again ... Thou **hypocrite**" (Matt. 7:1-5).

The Lord is referring here to a rash or *hypocritical* decision, not to wise judgment based on Scripture. In particular, He is telling us not to look down on someone for ungodly behaviour *that we share*. Similarly, it would be very easy to quote the first half of Romans 2:1 about not judging, while omitting the rest of the verse which shows that it is *hypocrisy* which is being condemned, because: "thou that judgest **doest the same things**". The Bible condemns hasty, superficial, judgment; hence the Lord said "Judge not **according to the appearance**, but judge **righteous** judgment" (John 7:24). There is good and bad judgment, not merely bad.

Let's see what the rest of Scripture has to say on this subject. For anyone who wants to dwell on the Lord's words "I judge no man", He also said "as I hear, I **judge**" (John 5:30). We are also told, "He that is **spiritual** judgeth **all** things" (1 Cor. 2:15). (The explanation for the phrase "I judge no man" is given by its context. The Lord did not judge in the same *way* the Pharisees did, nor in the same sense they thought He would.) Indeed, the following scripture shows Paul's astonishment that the Corinthians were *not* judging people in their church:

> "But now I have written unto you not to keep company, if any man that is **called a brother** be a fornicator, or covetous, or an idolater, or a railer, or a drunkard, or an extortioner; with such an one no not to eat [i.e. don't even sit at the same meal]. ... [D]o **not ye judge** them that are **within** [the Fellowship]? But them that are **without** God judgeth. Therefore **put away [expel] from among yourselves** that wicked person" (1 Cor. 5:11-13). (Here

again we have the exhortation to safeguard the rest of the Body by purging out false ways. You need to judge a person as wicked before you can expel them.)

"Know ye not that we shall judge **angels**? how much **more** things that pertain to **this** life?" (1 Cor. 6:3). See also the verses surrounding this one.

If we are *not* (carefully) judging the true spiritual state of those around us (as well as ourselves) then we are hardly being a good brother or sister. We need to be watching out for each other, caring for the spiritual welfare of all - as well as seeking to ensure that no *false* brethren have "crept in unawares" (Jude 1:4) for "**many** deceivers are entered into the world" according to 2 John 1:7. On Alpha, Nicky never discusses the possibility of anyone we meet being a false brother, apparently expecting us instead to accept anyone and everyone:

"The Father loves **all** his children. We should say 'we accept as our brothers all those you receive as your children'" [Talk 14].

Note, however, that this demands we be able to *determine* those whom God has "received" i.e. those who are true children of God, yet Nicky elsewhere demands that "we must stop judging each other" - so we cannot! Much of the church is happy to blindly accept people as true Christians just because they say they are and because they come along to meetings, yet it chastises anyone who claims that brothers can tell whether someone is, or is not, truly of God. Scripture is on the side of the latter. Bizarrely, Nicky elsewhere talks of the admission by one man that he had been a bishop for fifteen years *whilst still an atheist*.[1] Nicky would seemingly have banned the brethren from questioning, during all those years, whether the man in charge of their Fellowship was a true believer!

It is insanely risky to assume, just because someone claims to be a believer, or says they "love Jesus", that they must necessarily be the genuine article. Many who claim to follow the Lord, and *even* some that genuinely *believe* they do, are not true Christians:

"Wherefore by their fruits ye **shall know** them. **Not** every one that saith unto Me, **Lord, Lord,** shall enter into the Kingdom of Heaven" (Matt. 7:20-21).

---

[1] Talk 9.

"**Beware** of false prophets, which come to you in **sheep's** clothing … Ye **shall know** them by their fruits" (Matt. 7:15-16).

For those who refuse all this on the basis that "we can never know someone's heart":

(1) Scripture says the person's true nature *will* be evident – e.g. from the things they say: "for of the abundance of the **heart** his mouth speaketh" (Luke 6:45, see also Matt. 12:34),
(2) The Lord *can* make us directly aware of the person's heart condition (see, for example, Acts 5:3 & 8:21), and
(3) The truth is that we *can* know their *spiritual* state: "He that saith, I know Him, and **keepeth not** His commandments, **is a liar**, and **the truth** is **not in him**" (I John 2:3-4).

The apostle John devoted his *entire* first epistle to showing how we can distinguish the real brother from the counterfeit. (For a vivid description of what false - or apostate - brothers will do to true believers if they remain undetected, see Matt. 24:3-13, Luke 21:12-16 and Matt. 10:16-23).

18:3 DANGER OF DEATH! Scripture tells us to "beware" of false teachers / prophets. We are also warned to separate from those among us who demonstrate that they are not "of God" (see 2 Thess. 3:6, 2 Tim. 3:2-5, 1 John 4:1). We are also told to avoid fellowshipping with fools (Prov. 13:20, Prov. 23:9 etc). How can we hope to obey these commands if we are not allowed to make any judgments? Again, how can a church possibly identify and cast-off "heretics" (as per Titus 3:10) if it is not permitted to determine who is and isn't one? We are failing God and His true People if we do not do these things. What has a true disciple to fear from wise, *biblical*, assessment by his brothers? Who benefits when we turn a blind eye to serious error within the Church?

In fact there is indeed a sense in which we are not to judge others: for the *Word of God* gives the judgments, we merely apply them (as per Exo. 24:3 and 1 Ki. 6:12). The Psalmist said:

"I have refrained my feet from every evil way, that I might keep Thy **Word**. I have **not departed** from Thy **judgments** … How sweet are Thy words unto my taste! yea, sweeter than honey to my mouth! … Thy **Word** is a lamp unto my feet, and a light unto my path. I have sworn, and I **will** perform it, that I will **keep** thy righteous **judgments** … [Q]uicken me, O LORD, according unto

Thy **Word** ... and teach me Thy **judgments**" (Psa 119:101-108).
See also vv6-8, 12-16, 19-21, 30-31, 38-40, 62-63 etc.

And Christ Himself said:

"...the **Word** that I have spoken, the same shall **judge him**"
(John 12:48). The Greek term, once again, is "logos" here.

Scripture lists the criteria for determining God's judgment about a
person. It exposes, for example, the telltale signs of a "fool" (e.g. in Prov.
10:18 and Prov. 28:26). It gives the basis on which to identify false apostles
(2 Cor. 11:4-13) and so on. We must simply, and carefully, follow God's
guidance, and resolve to agree with the conclusion He gives in His Word,
whatever that might be.

According to the following Scriptures, if the habitual 'fruit' in
someone's life is any of the things mentioned below, then the Bible forces us
to judge that the person is not abiding in Christ. And the Lord plainly told
us, e.g. in John 15:4-10, what will happen to those who do not "abide in"
(i.e. walk with) Him. If we close our eyes to these Scriptures, we are
effectively consigning the wayward soul to destruction and the rest of the
Fellowship to peril. Below are a number of examples, almost all of which
were written to *churches* and are therefore definitely directed to believers.

We are saved through faith alone, but unrepentant sinfulness is
incompatible with living by faith. Thus, according to the Bible, someone's
salvation must be gravely doubted if they are repeatedly or unrepentantly...

- Unrighteous (Gal. 5:19-21; Eph. 5:5-7; 1 Pet. 4:18), or unholy (Heb.
  12:4; 2 Pet. 2:20-22; Col. 3:1-6);
- Unfaithful to God (1 Tim. 5:12; Matt. 24:48-51; Heb. 3:11-14), or
  rebellious toward Him (Heb. 10:26-29; 1 John 3:6-8; Heb. 5:9);
- Lukewarm toward God (Heb. 2:3; Rev. 3:16; Luke 14:27), or spiritually
  unfruitful / unprofitable (John 15:2; James 2:20-26; Rom. 11:20-23)
- Unforgiving of personal trespass (Matt. 6:15; 18:23-35; James 5:9), or
  unmerciful (Jas. 2:13; Rom. 2:5; Matt. 5:22), or hypocritical (Rom.
  2:1&3);
- Greedy (1 Tim. 6:7-12), or lustful (Jas. 1:12-15), or idolatrous (1 Cor.
  10:6-14).

Note that several of the above sins reappear (alongside references to
behaviour we have not mentioned, such as lying, fornication and sodomy) in
other damning passages, like Ephesians 5:5-7...

"For this ye know, that **no** whoremonger, **nor** unclean person, **nor** covetous man, who is an idolater, hath **any** inheritance in the kingdom of Christ and of God. Let **no** man deceive you with vain words: for because of **these things** cometh the wrath of God upon the children of disobedience. Be **not** ye therefore partakers with them". See also Rev. 21:7-8; Rom. 1:20-32; Gal. 5:19-21; and 1 Cor. 6:9-10.

Note also that we cannot claim to have any moral authority if we are guilty of the same things! To repeat: if people do (or don't do) certain things, then God's Word supplies His judgment about them and thus informs us of the deductions we must draw. We are simply to compare behaviour to the scriptures and accept what God says about it.

Interestingly, God reserves most such damning passages for those who are *unfaithful to His Word.* See especially: John 8:31; 1 Cor .15:1-2; 1 Tim. 4:1-2; Rev. 22:18; Rom. 2:8-9; & 2 Pet. 3:16-17.

18:4   HOW CAN WE KNOW ERROR AND FALSE TEACHERS?

The answer to this should be easy to infer from the material given so far in this Part. We know a teaching *must* be erroneous if it does not line up with Scripture *when taken as a whole*, but instead leaves inexplicable 'problem' passages that disagree with it. Many teachers try to sweep these scriptures under the carpet. Psalm 119 tells us that God does not allow His Word to be so disrespected:

"**[A]ll** Thy commandments are righteousness" (v172).

"Then shall I not be ashamed, when I have respect unto **all** Thy commandments" (v6).

"I **love** Thy commandments above gold; yea, above fine gold. Therefore I esteem **all** Thy precepts concerning **all** things to be **right**" (v104). See also verse 88.

Sound doctrine is that which is totally *biblical.* Any true teacher will live by this.

"**Holding fast** the **faithful Word** as he hath been taught, that he may be able by **sound doctrine** both to exhort and to convince the **gainsayers**" (Titus 1:9). Note: This verse shows that a genuine Christian is not necessarily one who has a very sound

21

understanding, but one who is so committed to the Bible that they will change their understanding if the scriptures demand it.

The original Alpha videos agreed on this point. Nicky said of the Bible that "it's how we know if something is wrong". We can determine a false teaching if we "put it alongside the Bible ... and **test** it" [Talk 5, 1st Edn]. In the replacement videos however, Nicky restricted the Bible's helpfulness to confirming "belief" (instead of belief *and practice*), and he removed the word "test" for some reason. But in neither video set did he mention the possibility of false *teachers* in the Church.

A teacher isn't necessarily sound because he dresses well, or has a good sense of humour or a fine singing voice. The test of a sound teacher is not even that he has an impressive healing ministry or a large congregation. The Church can recognise false *teachers* because they teach an unbalanced view of Christianity by promoting an inconsistent interpretation of God's Word. (Note that *unrepresentative* teaching of the Word is also a bad sign. If, for example, the Bible describes God's Kingship twenty times more often than His Fatherhood, then a similar ratio ought to be present when someone teaches about Him at any length – especially when teaching those who do not already know the Bible, or when trying to convey an overview of Him.) Let us prove this principle categorically by looking at what God has stated regarding this matter:

> "**To the law and to the testimony** [i.e. the Bible]: **if they speak** not **according to this Word**, it is because there is **no** light in them" (Isa. 8:20).

> "If **any** man **teach otherwise**, and consent not to ... **the words of our Lord Jesus Christ**, and to the **doctrine** which is according to **godliness**; He is proud, knowing **nothing**" (1 Tim. 6:3-5).

> "Whosoever transgresseth, and **abideth not** in **the doctrine** of Christ, **hath not God**. He that abideth in the doctrine [singular again!] of Christ, he hath both the Father and the Son" (2 John 1:9-11).

In essence, if someone is going to teach on a given subject, then they must know what the Bible says about that subject, else they will be in danger of teaching error. Of course, genuine *minor* mistakes can happen, but these should be few in number for a godly teacher who takes seriously the heavy responsibility they have to the Body. If someone *does* know what the Word says, but then interprets it in a way incompatible with the rest of

Scripture, they are not 'dividing' the Word rightly and must be challenged. If they persist in doing so then they must be adjudged a false teacher.

Regardless of whether a given teacher of falsehoods is a *deliberate* deceiver or is just himself deceived, we still need to identify and expunge his untruths before they spread and mislead our brothers and sisters. (We also need to be on the lookout for teachings that are so worded that they could be interpreted differently by different audiences.)

We must learn to be wise and to weigh *everything* that a teacher says. Just because they know their Bible backwards does not mean they are 'okay'. The ability to reel off two dozen scriptural names for Jesus does not relate to their soundness. Just because they firmly oppose a particular heresy does not mean they are correct on other issues. No matter how strongly a teacher may *claim* to 'love Jesus', the *proof* is that they are truly committed to His Word (and hence obey it). And we still need to remain vigilant even when we *do* know a teacher to be sound – for there is no guarantee that his teachings will remain that way.

Alpha does not do much to warn its babes to watch for such things, and Satan is surely certain to make the most of this omission.

18:5 HOW SHOULD WE FEEL ABOUT FALSEHOOD? Whoever
we are, and whatever the circumstances, we should be committed to the precepts of God's Word and *detest* false things being taught to the Church. The Psalmist asserted that, because the scriptures are so hugely valuable, he abhorred unbiblical teachings: "Through Thy precepts I get understanding, therefore I **hate** every false way" (Psalm 119:104). He went even further in verses 127-8, saying that he *loved* God's Word - and therefore despised unscriptural beliefs.

We should thus stand very boldly for the truth, for the sake of all concerned: "Therefore, brethren, **stand fast**, and **hold** the traditions [i.e. not man's traditions but those taught by the apostles as recorded in Scripture] which ye have been taught, whether by word, or our epistle" (2 Thess. 2:15, see also Jude 1:3), "I have chosen **the** way of **truth**: Thy **judgments** have I laid before me. I have **stuck** unto Thy **testimonies**: O LORD, put me not to shame" (Psa.119:30-31).

We should be very zealous for God and be thoroughly opposed to anyone who would mislead the flock. For a powerful *physical* picture of this important spiritual truth, see how Phinehas reacted, in Numbers 25, to the

People of God being seduced into following false ways. Note also God's great jealousy and wrath at seeing His People led from His ways.

Paul was similarly enraged by those in Galatia who were teaching the church there that Christ's atoning work was not enough and that we have to do things to help make atonement for our own souls (just like Rome). He said to those who had accepted this falsehood that "Christ is become of **no** effect unto you ... [Y]e are fallen from grace" (Gal. 5:4), and, of those who were teaching such heresy, "I would they were even **cut off** [i.e. cut off from hope]" (Gal. 5:12). These men were misleading – or "troubling" - the sheep. *Anyone* who troubles God's flock is risking terrible recompense from Him (2 Thess. 1:6). We should be just as consumed with ardent desire as Phinehas and Paul were that the Lord be given a pure Bride who is taught the full truth about Her Betrothed and Her King. Yet Nicky shows little such desire. He says:

> "A body is one, so the Church is one. We all belong to the body, but ... there is **diversity** within the body of Christ" [Talk 14].
> (Note the ambiguity of Nicky's statement. Why can he not be clearer?)

Does it *really* not matter if a church is being taught lies? Where in Scripture does it say that diversity of doctrine is acceptable? Diversity of belief really means confusion, disorder and doubt. Nicky's choice of term puts an unbecomingly positive 'spin' on a terrible disease in the Body of Christ. In truth, the Bible *condemns* diversity of beliefs, so why does Alpha appear to sanction it?

> "My people are **destroyed** for [i.e. due to] lack of **knowledge**"
> (Hos. 4:6).

Every church has its flaws of course, but is it really too much to ask for one which (a) has put a stop to any more teaching coming in untested, (b) has decided to try and steadily remove the error already present, and (c) has determined to live by the light it already has? Is it unreasonable to expect supposedly 'evangelical' Fellowships to be *genuinely* committed to God's Word – i.e. studying God's precepts and instructions, and seeking to operate by *all* the church principles set out in the Greek scriptures?

18:6 HOW SHOULD WE REACT TO FALSE TEACHERS? Follow-
ing on from this, it is appropriate to look at what God commands us to actually *do* about any false teachers in our midst. Note that the Lord calls *us*

to be responsible for the running of Fellowships. We have to *actively* stand up for the truth. He will not do our job for us. He has already equipped us, with His Word and His Spirit - and with the call, figuratively, to 'battle' for the truth. Once we are sure that falsehood is being taught (and we must ourselves be *completely* open to correction and change our own doctrine immediately if the teaching turns out *not* to be false) we are constrained by *biblical* command to act.

The action we need to take will depend on the circumstances. (The Bible, as always, gives the instruction we need, but please note that the Matthew 18:15-17 injunction to go to your brother first does *not* apply here, because this passage refers to someone in our Fellowship *trespassing* against us personally, rather than to that person *teaching falsehoods* to the Church.) The right response will vary depending on factors like:

- The seriousness of the error, and how dogmatically it is being taught,
- Whether or not the teacher involved has already been challenged or is known to be open to correction,
- How old we (and they) are in the faith, and
- Whether or not we (or they) are a deacon or elder.

Needless to say, the *first* step in bringing correction should always be prayer. But thankfully the Lord has already given us guidance in the form of scriptural commands regarding such situations. For example, if we are in a position of authority and the degree of error which the teacher is giving out is not *too* great:

> "I **besought** thee to abide still at Ephesus ... that thou mightest **charge some** that they **teach no other doctrine**" (1 Tim. 1:3).

> "For there are **many** unruly and vain talkers ... Whose mouths must be stopped, who subvert whole houses, **teaching things which they ought not** ... Wherefore **rebuke them sharply**, that they may be sound in the faith" (Titus 1:10-13).

But even regarding a teaching which some folks might have tried to claim was a "secondary" matter, i.e. the question of whether Christians needed to be circumcised, "Paul and Barnabas had **no small dissension and disputation**" with those who taught that it *was* necessary (see Acts 15:2). Note that, far from turning a blind eye to this "diversity" of opinion, the matter was carefully followed up. The church went to great lengths to determine (and then publicise and insist on) the *true* teaching, i.e. that circumcision was only a physical prefigure of what our spiritual condition towards God should be, and that it meant nothing now that Christ had come. Let's dwell on that for one more moment. The addition of one tiny thing to the gospel of Christ led Paul to start a major dispute. Would this not be branded "extreme", or "very very bigoted" by HTB and others today?

(Interestingly, a parallel state of affairs exists today with Seventh-day Adventism – a denomination which insists Christians *must* observe the Sabbath if they are to be saved. "**[A]ll Ten** Commandments are **binding** in the Christian dispensation ... One of these commands is the observance of the **seventh day** as the Sabbath".[2] But this is likewise adding human work to the gospel of salvation through faith alone. According to Adventism, we are no longer saved by grace *alone*, but rather by observing aspects of the symbolic Old Covenant too! But see Rom. 11:6; 3:21-28; and 2 Tim. 3:15. SDA teaching also implies that Christ did not completely fulfil the law as He claimed. But see Matt. 5:17-18; or 2 Cor. 5:18-21. Far from having "no small disputation" with the denomination propagating this dangerous lie, the Alpha organisation seems only too happy to *promote* it - see *Alpha News*, Jul - Oct 1998, p10.)

If a teacher is dogmatic about their heretical teaching, i.e. if they claim that we *must* believe this teaching in order for us to be part of the true church, and if they won't repent on being challenged, then Scripture says:

> "A man that is an heretic after the first and second admonition **reject**; Knowing that he that is such is **subverted**, and sinneth, being condemned of himself" (Titus 3:10-11).[3]

If we are young in the faith then we might sensibly consult with someone who is "older in the Lord" and who knows God's Word better. Such a person will usually be better placed both (a) to determine if the teaching *is* false, and (b) to challenge the teacher effectively if so. (Scripture commands that we "Rebuke not an elder, but entreat him as a father" (1 Tim. 5:1a). However, this passage does not say we can't approach an elder at all. Nor does the Bible require us to hold a particular 'post' within a Fellowship before we can entreat such a person. Ignoring error is not an option.)

Whoever we are, we must recognise that it is a really grave matter to be taught error, and it will certainly lead to problems for us (*and* for the

---

[2] *Bible Footlights*, p37.

[3] Note: the Greek word *hereticos* - translated "heretic" here - implies someone who is dogmatic *about his heretical teaching*. Modern Bible versions often hide the central *heretical* aspect. They do the same in 1 Cor. 11:19. But 2 Pet. 2:1 shows the primary meaning of the word.

rest of the brethren) if we continue to expose ourselves to it. If the falsehood is potentially serious and the teacher refuses to back down, then, as we have already seen, we are instructed to "withdraw" ourselves from him. In 2 John 1:9-11 we are even charged about such a person: "receive him **not** into your **house**". But the passage doesn't stop there. We are also commanded not so much as to *greet* him - for in so doing we would be legitimizing his ministry in the eyes of anyone who was to witness it. Due to the fact that this might encourage others to listen to his false teachings, greeting him would even make us a "**partaker** of his evil deeds" (v11).

Even the *smallest* errors should, in love, be challenged. If someone is getting one area wrong then it is almost certain that they are incorrectly interpreting other matters too. We are actually *serving* our teachers if we, gently and respectfully, bring them correction and true doctrine.

(Some readers will oppose the idea of rejecting a heretic, because they believe that the parable of the 'wheat and tares' prohibits it, despite all the gainsaying verses we have already studied. These folks fail to appreciate that the "field" in this parable does not represent the professing Church but the whole WORLD (Matt. 13:38). We only serve the enemy's purposes if we leave these people to do what they want.)

18:7 SHOULD WE NAME NAMES? It is perhaps surprising, in light of what we are often taught today, that there are numerous examples (in the Greek scriptures alone) of God's People 'naming names' of people so as to warn others about the false teachings they are dispensing:

> "**Study** to show thyself **approved** unto God, a workman that needeth not to be ashamed, **rightly** dividing the **Word of truth**. But **shun** profane and vain babblings: for they will increase unto more ungodliness. And their word will **eat as doth a canker** [i.e. will grow like a cancer]: of whom is **Hymenaeus** and **Philetus**; Who concerning the truth have **erred** ... and [thus] **overthrow** the faith of some" (2 Tim. 2:15-18).

Such specific warnings achieve other things too. They demonstrate that *no man* is infallible and that significant slips in the doctrine of *anyone*, no matter how 'sound' they are, need to be noted and taken seriously. Such warnings also remind us that even the most 'anointed' teacher needs to have his words tested against Scripture. *Any of us* can go wrong at times (see Gal. 2:11 or James 3:2).

In the case of a false 'brother', just because he has not succeeded in infiltrating *one* Fellowship with his falsehoods does not mean he will not try elsewhere, nor that we should not alert our brethren in other localities to his false ways. Quite the reverse. But let's see more proof that 'naming names' is sometimes a required step:

> "This thou knowest, that all they which are in Asia be **turned away** from me; **of whom** are **Phygellus** and **Hermogenes**" (2 Tim. 1:15). See also 3 John 1:9-10.

> "**Alexander** the coppersmith did me much evil: the Lord reward him according to his works: Of whom **be thou ware** also; for he hath greatly withstood our words" (2 Tim. 4:14-15).

> "Holding faith, and a good conscience; which some, having **put away** concerning faith, have **made shipwreck**: Of whom is **Hymenaeus and Alexander**; whom I have delivered unto Satan, **that they may learn** not to **blaspheme**" (1 Tim. 1:19-20).

Once again, if someone's teaching or behaviour is a threat to the rest of the Body, then the Body needs to be warned. Let us not only consider the needs of the dangerous 'teacher', but also our wider duty to a vulnerable flock.

How, then, does all this compare with what Alpha teaches? Sadly, either Alpha or the Bible must be wrong here...

18:8 NEVER CRITICISE?   In the "Family of God" section of Talk 14, Nicky says "I make it a rule, and I hope I keep to it, **never** to criticise another Christian". Laudable though this seems, is it a "rule" taught by God or by man? Does the following not sound like criticism?

> "But Peter said unto him, **Thy money perish with thee**, because thou hast thought that the gift of God may be purchased with money ... **[T]hy heart is not right in the sight of God**. Repent therefore of this **thy wickedness**..." (Acts 8:20-22).

Nicky doesn't tell us what he means by "criticise", but it apparently doesn't preclude him calling certain Baptist ministers "very, very bigoted and arrogant",[4] nor prevent him saying that "in some churches ... they have

---

[4] For the full quote see section 12:1 of this book, which appears in the 'World' volume.

lost God".[5] Nicky should have made clear that admonition, reproof and even rebuke (which actually sounds *stronger* than "criticism") are all vital parts of a healthy church. Not only are we all meant to be **"able** ... to admonish **one another"** (Rom. 15:14), but the Bible says we are *supposed* to be "teaching **and** admonishing **one another"** (Col. 3:16, see also 2 Thess. 3:15).

In fact, we are *encouraged* to challenge and correct our brothers when they err: **"Rebuke** a wise man, and **he will love thee"** (Prov. 9:8b), "He that **rebuketh** a man afterwards shall find more **favour** than he that flattereth" (Prov. 28:23), and **"Take heed to yourselves**: If thy brother trespass against thee, **rebuke him"** (Luke 17:3a).

Of course, all correction must be *biblical* (2 Tim. 3:16-17) and done with love. But there is no conflict here. We in the West just get given an impoverished idea of what love really means. According to Proverbs 13:24, it is actually *unloving* not to discipline. Indeed, Scripture likens refusal to rebuke our brethren to *hating* them, because we are not rescuing them from their erroneous ways: "Thou shalt **not** hate thy brother in thine heart: thou **shalt in any** wise **rebuke** thy neighbour, and **not suffer sin** upon him" (Lev. 19:17). But again Nicky insists, with the usual lack of Scriptural support,

"We are **not** to criticise one another" [Talk 14].

It is beneficial to an individual if he is challenged before he has a chance to compound his error, but this is also an important way to maintain righteousness in a church: "Them that sin **rebuke** before **all**, that **others also** may fear" (1 Tim. 5:20). As we have already seen in Titus 1:10-14, such challenges are crucial to maintaining sound doctrine and thus the safety of all.

The church is undeniably in the miserable state it is partly because people have not been properly led in the way of truth but have instead been allowed to come up with, and keep, their own man-made ideas without being criticised; thus moves of God have come to a halt. If there is still any doubt about this matter, the directness and seriousness of the following passage should make for sobering reading:

"**I charge thee** therefore **before God**,... Preach the word; be instant in season, out of season; **reprove, rebuke, exhort** with ... **doctrine**. For the time **will** come when they will **not** endure **sound doctrine**; but after their own lusts shall they heap to

---

[5] Talk 14.

themselves teachers, having itching ears; And **shall turn away** their ears from the **truth**, and shall be turned unto **fables**" (2 Tim. 4:1-4).

The fact is that we all need to be admonished and rebuked at times - even the apostle Peter. Paul not only **"withstood him to the face**, because he **was to be blamed"** but told the church in Galatia about it too.

18:9 WHAT IS THE CORRECT ATTITUDE TO CRITICISM?   Nobody likes to be criticised. It hurts our pride and forces us to accept that we may have been wrong. Our carnal side wants to rebel. The flesh does not like to be corrected. But those who try to live by the *spirit* rather than the flesh know that rebuke can be of great value: "As an earring of **gold**, and an ornament of fine gold, so is a wise **reprover** upon an obedient ear" (Prov. 25:12). As such, we should always be open to correction and be receptive to being put right:

> "Reprove one that hath **understanding**, and he will understand knowledge" (Prov. 19:25b).

> "He that regardeth [i.e. who values] reproof is **prudent**" (Prov. 15:5b).

We should be mature and realise that being criticised is actually a blessing: "It is **better** to hear the **rebuke** of the wise, than for a man to hear the song of fools" (Eccl. 7:5), and "**Open rebuke** is **better** than secret love" (Prov. 27:5). It is a blessing because it helps to keep us from sin and error. It is therefore very disturbing for Nicky to imply, as he has done, that he doesn't take his critics seriously.[6] In contrast, Scripture has some solemn things to say about those who think they know it all and who look down on reproof:

> "Whoso loveth instruction loveth knowledge: but **he that hateth reproof is brutish**" (Prov. 12:1).

> "Poverty and **shame** shall be to him that refuseth instruction: but he that **regardeth reproof** shall be **honoured**" (Prov. 13:18).

---

6 See Ruth Gledhill, The Magnet of Alpha, *The Tablet*, 27th June 1998, p840. Note also the way in which Nicky 'permanently' mislaid' his copy of Stephen Hunt's first critique of Alpha after only reading half of it. In other words, there is no sign that Nicky replaced it. (We document further examples elsewhere.)

"Seest thou a man wise in his own conceit? there is **more hope** of [i.e. for] **a fool** than of him" (Prov. 26:12).

The same message also appears in Prov. 6:23, 10:17, 17:10, 29:1, 15:10, 5:12-13, Amos 5:10, Jer. 5:3-4 and Jer. 7:27-28.

Regarding those who criticise us, it is completely useless to ignore their comments and just 'love' them back. In fact, the *truly* loving (not to mention wise) thing to do would be to take the comments seriously and to humble ourselves before God and check whether they are justified. If Nicky dismisses those who challenge him, then what encouragement will they have to help restore him to the right path if he needs correction in the future?

'No man is an island'. Our walk with God impacts on everyone around us. If we truly love those whom our lives affect then we must weigh all criticism received, regardless of the manner in which it is presented. When reproved, we need to examine ourselves to ensure that we have not inadvertently departed from the faith at all (2 Cor. 13:5). Ultimately, no-one is responsible before God for our walk but us. We must therefore never dismiss scriptural admonition. Otherwise those souls who *are* obedient to God's Word will be forced to reject us in order to protect themselves and any others whom we endanger by our unbiblical attitudes and beliefs.

18:10 "TOUCH NOT MINE ANOINTED" Before we examine a few of the errors with which the church has had to contend in recent years, we will need to deal with the oft repeated cry "Touch not mine anointed, and do my prophets no harm" (1 Chr. 16:22, Psalm 105:15). This is used to brush aside any criticism of certain teachers and to threaten with Divine retribution any folks who would question them. But is this right?

1 - As always we must look at the context! Both passages actually refer to *physical attack*, not to *biblical criticism*. Furthermore, the "anointed" in these verses refers to the entire People of God. Besides, *real* men of God love the truth and have no problem at all with seeing their teachings weighed against Scripture and themselves being taken to task where necessary - as Peter was. They can see that there is no "harm" in it. In fact they will be grateful for it.

2 - If someone *is* teaching unbiblical things then they can hardly claim to be "God's anointed", since doctrinal purity is a mark of a representative of God. If they *are* especially godly then they will also be especially mature and humble. They won't 'lord it' over their hearers but will actually *encourage*

their audience to test what they say by God's Word, and to question apparent discrepancies – as Paul did.

3 – Such an argument is a mis-use of Scripture, patently at odds with many others, and simply serves to frighten, oppress and cow the people of God and thus to control them. This is not the behaviour associated with the meek and gentle true shepherds in Scripture but is, rather, one of the practices of the Nicolaitans (i.e. those who subjugate the people) – something God hates (see Rev. 2:6 and 2:15 also Luke 22:25-26). After all, every believer is part of the priesthood now (1 Pet. 2:5 and 2:9). We should not be frightened of any man: "The fear of man **bringeth a snare**: but whoso putteth his trust in the LORD shall be safe" (Prov. 29:25). In other words, we should not fear these 'super-apostles' – and *they* should trust in the Lord, instead of their own attempts to subjugate men, to keep them from "harm".

(In fact it is a well-known mark of *cultic* movements that a small number of people in a group claim special anointing and demand that their words not be judged against *God's* Word. The truth makes us *free*, but these people engender fear and bondage instead.)

CHAPTER **19**

$\mathscr{F}$AITH TOWARD...?

19:1 INTRODUCTION   In Part One of this book, i.e. in the 'World' volume, we saw that those who overtly reject the Bible cannot be classed as Christian, and that their religion (if any) must be false. But even apparent attachment to the Word of God does not necessarily mean anything, for by exploiting a handful of verses one can invent a whole range of doctrines. Even Moonies can 'justify' their faith using this method. (We can be certain that there is a pressing problem when someone is dogmatic about a teaching heavily founded on *ambiguous* verses.) Among the enemy's various subtle tactics to undermine the Church is the use of actual Scripture - *but always in an unrepresentative way*. That is why we need a good working knowledge of God's Word so that we can detect those doctrines which are at odds with the overall direction of Holy Writ.

It is probably a lack of precisely this working knowledge which has led to the Church opening its doors to teachers who tell us that the Bible is not enough, that God failed to include some important material in it, and that they possess that missing information. (This despite the very dire warnings in the Bible about adding to it). The following sections reveal one such set of teachers around today.

There are several reasons for including this material:

1. It is a good illustration of the sort of thing about which Alpha should be warning unsuspecting folk,
2. It has infiltrated the teachings of much of the church - including HTB and thus, to an extent, Alpha itself,
3. It has a direct spiritual link to Alpha which we shall look at in the final Part of this book, and
4. It is so significant that it needs to be exposed when an opportunity like this arises.

The entire Body, and even the public at large, are endangered by these teachings. Therefore we are obliged to sound *public* warnings about the people who dispense them.

19:2 A PRELIMINARY LOOK AT GOD   It is crucial to a Christian's walk that he have an accurate view of God. If someone is dissatisfied with their Christian life it is probably because they have been taught a distorted view of what the Lord is like.

The Scripture "Where there is no vision, the people **perish**: **but** he that keepeth the law [torah], **happy is he**" (Prov. 29:18) has been badly misinterpreted by many in the modern church. They ignore the latter words and make the verse out to mean that, unless the church members are all busy with some grand project, or are all working towards some particular social target, then they will fall away from God. The word translated "vision" here refers to a revelation *of God*, hence the second part of the verse. Those who are truly committed to God's "law" (i.e. who know and obey His Word) will gain an accurate picture of the Lord and thus know a joyful walk with Him.

(Note: We must not confuse the symbolic laws placed on Israel with God's wider "torah" - or "direction".)

Unfortunately, the God described by certain professing believers is a far cry from the one described in the Bible. Before we investigate further, let's take a glimpse at how wonderful the true God is:

> "**Great** is the LORD, and **greatly** to be praised; and His greatness is **unsearchable**" (Psa. 145:3).

"The LORD [i.e. YHWH or "Jehovah"] is the **true** God, He is the living God, and ... everlasting King: at His wrath the **earth** shall tremble, and the nations shall not be able to abide His indignation" (Jer. 10:10).

"With God is **terrible** majesty. Touching the Almighty ... He is excellent in power, and in judgment ... Men do therefore fear Him" (Job 37:22-24).

"Consider the ... **severity** of God" (Rom. 11:22). For just a few instances of His severity, see 1 Kings 13, or 1 Sam. 6:19 or Num 11:31-34. We will visit further examples later, but just consider that God "sought to **kill**" Moses simply for not circumcising his son (Exo. 4:24-26). Consider too that the Lord killed seventy *thousand* of His People purely because David numbered them (1 Chr. 21). Disobeying God, or lacking faith in Him, is something He takes extremely seriously.

19:3   THE FEAR OF GOD IS?   Scripture frequently and unreservedly shouts to us to fear God. Indeed, the wisest mortal man ever to live summed up the *entirety* of his findings on wisdom by saying, in Eccl. 12:13, "**Fear God**, and keep His commandments: for **this** is the **whole** duty of man", and Moses reached the same conclusion (in Deut. 8:6 & 10:12). Now, many people protest that all such passages just mean 'have reverence for'. But if that is all that is meant, why does Scripture use the word "fear" instead? The Bible employs the word "reverence" numerous times elsewhere, so why not in these places? The truth is that we need to approach God in full awareness of His terrifying majesty and power...

Even an innocent person feels nervous in a High Court because of the authority possessed by the Judge. Even a nation's most loyal subject is cautious when in the presence of his King. Should *we* not quake, knowing that the "Judge of all", the "King of kings", the "Most High God" is near - and that we are far from innocent? To exhibit fear of one's King is very honouring to him before his courtiers, and is going to improve the chances of the King bothering to take notice of us and our supplications. Remarkably it is even stated of God's *own Son* that His praying "was heard in that He **feared**" (Heb. 5:7 – see also Isa. 11:2-3). How much more should *we* fear Him! "Sanctify the LORD of hosts Himself; and let Him be your **fear**, and let Him be your **dread**" (Isa. 8:13). See also 2 Cor. 5:11 or Num. 14:32-37.

Imagine you are sitting in the capsule atop a Saturn 5 moon-rocket. Or are standing next to an armed, multi-megaton, atomic bomb. Or are at the edge of a huge, active volcano. Or are in the direct path of a collosal tornado. Most people would be frightened to death by recognising their own puny power compared to the awesome destructive capacity of such things. We need to behave that way before Someone who could destroy the universe in a moment! "Fear ye **not** Me? saith the LORD: will ye not **tremble at My presence?**" (Jer. 5:22). (To help a believer appreciate God's greatness and majesty, we recommend they get out into the open country and look at the sky. It helps to give us an - albeit minuscule - idea of His magnificence and glory, as per Psa. 19:1 and Psa. 97:6.)

If we are still in doubt that to "fear God" means more than just 'revere' Him, perhaps we should consider the following passage:

> "[The Lord Jesus Christ] called unto Him **His twelve disciples** ... and commanded them, saying, ... **[F]ear Him** which is able to **destroy both soul and body in Hell**" (Matt. 10:1,5,28).

Please Note: The Lord was not talking to unbelievers here, but to *disciples*. No wonder Php. 2:12 commands us to work out our salvation "with fear and **trembling**". There are plenty more Scriptures showing that believers need to fear God:

> "My Covenant was with him [Levi] of life and peace; and I gave them to him **for** the **fear** wherewith he feared Me, and was **afraid** before **My Name**" (Mal. 2:5); "**Serve** the LORD with **fear**, and rejoice with **trembling**. Kiss the Son, **lest He be angry,** and **ye perish** from **the way**, when His **wrath** is kindled **but a little**" (Psa. 2:11-12).

> "Thou, even Thou, **art to be feared**: and who may stand in Thy sight when once Thou art angry? Thou didst cause judgment to be heard from Heaven; **the earth feared, and was still** ... [L]et all that be **round about** Him bring presents unto Him **that ought to be feared**" (Psa. 76:7-11).

And, if we *still* question whether believers need fear Him much, we should remind ourselves that "God is **greatly** to be feared in the **assembly** of the **saints**" (Psa. 89:7a) and that we must seek to "serve God acceptably with reverence **and** godly **fear** [note the distinction]: For our God is a **consuming fire**" (Heb. 12:28-29, see also Deut. 4:10-11 and Psa. 34:9-11, Deut. 5:29, 1 Sam. 12:24, Psa. 34:9-11, and Acts 9:31).

Remember how even Abraham, "the Friend of God", was hesitant and fearful as he talked with the Lord about Sodom's fate: "And Abraham answered and said, Behold now, I have taken upon me to speak unto the Lord, which am but **dust and ashes** ... Oh let not the Lord be angry, and I will speak yet but this once" (Gen. 18:27-32). Consider too how very fearful Queen Esther, a prefigure of the Bride of Christ, was about petitioning the King (see Esther 4). Sadly, Alpha engenders no discernible fear of God at all.

> "**Behold**, the **fear** of the Lord, **that** is wisdom" (Job 28:28).

> "The fear of the LORD is the **beginning** of knowledge" (Prov. 1:7).

19:4 A POPULAR TEACHING Having laid this groundwork, we can now come to the main topic of this Chapter. Let us consider the following Scripture:

> "**Thine**, O LORD, is **the** greatness, and **the** power, and **the** glory, and **the** victory, and **the** majesty: for **all** that is in the Heaven and in the earth is Thine; Thine is the Kingdom, O LORD, and Thou art exalted as head above **all** ... Thou reignest over all; and in **Thine** hand is **power and might**" (1 Chr. 29:11-12).

A common doctrine that has steadily come into parts of the Church in recent years has been the idea that faith is a "force" and that, provided we have "faith in our faith" and we don't doubt that what we have asked for will come to pass, it will. But, attractive as this belief sounds, is it true?

While we must certainly have faith, it is faith *in God* that is always in view in Scripture, not faith in some impersonal "force". The Word says "Commit thy way unto the **LORD**; **trust** also in **Him**; and **He** shall bring it to pass" (Psa. 37:5, see also John 14:10). We need to put our trust in *God*, "Trust in **Him** at **all** times" (Psa. 62:8a) not in ourselves. Indeed, according to Jer. 17:5, such self-reliance could actually bring a curse on us. God tells us to "Trust in the **LORD** with **all** thine heart" (Prov. 3:5a) and to "**rely** on the **Lord**", not on some 'force of faith' (see 2 Chr. 16:8).

Yes, the Lord Jesus required those folks who needed a miracle of Him, to have "faith". But the faith in question here was a strong faith (i.e. "belief") in Jesus' Messiahship - and His resultant ability to perform the miracle - not a faith in the recipient's own capacity to imagine receiving the miracle strongly enough:

> "And when he was come into the house, the blind men came to Him: and Jesus saith unto them, Believe ye that **I am able** to do this? They said unto Him, Yea, **Lord**. Then touched He their eyes, saying, **According to your faith** [i.e. your solid faith in My Lordship and thus My ability to do heal you] be it unto you" (Matt. 9:28-29).

Similarly, the lame man who was healed "in the Name of Jesus Christ of Nazareth" in Acts 3 was healed "through **faith** in **His Name**" i.e. through faith in Christ's Godhood and power, *not* through "faith in faith". We should have "faith in the **Lord Jesus**" (Eph. 1:15), a steadfast "faith **in Christ**" (Col. 2:5, Acts 24:24).

Some teachers put great store in the woman with the issue of blood in Matthew 9. The Lord said to the woman "thy faith hath made thee whole" (v22); but it was her faith *in the Person she touched* which was rewarded. Her choice of action indicated her faith in the Lord's Christhood, since it was a tradition in Israel (derived from Malachi 4:2) that the prayer-shawl of the promised Messiah would have healing power. (Hence the many other people who did exactly the same thing to Him in Matthew 14:36.) It was the woman's faith *in His Messiahship* that led to her healing, as it demonstrably also was - just one chapter earlier - for both the leper (in 8:2) and Centurion (in 8:8).

Another favourite passage used by proponents of this "faith in faith" idea is Matthew 11:23-24 where Christ appears to be teaching that, provided a person does not "doubt in his heart ... he shall have **whatsoever** he saith". However, such teachers are then forced to hide, or at least twist, the *immediately preceding* verse where Christ says "Have faith in **God**", showing that it is steadfast belief in *God*, and His ability to perform the miracle, which is central. Likewise they will freely quote 1 John 5:15 which refers to getting "whatsoever we ask", while conveniently omitting the verse before it which assumes that we have only asked for those things that are "**according to His will**".

When God gives us a specific promise, rather than when we decide we want something, we should (a) trust in His *faithfulness* that He will fulfil His promise, and (b) trust in His *ability* to fulfil it. It is *He* whom we must not doubt. He is, after all, the Almighty God, the Creator of *all* things (see, for example, Prov. 26:10, Jer. 10:16, Ezek. 10:4-5 and Eph. 3:9).

> "Thus saith the LORD, thy Redeemer, and He that formed thee from the womb, I am the LORD that **maketh all** things; that

stretcheth forth the heavens **alone**; that spreadeth abroad the earth **by Myself**" (Isa. 44:24).

"Blessed is the man that **trusteth** in **the LORD**, and whose hope **the LORD** is" (Jer. 17:7).

This doctrine of the 'Faith' movement has somehow managed to slip the notice of some godly folks in the Church, yet it is *identical* to the teachings of New Thought metaphysical cults like the "Christian Science" and "Religious Science" movements.

19:5 THE FAITH OF GOD   The 'Faith' movement goes on to teach that God created the universe by speaking "faith-filled words". However, it was *not* a matter of His having "faith" that caused things to happen (who or what is GOD supposed to have faith *in*?). It was because He is, according to more than sixty individual scriptures, the *Almighty* God, and has *complete* power. He does not need to rely on some "force of faith".

'Faith' teachers point to scripture phrases like "the faith **of** God" or "the faith **of** Christ", and insist that these can mean nothing else but that God "has faith". Yet this is patently inconsistent for they do not claim that the phrase "the *fear of God*" (or even "the *terror* of God" – Gen. 35:5) means that God has fear! The phrase "of God" appears throughout Scripture:

- It can mean "from God" e.g. "If this **man** were not **of God**, he could do nothing", and "So they read in the book in the **law of God** distinctly", or
- It can mean "regarding God" e.g. "for thou savourest not the **things** that be **of God**", and "Thou art true, and teachest the **way of God** in truth", or
- It can mean "toward God" e.g. "For this is the **love of God**, that we keep His commandments", or "He that ruleth over men must be just, ruling in the **fear of God**."

Hence phrases like "faith of God" will, depending on context, mean 'faith *from* God', 'faith *regarding* God' or 'faith *toward* God'.

Note the way such 'Faith' teachers clutch at a handful of verses and resolutely ignore all the others on the same topic. The universe was created not by the "force of faith" but by God's own power: "The heavens are the **work** of **Thy hands**" (Psa. 102:25), and "**He** hath made the earth **by His power**" (Jer .10:12). God, who "**by** His **strength** setteth fast the mountains" (Psa. 65:6), has no need to be subservient to some mystical other force! (See also Gen. 2:4b, Deut. 3:24, Psa. 8:3a, Isa. 64:8 etc). The following will also help to settle the question:

> "For thus saith **the LORD** that created the heavens; God **Himself** that formed the earth and made it; **He** hath established it ... I am the LORD; and **there is none else**" (Isa. 45:18).

It is *God*, not "faith in our faith", which is our fortress. It is *God*, not some "formula" we can employ, or "force of faith" we manipulate, that is our strong tower. *God*, not some mysterious set of spiritual laws, is our Deliverer from the enemy. The *Lord* is our shield and defence; it is nothing of ourselves. We just walk humbly with Him and He keeps us.

(People often read the wonderful promises in Psalm 91 but neglect to notice the prerequisite for them. Those pledges of protection are made to those who "**dwell** in the secret place of the Most High", that "**abide** under the shadow of the Almighty", not who master some technique. We need to look to *God*, not to ourselves or some impersonal power source. As 2 Sam. 22:33 has it, "**God** is my strength and power".)

19:6 VISUALISE THIS   Many churches now teach that, by visualising what we ask for, we can obtain it - depending on our powers of visualisation. But this is to have faith in one's *self*; i.e. faith in one's own ability to conjure up and maintain realistic images, rather than holding a simple, childlike trust in *God*.

There is a very big difference between 'visualising something into being', and having the 'eye of faith'. (The latter is where God has confirmed to someone that their petition has been accepted by Him, and thus their view of the world is changed by His promise.) In the same way, there is a huge gap between a person who is resting in the knowledge that the Lord has heard and accepted their request and will bring it about in due time, and the person who is striving to create an answer by force of will or effort.

A favourite Bible passage used to support visualisation is Genesis 30:37-39. Here, cows gave birth to "streaked, speckled and spotted" calves after being made to gaze on rods of wood that had been marked with streaks. But do these few verses really teach Christians to use visualisation?...

(1) These lone verses are unlikely to be the sole representatives of a truth that is supposedly so vital to our Christian lives. There surely ought to

be more, and clearer, precedents if visualisation is so fundamental to our prayers?[1]

(2) The differences between this passage and the teaching from the 'Faith' movement on visualisation are very striking. For example, it was the *Master* of the herd who created the streaks - whereas 'Faith' teachers tell us to generate *our own* 'image'. Furthermore, it was the *Master* of the herd who controlled the presence of the streaked wood – whereas *we* are meant to be the ones in control of our 'images'. Finally, it was the *Master's* will which was only ever in view in the passage – the animals had no real choice at all. Whereas, in visualisation, we are taught to decide for ourselves what *we* want.

(3) The practice of gazing at images, whether mental or otherwise, for some mystical purpose, is a thoroughly pagan activity. We are to meditate on God's Word, or His attributes, or His deeds, but meditating on *images* - whether of God or anything else - is *nowhere* encouraged in Scripture. In fact it is roundly indicted (e.g. in Exod. 20:4-5; Lev. 26:1&27-32; Deut. 4:15-26; Deut.16:22; and Ezek. 6:6-7).

The "streaked" wood is an allusion to, or 'prefigure' of, the cross of Christ. The point of the passage is that, if Christians focus on the wooden cross (which our Master streaked with His own blood), and if they always keep in mind what He did for us on it, then they will bear Christ-like fruit.

Please note: When we use the word 'visualisation' here we are not referring to passively picturing some non-religious item or scene (e.g. remembering a happy holiday or solving an engineering problem through imagining it spatially). We are instead referring to any attempt to visualise spiritual beings as part of a religious act, or attempting to change physical reality directly through the power of thought. So, redesigning a bedroom in your mind's eye is fine, but trying – for instance - to heal yourself through thought-power is not.

Worryingly, and on several occasions, Nicky encourages Alpha's guests to visualise Jesus. (He even shows a painting of Him, complete with halo.) In reality, such acts are demonic, not scriptural. Shamans get results

---

[1] The only other verse we know of which is used in support of visualization is Proverbs 23:7. But, when read in context, the meaning is rather different: "Eat thou not the bread of **him that hath an evil eye** ...: For as **he** thinketh in his heart, so is he" (vv6-7a). This passage deals with a specific situation. People can bring curses on themselves through evil thoughts, but this passage plainly does not teach that we can be *blessed through visualization*.

because they are operating in Satan's ways and so access the enemy's help and power. Christians may also obtain results from visualisation - for the very same reason. Satan loves to reward people for straying from God's ordinances – although any such 'reward' is always accompanied by a greater curse. (A family friend visited the 'Marian shrine' at Walsingham and was healed of her neuralgia only to have it replaced by a most vicious form of M.S. which left her blind.)

It is rightly sobering and humbling to realise that neither our faith nor our prayers have any *intrinsic* power. God alone has all the power. The only 'positive thoughts' which achieve truly positive results are those about the Lord's greatness, faithfulness, goodness etc.

19:7 GOD IS SOVEREIGN   God is *God*. He is the ruler of the Universe and does as He pleases (Eccl. 8:2-8, Psa. 115:3). We are His (unprofitable) servants and we exist for His pleasure, not the other way around. We do *not* deserve *any* blessings from Him. He is perfectly at liberty to withhold things from us for whatever reason He likes - and not only for the good of His Name and Kingdom. See, for example, Romans 9:20-21 and Job 2:10. So to teach that the Most High God is ever *obliged* to do things for us is a serious error, because it demeans God and instead exalts man.

Out of His *mercy* God has made some wonderful promises to those who *fear* Him (as opposed to those who think He is somehow at their beck and call) but we cannot *make* Him do anything. We are not our own, we are *His* property (1 Cor. 6:19-20). It is vanity to believe that we can claim "rights" or manipulate God, yet these are exactly the things being taught by the 'Faith' movement. Its leaders deny God's sovereignty by teaching that, through utilizing certain spiritual laws, we can actually "write our own ticket with God" (as Kenneth Hagin Snr. put it[2]). But, as other ministries have observed, God is no bellhop, despite Kenneth Copeland's claim that "As a believer, you have the **right** to make **commands** ... Each time you stand on the Word you are **commanding** God".[3]

> "Thou art worthy, O Lord, to receive glory and honour and power: for **Thou** hast **created all things** [including us!], and **for Thy pleasure** they are and were created" (Rev. 4:11).

---

[2] Hank Hanegraaff, *Christianity in Crisis*, (Nelson Word, 1995), pp74-75. (We cannot endorse Hank's ministry however. See our Recommended Reading section for several reasons.)
[3] *Christianity in Crisis*, (hereafter 'C in C'), p384 fn 58.

> "Sing forth the honour of His Name: make His praise glorious. Say unto God, How terrible art Thou in Thy works! ... **He ruleth by His power for ever** ... [L]et **not** the rebellious **exalt** themselves" (Psa. 66:2-7).

19:8 HEALTH INSURED?   Two of the "rights" we are supposed to be able to demand are health and wealth. God undoubtedly likes to prosper us in this life (although it is crucial to remember that prospering can take forms other than material ones). But the Lord is far more interested in our *eternal* welfare - and that of those around us - than in our temporal conditions. So, when these interests clash, it is *spiritual* health and wealth which will take precedence. An obvious example is the rich young man in Matt. 19:20-24. This principle is confirmed again and again in Scripture in the lives of even the greatest heroes of the faith – including those living under the Abrahamic Covenant on which the 'Faith' teachers focus so heavily - like Moses, David and Elisha.

Let us look primarily at sickness for a minute. The man in John 9 who was born blind shows that God has purposes for sickness well beyond chastising our sins. He may use it, for example, to glorify Himself (as in this case and also with Lazarus), or to bring the gospel (as he did through Paul's illness – see Gal 4:13), or to prove us (as He did with Job), or to educate us (as He did with Timothy). For some strange reason, God neglected to tell *any* of these servants to "positively confess" their healing!

Although it is entirely appropriate to proclaim my healing in faith - if God has *specifically* promised it to me – it is nevertheless presumptuous for me to do so otherwise. Is there anyone among us who would not benefit from further sanctification or additional humility or greater reliance on God – all of which He may choose to achieve through affliction (as He did with Jacob)? Certainly it is true that God "doth not afflict **willingly**" (Lam. 3:33) but neither will He hesitate to if it will benefit His Kingdom.

Stripes

Certain teachers hang on to the part-verse "with His stripes we are healed" as proof that, through the Lord's sufferings, none of us ever need experience any illness. But the context in both Isaiah 53:5-6 *and* 1 Peter 2:24-25 (plus the Lord's respective choice of *figurative* Hebrew and Greek words for "healed"), shows that it is healing *spiritually* which the Lord's suffering achieved:

"He was wounded for our **transgressions**, He was bruised for our **iniquities**: the **chastisement of our peace** was upon Him" (Isa. 53:5).

Even a peremptory reading of 1 Peter 2:24-25 will substantiate this. It is our *alienation from God*, due to our fallen nature, which has been healed by Christ. Other passages which refer to the "healing" of our *souls* - rather than our bodies - include Jeremiah 17:14 and 51:8-9; also:

"Thine **iniquity** is taken away, and thy **sin** purged ... Make the heart of this people fat, and make their ears heavy, and shut their eyes; lest they ... **convert**, and be **healed**" (Isa. 6:8-10). See also Mark 2:17.

But what about Matthew 8:16-17, where Christ healed *all* that were brought to Him "that it might be fulfilled ... Himself took our **infirmities**, and bare our **sicknesses**"? Surely this passage disproves our claims above? Actually, it serves to confirm them, because all the people in the Matthew 8 passage were *demoniacs* – i.e. they were sick as a result of demonic activity which had come in through sin. Hence, when they were delivered of their demons (i.e. were *spiritually* healed), the resulting sicknesses were removed too. Sicknesses that have been given *to reflect sinful activity* will obviously disappear, through Christ, if the sinfulness in question has been properly repented of.[4]

Other Favourites

Certainly God heals. But over-dependence, for example, on God's promise made to physical Israel, to "put none of these diseases upon thee, which I have brought upon the Egyptians" (Exo. 15:16) is unwise. This is partly because the promise was conditional on God's People observing the many strict hygiene regulations and dietary laws that God had laid down, as well as keeping "**all** His statutes". But we must also recognise that "none of **these** diseases" does not equate to "no diseases at all".

---

[4] If a person is afflicted due to spiritual wrongdoing then they can be spiritually healed through Christ. That, for example, is how generational curses can be broken. We can be healed of these by renouncing the cause and trusting in Christ Jesus for deliverance. Hence the promise in Jer. 31:29-30, repeated in Ezek. 18:2-3, that there would come a time when generational curses need not be 'put up with'. Provided we *take advantage of* the spiritual healing that we can obtain through Christ's cross, then we can be set free from any sickness resulting from such curses.

(Note: Those who exploit this text are often the same people who normally refuse to listen to doctrinal statements based on "Old Testament" verses! Likewise they make much of Psalm 103:2-3 which says: "Bless the LORD, O my **soul**, and forget not all His benefits: Who forgiveth all thine **iniquities**; Who healeth all thy diseases". But David is addressing his *soul*; it is diseases *of the soul* which are in view (as in Deut. 28:28, Matt. 4:24 etc). The surrounding verses are not about the physical body, but are instead all about redemption, righteousness, judgment and sins – i.e. the soul – hence the mention above of forgiveness. The soul is forgiven, not the body.[5])

If we are suffering, then first of all we should *thank* God: "In **every** thing give thanks: for this is the will of God in Christ Jesus" (1 Thess 5:18, Eph 5:20), and we should stand on God's Word which says "**all things** work together for good to them that love God" (Rom. 8:28a). We should seek God for insight into the cause. Then we are in a position to pray sensibly. At no point do we *command* Him!

Paul

Paul's "thorn in the flesh" is an excellent example of this. The 'Faith' teachers have to belittle Paul by claiming that he was given the thorn because of sin, i.e. he was "**very prone** to brag"[6] (a somewhat hypocritical statement in view of the boastful remarks given by some of these teachers about themselves – see later). The truth is that Paul lived a thankful life; learned ("in whatsoever state" he was in) "to be content" (Php. 4:11); had the wisdom to grasp the reason for his thorn and, despite praying three times for its removal, got a "negative" response. Please note how his testimony contrasts totally with the 'Faith' message.

> "And **lest** I should be exalted above measure **through** the **abundance of the revelations**, there was given to me a thorn in the flesh, the messenger of Satan to buffet me ... For this thing I besought the Lord thrice, that it might depart from me. And He said unto me, **My grace is sufficient** for thee: for My strength is **made perfect** in **weakness**. Most **gladly** therefore will I rather glory in **my infirmities**, that the **power of Christ** may rest upon me. Therefore I take **pleasure** in **infirmities**, in reproaches, in

---

[5] If the passage *does* relate to any bodily diseases – again the word also means 'infirmities' - then it refers to those diseases which are suffered *as a result of iniquities*. As the passage implies, these will be healed when the person is forgiven that sin.

[6] Fred Price, *C in C*, p405, chap. 23 fn6. (Price is a protégé of Hagin and is an alumni of Hagin's Rhema Bible Institute).

necessities, in persecutions, in **distresses** for Christ's sake: **for when** I am **weak,** then am I **strong**" (2 Cor. 12:7-10).

For a 'Faith' teacher to say, as one of them has, things like "we don't allow sickness in our home"[7] is: (a) unbiblical, (b) boastful, and (c) untrue - that man's own wife sadly developing cancer. Even if the 'Faith' doctrine were correct, i.e. that God only gives ill-health to those who are in sin, the above claim would mean that no-one in that household ever sins... yet, according to 1 John 1:8-10, we *all* do!

Christians can undoubtedly get miracles from the 'Faith' formula. But, as noted, this only works (as with the anti-Christian movements which use the very same techniques) because the enemy is perfectly happy to use his resources if they will beguile people and draw them away from the truth. He loves to tempt us with pleasant, temporal things if it will encourage us to subject ourselves to him - just as he managed with Eve and tried to do with the Lord Jesus Christ. But "what is a man profited, if he shall gain the whole **world**, and lose his own soul?" (Matt. 16:26).

Tragically, people are also losing their *lives* by their determination to insist on their "right" to healing. While Hagin taught that "**no** believer should ever be sick",[8] and "that's the way I pray: 'I **demand** my **rights!**'",[9] the faithful followers of this idea are dying because they are ignoring their symptoms instead of seeking God over the cause of those symptoms. Returning to Alpha, Nicky unwisely teaches his hearers that "God **promises** healing to his People".[10] Later in the talk he strongly intimates that the sole reason that "not **all** are healed" is because "the Age to come is ... not **fully** realised" – even though this implies that God is unfair and/or limited.

The notion that health is our *right* - and thus that we only need to believe strongly enough that we are healed for it to come to pass - is simply not borne out in the lives of the men and women of great faith in Scripture, including those who *wrote* the scriptures. No wonder the proponents of the "name it and claim it" doctrine have to make themselves out to be better and more "anointed" than Job or David or Hezekiah or Paul. Indeed, the primary message of the Book of Job is that no man, however faithful, upright, and godly he is, deserves *any* good thing. Rather, we *all* deserve the torments of Job. We rely entirely on God's grace even for our very breath. We fool

---

[7] Fred Price, *C in C*, p237.
[8] *C in C*, p248.
[9] *C in C*, p406 fn2.
[10] Talk 13.

ourselves if we think we deserve anything but Hell - even as believers. It is only thanks to the Lord's kindness that we ever get blessings (Lam. 3:22-23). God, purely out of His *goodness*, gives His saints *spiritual and mental* health, but not necessarily *physical*!

19:9 REAL REPENTANCE?   Before we mention any other elements which comprise this "diversity" of teaching, there is one important point to make. As a direct result of many people beginning to 'wise-up' to these falsehoods and starting to expose them, the proponents of this gospel have used a number of tactics to minimise damage to their influence and income:

- One favourite ruse of these leaders is to claim that they have been "mis-quoted". But they have often had their messages taped, and the evidence is there for all to hear.[11]

- A second explanation given is that these folks have been "quoted out of context". However, (a) it is hard to think of ANY context in which most of their quoted remarks would be reasonable, (b) these 'out of context' teachings all fit neatly together into a complete (albeit false) gospel, and (c) again, the tapes are available for all to hear; the context of the quotes is unchallengeable – which is presumably why we have never heard any of the names we focus on here attempt to prove their claim.

- For those 'teachers' who know that the above excuses won't ring true, but who cannot bring themselves to admit they were wrong and thus lose face (and finance), the strategy has been to claim that they have now "come to a deeper understanding" of matters. The problem is that their previous teachings were not true at *any* depth. They were not superficial, they were plain *wrong*.

- The last group comprises those who have apologised. But, regrettably, and despite the harm that their teachings have done to many thousands of people, they seem consistently to have given the *minimum* apology they felt they could get away with. Their followers are adamant that these teachers have repented, but all of the apologies fall *far* short of *biblical* repentance...

  Rather than make any restitution for the money they have cajoled from people (like Zacchaeus did), they appear to have simply replaced their Rolls Royces with fractionally less luxurious cars. Rather than replace

---

[11] All quotes are thoroughly documented and cross-referenced in the sources we cite.

their past falsehoods with the *truth*, they have simply toned them down. Some have invented new falsehoods or have merely switched focus and now concentrate on other aspects of the same "gospel". Some have even carried on with no change (except for the 'security' personnel who now frisk people at the door prior to those meetings they don't want anyone to tape).

Note that, despite having proved all too fallible, these same people continue to insist that their pronouncements are never to be questioned and that they themselves are above any criticism.

19:10 WANT WEALTH?   Financial want is another tool used by God not only to bring correction but also to purify us and teach us - and enable us to relate to the poor. The Lord wants to see if we love Him or Mammon. (Both Luke 16:11 and Rev. 2:8 show that **"true"** riches" are *not* material.) Regrettably, all the 'Faith' teachers show an inordinate love of unrighteous Mammon, and their covetousness - and encouragement of it in others - is as unbiblical as it is offensive. Compare:

> "You can talk to me all you want while I'm **driving by in my Rolls Royce that's paid for** ... talk all you want ... Doesn't bother me";[12] and "The reason why I drive a **Rolls Royce**; [is] I'm following Jesus' steps".[13]
>
> with:
>
> "Let your conversation be **without** covetousness; and **be content with such things as ye have**" (Heb. 13:5). See also Eph. 5:5.
>
> and:
>
> "Take **heed**, and **beware** of covetousness: for a man's life consisteth **not** in the abundance of the things which he possesseth" (Luke 12:15). See also Exod. 20:17 &.
>
> and:
>
> "**Love not** the world, neither the **things that are in the world**. If any man love the world, the love of the Father is **not** in him. For all that is in the world, the lust of the flesh, and the lust of the eyes, and the pride of life, is **not** of the Father, but is of the world" (1 John 2:15-16). See also Prov. 17:5.
>
> and:
>
> "They that **will** [i.e. desire to] be rich fall into **temptation** and a **snare**, and into **many** foolish and hurtful lusts, which **drown** men in **destruction and perdition**. For the love of **money** is the

---

[12] Fred Price, *C in C*, p191. Price is a protégé of Hagin and is an alumnus of Hagin's Rhema Bible Institute.
[13] Fred Price, *C in C*, p187.

root of **all evil**: which while some **coveted after**, they have **erred from the faith**, and pierced themselves through with many sorrows" (1 Tim. 6:9-10). See also 1 Tim. 6:17a.

Despite the efforts of the 'Faith' teachers to prove otherwise, Christ was *not* materially rich. He was "meek and lowly" and wanted people to be attracted by His *character* and *message* rather than by any wealth or other outward attractiveness – hence His 'working-class' profession and His very humble background.

Just because Christ Jesus possessed one decent garment does not prove that He "wore designer clothes" as some have taught.[14] Indeed the episode with the "very costly" ointment shows that Christ's disciples were *not* used to Him having expensive things (see Mark 14:3-8). Again, the idea that Christ was wealthy makes a mockery of His conversation with the rich young man - and would make many of His other statements, e.g. where He teaches people not to lay up treasures on earth, *very* hypocritical (see Matt. 6:19-21 and 25-34).

Even the Alpha Course implies that Christ was outwardly attractive. Nicky says, with seemingly deliberate ambiguity - but without providing any scriptural proof:

> "Jesus on earth was so **attractive** ... he was magnetic, so the church of Jesus Christ, His body now on earth, should be **so attractive** that people are drawn to it" [Talk 14].

Whereas a more accurate statement of how the world actually saw Jesus is:

> "He hath **no** form nor comeliness; and when we shall see Him, there is **no** beauty that we should desire Him. He is **despised** and **rejected** of men; a man of sorrows, and acquainted with grief: and we **hid** as it were our faces from Him; He was **despised**, and we esteemed Him **not**" (Isa. 53:2-3).

Jesus on earth was so 'magnetic' that he was cast away by the world and put to an horrific death before He had even reached the age of 34.

---

[14] John Avanzini, *C in C*, pp187,208. (Avanzini taught this on *Copeland's* 'Believer's Voice of Victory' TV program.) Why would the Lord Jesus say "behold, they that wear soft [i.e. costly] clothing are in **kings' houses**" (Matt. 11:8) if he too wore such clothes?

The 'Faith' teachers, apparently determined to convince us that, as one of them put it, "being poor is a **sin**",[15] and intent on promoting self-indulgence rather than self-control, turn their attention to Paul. They claim he *must* have been rich because his captor, Felix, hoped "that money should have been given him of [i.e. from] Paul, that he might loose him" (Acts 24:26), but:

- In the preceding verse, Paul is reported as standing for *temperance* - not excess wealth. Paul also pointed out that, for the sake of Christ, he had "suffered the **loss** of **all** things" (Php. 3:8-9),
- Felix knew of Paul's huge influence among Christians. No wonder Felix imagined that money could be obtained for his release. Remember that Paul had previously passed on substantial offerings from one church to another and was in Jerusalem to do that very thing again (v17),
- Paul's standard sufferings do not exactly suggest wealth. He spent His walk: "In weariness and painfulness, in watchings often, in **hunger** and **thirst** ... in **cold** and **nakedness**" (2 Cor. 11:27; see also Php. 3:10-21; and 2 Cor. 6:4),
- Paul sometimes lacked necessities (2 Cor. 6:4) and was known as being "**poor**, ... [and] as having **nothing**" (v10).[16]
- While we're on the subject of the apostles, Acts 3:6 hardly indicates that *Peter* was 'rolling in it' either.

Now, it is true that God promised to bless Abraham and his seed, and to "multiply" Abraham. Scripture also says that "if ye be Christ's, then are ye Abraham's seed, and heirs according to the promise" (Gal. 3:29). The 'Faith' teachers argue that we are therefore entitled to tremendous material prosperity - just like Abraham enjoyed. But there are major faults with this rationale:

The most obvious flaw here is that Abraham's physical blessings translate into *spiritual* ones in the Church – we are *spiritual* heirs. But another problem is that physical riches were never part of the Abrahamic **_Covenant_**. In other words, God gave Abraham wealth but never *promised* it to him. The *promised* blessing was that: **(1)** God would give Abraham a (miraculous) son, **(2)** God would, through Abranham's seed, make a *nation* arise (hence the word "multiply"), **(3)** God would make sure that Abraham's offspring would ultimately possess a homeland forever, and **(4)** the Lord

---

[15] Robert Tilton, *C in C*, pp186,214.
[16] Since it is impossible for Paul to have possessed "**all** [*material*] things", his references in the rest of this verse to 'making many rich' and 'possessing all things' must refer to *spiritual*, rather than physical, wealth.

would "be their God" (see Gen. 17:1-8 and Hebrews. 6:14-15). Abraham's physical prosperity was incidental - he was rich well before God made the Covenant. Below is the *actual* reward for Abraham's faith:

"The word of the LORD came unto Abram in a vision, saying ...
I am thy shield, and thy **exceeding great reward**" (Gen. 15:1).

We believers do indeed share in Abraham's *promised* blessing, for God has given *mankind* a miraculous Son – the Son of Man (Acts 13:23; Gal. 3:19), and, through Him, a nation has been multiplied (Acts 6:7; Eph. 3:6). We will eventually inherit an eternal homeland (2 Pet. 3:13-14; Heb. 9:14-15). And the Lord is our God. The text in Hebrews 11:8-16 puts it all together.

We have undeniably all been given "exceeding great and precious promises" upon which we can stand. But they are *spiritual* promises, not temporal. They are: the promise of the Holy Spirit (Eph. 1:13; Luke 24:49); the promise of ultimate salvation (Acts 2:37-39; Heb. 10:34-39); and the promise of eternal life... "And **this** is the promise that He hath promised us, even **eternal life**" (1 John 2:25), whereas Nicky ambiguously promises us "all the riches of heaven"[17] and will only go so far as to say "There's no **guarantee** in Scripture that **every** prayer for an **Aston Martin** ... will **necessarily** be answered".[18]

According to God's Word, if we are not to be resurrected then we true Christians are "of **all** men most **miserable**" (1 Cor. 15:19). Why would we be the *most* miserable of *all* men if we can enjoy guaranteed health and wealth in this life?! There would be no reason for Paul to say this if the church was designed to live in material prosperity.

19:11 SOWING DISCORD   Now to the famous "seed-faith" principle whereby, so the 'Faith' teachers claim, we can assist our faith for material things by sowing materially - ideally by sending money to these very same teachers. Is this a concept *really* taught throughout Scripture? Certainly it is true that "they that plow **iniquity**, and sow **wickedness**, reap the same" (Job 4:8), and the Lord promises: "Sow to yourselves in **righteousness**, reap in **mercy**" (Hosea 10:12) but these are *spiritual* promises. If we sow anything into the Kingdom of God we will gain an hundredfold *spiritually*, but not necessarily materially. We should not sow for *worldly* gain but for spiritual:

---

[17] Talk 3.
[18] Talk 6.

> "Be not deceived; God is not mocked: for whatsoever a man soweth, that shall he also reap. For he that soweth to his **flesh** shall of the **flesh** reap **corruption**; but he that soweth to the **Spirit** shall of the Spirit **reap life everlasting**" (Gal. 6:7-8).

Some readers may well disagree with us, on the basis of 2 Cor. 9:6 - which states, in the context of financial offerings, that "he which soweth sparingly shall also reap sparingly; and he which soweth bountifully shall also reap bountifully". It is true that if we sow faithfully then we will gain reward *in heaven* (vv9-10), and we *can* expect to have sufficient resources to live and function as Christians. Unfortunately, the 'Faith' movement goes well beyond this, yet Paul never says that the reaping shall be *financial* – or even of a material nature at all.

If the reaping is indeed financial, how do we explain that the very person who wrote about this principle was himself financially "poor" (as we noted in some detail in the preceding section of this book)? How likewise are we to explain the "deep poverty" of the church in Macedonia if it was as godly as Paul makes out in the chapter immediately preceding this one (see vv1-2)? And how do we explain too the "poverty" of the church in Smyrna which God praises in Rev. 2:8-10? In fact, how do we explain all the other biblical points we have made so far on this subject? (We are not saying that all true Christians will inevitably be poor, but that there is no *guarantee* in Scripture that they will prosper financially either.)

Paul does *not* say that what we reap will be of the same *type* as the thing we have sown - else would he not be telling us to give to the kingdom for *material* reward? This would be a very shallow reason, at odds with the rest of the New Testament! Indeed, Paul says that the 'things' reaped are of a *spiritual* nature – we reap God's *love* (v7), and God's *mercy* (v8). Note too that this love and mercy may very well not be manifested in a material form at all. If we give materially, and thereby show faith in God, we will abound in the spiritual qualities listed in the preceding Chapter (see 8:7). In fact, the whole of this epistle is devoted to urging the church *not* to look for *earthly* wealth, but *spiritual* (see, for example, 4:16-18; 5:6; 11:8-9; and 11:27).

Some readers will want to point to Mark 10:29-30 at this stage:

> "Jesus answered and said, Verily I say unto you, There is no man that hath left house, or brethren, or sisters, or father, or mother, or wife, or children, or lands, for my sake, and the gospel's, But he

shall receive an hundredfold now in this time, houses, and **brethren**, and sisters, and **mothers**, and children, and lands, with **persecutions**; and in the world to come eternal life."

On the surface this does indeed seem to say that we shall, in this life, reap an hundredfold of whatever we sow. But, apart from all the verses we have already looked at which undermine this idea, there are other major problems with it. For a start, people do not inherit a hundred mothers in this life, so this passage cannot be speaking of what we think. (We only receive these things in the sense of becoming members of the worldwide Church which should have "all things in common".) Secondly, the reaping will be achieved through suffering "persecutions" – again not something the Word-Faith movement acknowledges!

(If the reader knows any Bible passages not specifically addressed in this book which appear to support the teachings we are arguing against, we urge them to double-check whether the passage comprises part of the ambiguous minority of evidence which God always supplies to cause those who do not love the truth to "believe a lie" (2 Thess. 2:10). New Testament references to becoming "rich" either refer to <u>spiritual</u> wealth or to material riches <u>after the Lord's return</u>. Certainly the Bible says that we can expect to "prosper" in this life, but it is <u>spiritual</u> prospering. Was Christ prospering physically on the cross? Hardly. Was Stephen physically prospering as he was being stoned to death? No.)

The promoters of the "prosperity" gospel seem continually to be inventing new and ever more imaginative ways of wheedling money out of their followers. And they will readily play on the guilt, gullibility or greed of anyone who will listen to them. For example, "If you neglect to pay attention" to one 'Faith' teacher's direct mailing for money, "then Satan will take advantage and hit you with bad things". Another rockhard-sell has been to claim that God was going to *take the life* of a particular 'Faith' teacher if his followers did not send him enough money.[19] But if the 'hundredfold' passage is true, why do these men not simply have faith in God to fulfil His promise rather than become so desperate that they resort to conning it out of others?

Some 'Faith' teachers claim they only seek money so that they can give to the poor. If that is true, why not simply let the poor sow and reap a hundredfold for themselves? Note the way in which the 'Faith' movement

---

[19] Oral Roberts, *C in C*, pp196-197. Copeland, Hagin and Hinn all cite Roberts as a significant influence on their ministries.

simultaneously teaches that 'being poor is a sin' – which may explain why they invariably keep the money for themselves rather than giving it to the poor. Such a teaching greatly discourages hearers from giving material help to needy brothers or sisters in the Lord – i.e. exactly the group which God's Word calls us to care for most of all![20]

> "Hath not God chosen the **poor** of this world rich in **faith**,[21] and heirs of the kingdom ...? But ye have **despised** the poor. ...If ye fulfil the royal law according to the scripture, Thou shalt love thy neighbour as thyself, ye do well: But if ye have **respect to persons**, ye commit **sin**"(James 2:5b-9a)

'Faith' teachers are adamant that gaining riches and worldly success implies godliness. Yet not even the most faithful believer is instantly perfect in every way; there are always things the Lord wants to improve in each of us. Hence, while He may bring correction for *sin*, He also does likewise for *sanctification* – i.e. even among those who are walking closely with Him. Thus the state of not outwardly 'prospering' can actually be a sign that God is moving a true disciple on in Him (see 2 Cor. 4:16-17). For instance, Rev. 2:10 indicates that the Lord allows righteous saints around the world to be put in prison, not to punish them for some sin or other, but simply to test and sanctify them - or to bring the gospel to those interned with them.

> "**All** that will live **godly** in Christ Jesus **shall** suffer persecution" (2 Tim. 3:12), and "We must through **much** tribulation enter into the Kingdom of God" (Acts 14:22).

As a result of the shameless scams of the 'Faith' apostles, the world is disgusted by - and *seriously* put off from - Christianity. And it laughs at us believers for allowing them to make merchandise of us. The Bible has some things to say about such teachers:

> "If any man ... consent not to ... the doctrine which is according to **godliness**; He is **proud**, knowing **nothing**, ... **supposing** that **gain** is godliness" (1 Tim. 6:3-5); "For there are many ... **vain** talkers ... teaching things ... for **filthy lucre's** sake" (Titus 1:10-11).

> "There shall be **false** teachers among you ... and **many** shall follow their pernicious ways; by reason of whom the way of truth shall be **evil spoken of**. And through **covetousness** shall they with feigned words **make merchandise of you**" (2 Pet. 2:1-3).

---

[20] See chapter 12 of our "Unofficial Guide" for more on this.
[21] Note how it is the *poor* who develop the most faith. You need much less faith if you are rich!

Unfortunately, the Alpha Course too implies that Christianity will bring a person temporal success. This is always an easier road than talking about things like salvation from an eternity in the lake of fire and the cost of walking with God. (The cost includes temporal *sacrifice* and *suffering* - and trouble and distress and rejection. See 2 Tim. 2:9-13, Php. 1:29, 2 Thess. 1:4-5, Rom. 8:16-18, Acts 14:21-22, John 16:33 & 15:19-20). Nicky says:

> "Our land desperately needs Jesus Christ … for marriages to be restored, for families to be reunited, for people to be healed".[22]

But he is missing the point. Our land desperately needs the Lord Jesus Christ because its people are currently *on their way to Hell*.

HTB is always promoting Alpha on the basis that, through it, 'God changes lives'. The changes touted always seem to be ones where the main change is temporal. In other words, Alpha is promoted as being able to help you with your health or wealth, your relationships and so on. But salvation is a far more important change God wants to make, and He may well bring a *deterioration* in your temporal circumstances for the sake of His Kingdom. Paul's circumstances remained humble - i.e. he remained a tent-maker.

(Please Note: One reason we use inverted commas when referring to the 'Faith' movement is that the reason these people want to be wealthy is because they LACK true faith. They don't have faith that God will supply their needs in a timely fashion, so they want to store up money in the bank instead of having a simple trust that God will give them what they truly require when they truly require it. They also reveal their lack of true faith in God when they use bodyguards in place of God.)

19:12 BE SPECIFIC   The 'Faith' teachers call for great specifics in our prayers – before we have even asked the Lord for His view. We should, apparently, decide in detail exactly what we want, then proclaim it until it becomes real. The obvious problem is that specifics in prayers imply we always know what's best, which is often not true. Might this explain the large number of less-than-specific prayers from men of great faith recorded in Scripture?

> "My thoughts are **not your** thoughts, **neither** are your ways My ways, saith the LORD" (Isa. 55:9). See also Eccl. 11:5.

---

[22] Talk 6.

"We know **not** what we should pray for" (Rom. 8:26).

For example, it is reasonable to ask God for 'the right partner', but who am I to say what *is* right for me? How many times have we come up with our own 'solution' to a need, only to discover that the Lord had a much better and wiser way? Why not let the Lord glorify Himself by allowing *Him* to decide what is best for us?

Christ Jesus did say, in John 14:14, "If ye shall ask **any** thing in My Name, I will do it." But:

(a) He was talking about extremely Christlike believers (see vv12 and 16) who had unwavering faith in Him, *and* were led by His Spirit;
(b) He twice said that the 'thing' requested must be asked for in His "Name" - which does not merely mean ending a prayer with the words "in Jesus' Name" but requires that the prayer be completely compatible with Christ's *character* – and thus His will; and
(c) He made clear elsewhere that we should seek *God's* will for our lives (see below for proof of this).

We *must* get into the habit of interpreting individual verses on a subject in the light of all the others on that subject. That is not to deny that there is a place for specific prayer; but this is possible only *after* we have come to know the *will of God* in the matter, through seeking Him diligently, and then only if He chooses to reveal His will to us. But this is not the same thing at all as the "name it and claim it" type of prayer. We can speak *curses* into our lives, but it does NOT follow that we can speak blessings into them too. *God* decides who to bless, and when, and how.

19:13 THY WILL BE DONE   The Lord Jesus Christ, when praying about His approaching beatings and crucifixion, repeatedly asked the Father to countermand His request if it was not His Father's will: **"If it be possible, let this cup pass from Me: nevertheless not as I will, but as Thou wilt"** (Matt. 26:39), **"Thy will** be done" (v42), "And He left them ... and prayed the third time, saying the **same** words" (v44). The Lord knew that it does *not* show a lack of faith in God to include an "if it be Thy will" in statements and prayers. Rather, it is showing real submission to God. It says that our wishes are subordinate to His.

Similarly, Paul wrote to the Corinthians: "But I will come to you shortly, **if the Lord will**", and "I trust to tarry a while with you, **if the Lord**

permit" (1 Cor. 4:19 and 16:7, see also Rom. 15:30-32). Paul knew that, unlike Christ, we mortals are far from infallible and that, unless the Lord has clearly prophesied an aspect of our future, we do not know what will happen in our lives. A quote to debunk the "health and wealth" teaching here is:

> "Ye that say, To day or to morrow we will ... [do this and that] and get **gain**: Whereas **ye know not** what shall be on the morrow ... [Y]e **ought** to say, **If the Lord will**, we shall live, and do this, or that. But now **ye rejoice in your boastings**: all such rejoicing is **evil**" (James 4:13-16). See also Prov. 27:1.

Unfortunately this all goes against the grain of the 'Faith' doctrine which says that you *must* have "faith in your faith"[23] and "speak into being" the things you desire.[24] So its proponents demand that we "**never, ever, ever** go to the Lord and say, 'If it be thy will...'".[25]

The problem is that we are prone to ask for things that are not God's will for us. And if we are *adamant*, then He may well give us over to them to suffer the consequences. Israel did exactly that when they asked for a King. It was an evil request (1 Sam. 12:19-20) and God said "they have rejected Me, that I should not reign over them". But, when they insisted, God gave them it. Hezekiah made a similar mistake when he prayed for a longer life without seeking God's will. The result was the birth of Israel's most depraved king (Manasseh). We must be careful not to overlook God's will and supplant it with our own ideas of what is best for us. Regardless of how much faith we have, if we are praying outside God's will then we are sinning and we will *not* prosper in the long run.

As we have seen, the 'Faith' teachers contend that it is our "faith in faith" which gets the results, so we can demand whatever we like. The Bible says *precisely* the opposite:

> "And this is the confidence that we have in **Him**, that, if we **ask** any thing **according to His** will, He heareth us. And **if** we know that **He hear us** ... we know that we have the **petitions** that we desired **of Him**" (I John 5:14-15).

---

23 Kenneth Hagin, *C in C*, p74.

24 Yonggi Cho, *C in C*, p84. Nicky is a big fan of Cho, who has spoken at HTB. See for instance *The Heart of Revival*, pp181-2, and *Challenging Lifestyle*, p157. Nicky encourages a similar mindset when he instructs us to TELL God "I now receive your forgiveness" [Talk 1; see also Talk 10] or to say "Thank you that you offer ... the gift of your Holy Spirit. I now receive that gift" [*Why Jesus?*, p18; see also Talk 3].

25 Benny Hinn, *C in C*, p11.

Christ's "negative", but righteous, confession that He would suffer and be killed was followed by Peter's "positive", but foolish, confession that these things would not happen (see Matt. 16:21-26). This led to the Lord's famous "Get thee behind Me, Satan" rebuke. Peter's mistake was to allow himself to regard "the things that be of **men**". Here is a lesson for us all, and one which occurs often in Scripture. The following is an illustration of how flawed the 'Faith' doctrine is. See if you can spot how godly the "negative confessions" are, how unhelpful the "positive confessions" are, and what the right conclusion is:

> "He took Paul's girdle, and bound his own hands and feet, and said, Thus saith the Holy Ghost, So shall the Jews at Jerusalem **bind the man that owneth this girdle, and shall deliver him into the hands of the Gentiles**. And when we heard these things, both we, and they of that place, **besought him not to go up** to Jerusalem. Then Paul answered, What mean ye to weep and to break mine heart? for I am ready not to be bound only, but also to die at Jerusalem for the name of the Lord Jesus. And when he would not be persuaded, we ceased, saying, **The will of the Lord be done**" (Acts 21:11-14).

In view of the fact that David, Paul and even Christ (among others) got "negative" replies to their prayers, consider how boastful and unbiblical the late Kenneth Hagin's words were when he said "I have not prayed **one** prayer in **45 years** ... without getting an answer - and the answer was **always** yes. Some people say, 'God always answers prayers. Sometimes he says, "Yes," and sometimes He says, "No".' I **never** read that in the Bible. That is just human reasoning".[26] Consider too that Alpha apparently has no problem with such teachers and that, according to Nicky, we should never judge them - or even criticise them.

---

[26] Hagin, *The Name of Jesus*, (Rhema, 1983), p16.

CHAPTER **20**

$\mathcal{T}$HE BIBLE'S VIEW OF GOD

20:1 THE FAITH FAILURE   According to the scriptures, God is, among many other attributes, "a mighty God and terrible", "clothed with honour and majesty", "the everlasting Father", "the only wise God". The opening sections of the previous chapter demonstrate that believers ought to fear God "greatly". But rather than do so - and "give unto the Lord the glory due unto His name" - the 'Faith' teachers take a dramatically different line. Consider the following examples:

- Kenneth Copeland announces "I was shocked when I found out who the biggest **failure** in the Bible actually is ... The biggest one in the whole Bible is **God**".[1] But God *never* fails (Zeph. 3:5)! He is Almighty and all-knowing, so He *can* never fail. Surely the *truly* shocking thing is that people follow Copeland and his failure of a god.

- Along with other 'Faith' teachers, Copeland further reveals that, when Adam sinned, God "**found Himself** in a peculiar position"[2] because He had 'lost control' of the Earth.[3] The 'Faith' movement teaches that Satan surprised and outwitted God and that God subsequently had to find "an

---

[1] *C in C*, p125.
[2] *C in C*, p126.
[3] *C in C*, p380.

avenue back into the Earth".[4]   They teach that He cannot foresee the future but that the prophecies recorded in Scripture were actually just Him "speaking things into being"…

But the true God cannot be surprised, for He knows "the end from the beginning" (Isa. 46:10, Acts 15:18) and knew how the whole of history would work out from "before the foundation of the world". Nor can God be outwitted, for He is absolutely "perfect in knowledge" (Job 37:16), "His understanding is **infinite**" (Psa. 147:5) and He is *all* powerful (Rev. 19:6, Exod. 6:3, Gen. 17:1). Nothing is too hard for Him (Jer. 32:17).

- Copeland and his colleagues go on to teach that God didn't have "any legal entrée into the Earth" because it 'no longer belonged to Him'.[5] As a result, God "can't do **anything** in this Earth realm except what we … allow Him to do"[6] - i.e. unless we give Him permission. To insist that, at any stage, the Earth "didn't belong" to the Lord is to fly in the face of explicit Scriptures like Psalm 24:1: "The earth is the **LORD's**, and the **fulness** thereof; the world, and they that dwell therein". And as for the idea that there is anything that (the *Almighty*) God cannot do… What sort of god does Copeland serve?

- God is omnipotent. He "doeth according to His **will** … [N]one can stay His hand, or say unto Him, What doest Thou?" (Dan. 4:35, Psa. 135:6). Hence, to teach - as the 'Faith' movement does - that the Godhead is subservient to some 'force' of faith, or that there are things that God "has no legal right to do anything about" for fear of being ruled unlawful by "the Supreme Court of the Universe", as various 'Faith' teachers claim, is to mislead the flock badly.[7]

- Not content with all this, Copeland (along with others) has the affrontery to teach that, God is "a being that stands somewhere around 6'2", 6'3", that weighs somewhere in the neighbourhood of a couple of hundred pounds".[8] Copeland obtains this remarkable information by assuming that the size of God's hand is the same as the length of an Old Testament

---

[4] *C in C*, p126.

[5] *C in C*, p132.

[6] *C in C*, p380.

[7] *C in C*, p134. The presence of suffering is the result of sinning against a **totally holy** God. Nicky's inability to properly explain the presence of suffering leads to one of two conclusions – either God is NOT omnipotent or He is subservient to some 'Supreme Court' and therefore has to follow its instructions.

[8] *C in C*, p121.

"span". Copeland is very thoughtful to inform us about his god, but it is not the God of the Bible who, since He is outside of His creation, does not have measurable dimensions...

Solomon knew the truth: "The heaven of heavens cannot contain Thee; how much less this house which I have built!" (2 Chr. 6:18, I Ki. 8:27 and Josh. 4:23-24, see also Jer. 23:23-24). When God says, in Isa. 48:13, "Mine hand also hath laid the foundation of the earth, and **My right hand hath spanned the heavens**", do we really suppose He possesses a nine-inch hand span? (The Hebrew original - not surprisingly, from the context - means that God 'stretched out' the heavens. The text nowhere suggests a nine-inch span. See Jer. 32:17 or Deut. 3:24 for a better idea of the mightiness of God's 'hand'.[9])

- Copeland et al seem determined to teach that God is just like us. In addition to God being a "failure", subservient to a greater force, and standing around six-foot three, Copeland says that our earth is just "a copy of the Mother Planet. Where God lives".[10] He further teaches that "Adam was not a **little** like God. He was not **almost** like God. He was **not subordinate** to God even".[11] But if that is so, why did the Lord give Adam *orders* (see Gen. 2, e.g. vv 8&15-17)? Why did he describe Adam as merely "dust" (Gen. 2:7 & 3:19). And why did He judge him?...

The 'Faith' position is deceitful, and it forgets the *true* God. The Lord has some very strong words about those who think that He is just like us: "Thou givest thy mouth to **evil**, and thy tongue frameth deceit ... **[T]hou thoughtest that I was altogether such an one as thyself**: but I will reprove thee ... Now consider this, ye that forget God, lest I **tear you in pieces**, and there be none to deliver. Whoso offereth **praise** glorifieth Me: and to him **that ordereth his conversation aright** will I shew the salvation of God" (Psa. 50:19-23).

How much does the 'Faith' movement encourage us to glorify our great God and to be in awe of Him?! But then, how much does Alpha do so in its current form? Nicky even teaches that *Satan* is the cause of "fear in the relationship" between us and God.[12]

---

[9] We must be careful not to take Scripture's anthropomorphisms too far.
[10] *C in C*, p379 fn7.
[11] *C in C*, p379 fn13.
[12] Talk 11.

20:2 DOES OUR IDEA OF GOD MATTER?   As we saw earlier, believers are supposed to fear God. Uncomfortable though it may be to our flesh to accept this, if we love the truth then accept it we must. And it is certainly worth getting right, as we shall now discover. For the blessings promised to those who *do* fear God are astonishingly great and manifold. That is why we have laboured this point.

Yet the 'Faith' movement teaches a small, fallible, emasculated, shadow of the true God. Who, in their right minds, would fear the 'Faith' teachers' God? As we look through the selection below of the unspeakably tremendous blessings that accrue to those who fear God, we might spare a moment to reflect that those who follow the 'Faith' movement are being robbed of each:

- The fear of God: "**prolongeth days**" (Prov. 10:27) and "is a **fountain** of **life**" (Prov. 14:27),
- "In the fear of the LORD is **strong confidence**: and his children shall have a **place of refuge**" (Prov. 14:26-27),
- "The fear of the LORD **tendeth to life**: and he that **hath** it shall abide **satisfied**; he shall **not be visited with evil**" (Prov. 19:23),
- "The **eye of the LORD is upon them** that fear Him, upon them that hope in His mercy; To **deliver their soul from death**, and to **keep them alive in famine**" (Psa. 33:18-19),
- "What man is he that feareth the LORD? him shall **He teach** ... his soul shall **dwell at ease**; and his seed shall **inherit the earth**. The secret of the LORD is with them that fear Him; and He will **show them His Covenant**" (Psa. 25:12-14),
- "The **mercy** of the LORD is from **everlasting to everlasting** upon them that fear Him, and **His righteousness** unto children's children" (Psa. 103:17).

See also Psa. 128, Eccl 8:12, Prov 3:7-8, Prov 22:4, Psa. 85:9, Psa. 103:11-13, Psa. 112:1-3, Psa. 145:19, Psa. 147:11, etc etc. Well might we say, with the Psalmist, "**Oh how great** is Thy **goodness**, which Thou hast laid up **for them that fear Thee**" (Psa. 31:19).

A study of the fear of the Lord quickly reveals a direct link between fearing God and obeying His Word. Arguably, the overriding problem with the church today is that it does not fear God nor "tremble at His Word" (Isa. 66:5). We are called both to "stand in awe of" God (Psa. 33:8) and to stand in awe of His Word (Psa. 119:161). Few today seem to be calling us to fear God, and yet God promises notable curses if we *don't* fear Him:

- "It shall **not be well** with the wicked, neither shall he prolong his days, which are as a shadow; because he **feareth not** before God" (Eccl. 8:13),
- "Know therefore and see that it is an **evil thing and bitter**, that thou hast forsaken the LORD thy God, and **that My fear is not in thee**, saith the Lord GOD of hosts" (Jer. 2:19),
- "And I will come near to you to **judgment**; and I will be a swift witness against … [those that] **fear not Me**, saith the LORD of hosts" (Mal. 3:5).

See also Prov. 10:27, 1 Sam. 12:24-25 and Deut. 28:58-62, not to mention all the unpleasant promises made to every person who lacks even the *beginning* of *wisdom*. Thus a church can teach much truth and yet still miss out VITAL elements. It can teach an apparently biblical gospel about Christ, but if it doesn't project a God who is to be approached with fear then, according to the scriptures, there is a deadly problem! If someone preaches a God to us who would never consign the faithless to the torment of eternal fire, then that person is preaching a *different* God, and we must not follow them. As Nicky rightly points out, it is "**Satan** [who] gives a false view of God".[13]

20:3 THE CHRIST OF THE FAITH MOVEMENT As with every cult, the 'Faith' movement misrepresents the written Word *and* the Word made flesh. Here are just some of their opinions about the Lord Jesus Christ which only serve to undermine His Deity - and their credibility:

- The 'Faith' teachers promote the idea that the Lord Jesus Christ was a *created* being. Because God's ('faith-filled') *words* supposedly created the universe, so it was that God *spoke* Christ into being in Mary's womb. The 'Faith' teachers utterly pervert the meaning of the phrase "the Word of God" and make the Second Person of the Trinity out to be a 'product' of God's "positive confession"…[14]

Compare this with the Lord's own words: "Verily, verily, I say unto you, **Before Abraham** was, **I Am**" (John 8:58). Compare it with the fact that "**In the beginning** was the Word, and the Word was with God, and the Word was God. The same was in the beginning with God. All things were made by **Him** [not "it"!]; and without **Him** was not any thing made that was made" (John 1:1-3). Compare it also with the fact that Christ

---

[13] Talk 11.
[14] *C in C*, pp141-142.

Jesus appeared to men *centuries* before His incarnation (e.g. in Dan. 3:25, Exod. 3:2-6 and Josh. 5:13-15).[15]

- They teach that Christ did not claim to be God - Copeland even quotes *his* Jesus as saying this very thing.[16] Yet, in *truth*, the Lord was regularly attacked by His own countrymen for claiming He *was* God. Throughout the Gospel of John, Christ Jesus used Hebrew idioms to announce His Deity. "Therefore the Jews sought the more to kill him, because He ... [said] that God was His Father, **making Himself equal with God**" (John 5:18); "**I and My Father** are one. Then the Jews took up stones again to stone Him ... saying, ... We stone Thee ... because that Thou, being a man, **makest Thyself God**" (John 10:30-33). Nicky helpfully refers to this latter passage, but an even more appropriate rebuttal to the 'Faith' claim that 'Jesus never claimed to be God' would be to remind people that what really matters is whether the *Bible as a whole* claims this – as, of course, it does in many places.[17]

When Christ said "I AM" (e.g. in John 13:19 and 18:4-8) He was using the covenant name of Jehovah. (The phrases "Son of man" and "Son of David" were both epithets for the Messiah, the only begotten Son of God. As Christ Jesus pointed out, in Mark 12:36-37, the Messiah is also God.)

- Perhaps the most horrific teaching from the 'Faith' camp is that the Lord became a *satanic* being on the cross. Benny Hinn has taught that Christ "became one with the nature of Satan"[18]. *(We will be examining Hinn's current position on the Faith doctrines in just a few moments.)* Hagin's phrase was that Christ had "Satan's nature".[19] Copeland, among others, promotes the identical doctrine.[20] They all point to the brass serpent that Moses lifted up on the pole in Numbers 21 as proof...

---

[15] A tiny number of verses do superficially suggest that Jesus is not truly God, but the rest of the Bible proves that Jesus is part of the Triune Godhead - just as a man's physical body is part of his whole being. Seemingly problematic verses are very easily explained on closer examination. See part 3 of our piece 'Chapter and Verse on Alpha's Jesus' for more.

[16] *C in C*, p138.

[17] Sadly, Alpha does not come out well when its teachings on the nature and deity of the Lord are examined carefully. For a very large set of ways in which the Deity of Christ is undermined on Alpha, see the article *Chapter and Verse on Alpha's Jesus*, available from the 'Rubies' section of our website (bayith.org).

[18] *C in C*, pp155-156.

[19] *C in C*, p156.

[20] *C in C*, p157.

But what Moses created and lifted up was not a *real* serpent, it was made of *brass*. It *looked* like a serpent on the outside, in the same way that Christ on the cross *looked* like a cursed being to the onlookers, but it (like Christ) had no venom, no poison. It did *not* have the "nature" of a serpent, just as Christ didn't. The spotless lamb of God remained holy to the Lord even after death - just as any sacrifice for sin did under the law (see, for example, Num. 18:10 or Lev. 7:5-6). Christ was only "made sin" in the sense that He took upon Himself the burden, the punishment, for our sins (Isa. 53:6; 1 Pet. 2:24). He was made the *offering* for sin, not the sin itself.

- Finally, the effect of the corrupt doctrine that Christ became "the essence of sin" is that demons "dragged Him down to the very pit of Hell itself" where they tortured Him for three days. He (allegedly) *died spiritually* and was then reborn (i.e. born again) in Hell.[21] This all requires no small amount of Scripture-twisting, not least to explain away just about every word the Lord said on the cross. He said, to the malefactor: "Verily I say unto thee, **Today** shalt thou be **with Me** in **paradise**" (Luke 23:43); He said, to His Father, in a rather non-Satanic way: "Father, **forgive** them" (Luke 23:34) and "into **Thy** hands I commend My **spirit**" (Luke 23:46); and He said, to all: "It is **finished**" (John 19:30).

Not only does the 'Faith' teaching deny that it was Christ's *body and blood* and thus His *physical* death that paid the price for our sins (Rom. 7:4, Eph. 2:13, Col. 2:14-15, 1 Cor. 1:17-18), but it also denies Christ's words when He said "I have power to lay down My life **and** I have power to take it up again" (John 10:18). God cannot die spiritually, He is "the **same** yesterday and to day and for ever" (Heb. 13:8).

New Hinn Information

In response to the inclusion of Benny Hinn's teachings within critiques of the 'Faith' movement, his fans often insist that he has repented of his attachment to this movement and its doctrines. There are some points worth making about this idea:

Has he really repented?

There are several reasons to doubt the extent of his repentence. To our knowledge he has still not withdrawn those books of his which promoted the errors of the 'Faith' movement, and neither have we ever heard him repent of his claim that "Those who attack **Kenneth Copeland** are attacking

---

[21] *C in C*, pp163,165,170-1.

the **very presence of God**.[22] Indeed, we are not aware that he ever even said the words "**I repent**" regarding 'Faith' teachings. He merely says they went "a bit too far".[23]

Another reason to doubt his sincerity here is that he only 'left' the movement in <u>1994</u> – i.e. after he had been in the ministry for <u>many</u> years and only after a very <u>popular</u> book had come out exposing the truth about the movement. (A number of other books had done the same in the preceding decade but didn't cause Hinn to 'repent'. Could it be that he ignored these because they were not popular enough to significantly threaten his ministry and income?)

If Hinn <u>has</u> really repented, then why has he not brought out a book which gives a thorough refutation of the 'Faith' position and which spells out where he now stands doctrinally?

The damage is already done

Thanks to all his erroneous books and videos, sold in their millions and still in circulation, the damage has already been done and continues to be done. Furthermore, as will be explained later, we are including Hinn because he was crucial to another movement which broke out BEFORE he distanced himself from his 'Faith' teachings.

The Word-of-Faith movement, in teaching their falsehoods about the grace of God and about His Son, fit the following scripture very well:

> "For there are certain men **crept in unawares**, who were before of old ordained to this condemnation, **ungodly** men, turning the grace of our God into **lasciviousness**, and **denying** the **only Lord God, and our Lord Jesus Christ**" (Jude 1:4). See also 2 Pet. 2:1-3.

We have now seen the 'Faith' teachers deny the fundamental truths about both the Father and the Son. What does that tell us? "Who is a liar but he that denieth that Jesus is the Christ? He is *antichrist*, that denieth the Father and the Son. **Whosoever** denieth the Son, the same hath not the Father" (I John 2:22-23). It is highly regrettable that Alpha takes a totally different line on heresy from that of the Word of God and never warns the sheep. For, while Nicky claims that "it sometimes almost breaks my heart to

---

[22] 'Benny Hinn' Program on TBN, 8:Jun:1992.
[23] The Many Faces of Benny Hinn (The Door, 2000). We understand that Hinn actually continues to *print* books which promote Word-Faith doctrines!

see how the Lord is portrayed",[24] he elsewhere makes this a very secondary concern:

> "The fourth (ministry) value is **harmonious relationships** ... We make it a rule on Alpha never to criticise another ... church or Christian leader".[25]

> "I long for the day when we drop all these labels and just regard ourselves as Christians with a commission from Jesus Christ ... Actually we must stop judging one another".[26]

It is even more tragic that Nicky himself portrays the Lord Jesus erroneously. For example, he states that "Jesus had **evil** thoughts" – giving the distinct impression that the Lord *entertained* evil thoughts.[27] (The Lord was *offered* temptations. He was *offered* evil thoughts by the enemy, but He rejected them all instantly.) Nicky also implies, from the occasion when Christ prayed twice for a – *faithless* - man's sight to be restored, that "even ... Jesus" was fallible.[28] He was not. (For very many further problems with Alpha's presentation of our Saviour, please see the series of articles entitled *'Chapter and Verse on Alpha's Jesus'*, available from our website.[29])

20:4 THE ULTIMATE HERESY   Because the enemy is behind the devious arguments of the Faith movement, there is a definite goal to them. Satan's plan in Eden was to convince Eve that she and Adam would "be as gods" (Gen. 3:5). His 'New Age' movement similarly teaches that men can be gods. The goal of the 'Faith' gospel is to teach that, if Christ was born-again, then (as Hagin put it) we become "**as much** an incarnation as was Jesus of Nazareth" when *we* are born-again.[30] Hagin explained it thus: "God made us the **same class** of being that He is Himself".[31] In the phraseology of Kenneth Copeland, "You don't have a god in you, **you are one**".[32] In the words of Benny Hinn, "You are a little **god**".[33]

---

[24] Talk 6.

[25] *Telling Others*, p114.

[26] Nicky Gumbel, The Spirit And Evangelism, *Renewal*, May 1995, p16. (See also Wallace Boulton, Ed., *The Impact of Toronto*, 1995, p83).

[27] Talk 11.

[28] Talk 13.

[29] See the 'Better Than Rubies' section of bayith.org for details.

[30] *C in C*, p175.

[31] *C in C*, p108.

[32] *C in C*, p110.

[33] *C in C*, p110.

Like Eve, we have a choice. We can succumb to the very attractive doctrine that 'we are gods'. We can focus on a minuscule set of ambiguous verses - all of which fail to support the doctrine when analysed seriously - or we can decide to look before we leap, and realise that the entirety of the rest of Scripture refutes the idea utterly. Before we make up our minds, here are a few handy hints that expose some fundamental problems with the 'Faith' position:

(1) There is only *one* God. We looked closely at this in Part One. "There is **one** God; and there is **none other** but He" (Mark 12:32). Satan is only called a "god" because of his power over unbelievers. Men are only "as gods" in the sense that they may have earthly authority over others.

(2) We are merely *adopted* sons into God's family; Jesus Christ is the only *begotten* Son of God (see John 3:16,18, John 1:14,18). We are mortal, only the *begotten* Son is Divine.

(3) While it is true that Christ *abides* in us, He said "**without Me** ye can do **nothing**" (John 15:5). Paul said we should *not* "think **any thing** as of ourselves" (2 Cor. 3:5). How god-like does that make us?! See also Heb. 2:7-9 in this regard.

(4) If Adam was "not subordinate to God" as Copeland states; if Adam was "an exact duplication of God's kind",[34] in other words if Adam and Eve were both *already* gods, then why did Satan bother to tempt them by saying "you **shall be** as gods"?

(5) The Psalmist said "What is **man**, that Thou art mindful of him?" (Psa. 8:4) and "What is man that Thou takest knowledge of him! ... Man is like to **vanity**" (Psa. 144:3-4). In view of these types of comments, how *can* we consider ourselves "gods"?

(6) We are as mere *clay* to a potter. God "remembereth that **we are dust**" (Psa. 103:14, see also 1 Pet. 1:24 and Gen. 3:19). Even the greatest men of God are nothing but "weak", "vile", sinners. To claim anything else only leads to pride; and we all know where *that* leads.

> "O man, ... what doth the LORD require of thee, but to ... walk **humbly** with thy God?" (Mic. 6:8).

(The philosopher Plato likewise taught the divinity of man. Sadly, Nicky endorses Plato, and he also implies we have a divine nature when he teaches us that we are to have "**high**" self-esteem rather than a biblical view of ourselves.[35])

---

[34] *C in C*, pp108-109.
[35] Nicky Gumbel, *30 Days*, pp75-76.

20:5 ARE *WE* CHRIST?   Finally, Kenneth Hagin used to assert that "the believer is called Christ ... that's who we are; **we're Christ**".[36] Presumably this is why Hinn taught that "You are **everything** He was and **everything** He is and **ever** He shall be",[37] and why Kenneth Copeland teaches that you should "pray to **yourself**".[38] Amazingly, the Alpha Course supports this by implying that we are Christ's *actual* body (see the quotes below).

The Church is continuing part of His earthly ministry, but that does not mean we *are* Christ. We are merely *representing* Him before the world; acting on His behalf. If someone is a servant of a master who goes away for a time, the servant may temporarily be made his master's representative; the servant may even have use of some of his master's tools, or be in touch with the master, but the servant is *not* the master in any real sense!

Christ abides in us, if we abide in Him, but this does not make us Christ - anymore than a plug abiding in a socket becomes the socket (or vice versa). Nor do the gifts which the Holy Spirit gives make us Christ. We should seek to become Christ-*like* in character, having our minds and hearts transformed to be more like His, but none of this makes us Christ. We are "one body **in** Christ" (Rom. 5:12) but we are not His actual body any more than we are *actual* stones or *actual* sheep or *actual* olive (or vine) branches. Despite what Nicky says below, Christ still has His own body; "For **in Him** dwelleth all the fulness of the Godhead **bodily**" (Col. 2:9; see also Heb. 10:12; Acts 1:11; Col. 2:9; and Php. 3:21).

Interestingly, Benny Hinn's remarkable words "Don't tell me you 'have' Jesus ... Don't say 'I have', say '**I Am, I Am, I Am, I Am, I Am**'"[39] are *specifically* prophesied and dealt with in Scripture. The Lord Himself warned us "Take heed that ye be not deceived: for many shall come in My Name, saying, **I Am** ... [G]o ye **not** therefore after them" (Luke 21:8).

Worryingly, even Nicky leans toward this idea:

"When Jesus ascended he changed **bodies**. Now the body of Christ is **still** on **earth**, but **we** are the body of Christ – the Church **is** the body of Christ".[40]

---

[36] *C in C*, p108.

[37] *C in C*, p382 fn44.

[38] Michael Horton, ed., *The Agony of Deceit*, 1990, p116.

[39] *C in C*, pp382-383 fn44.

[40] Talk 14. Nicky also says that bringing people to a church service is the same as bringing them to see Christ – which could easily be taken by his listeners as meaning that the Church is

"The Church is **the** place ... where he [i.e. God] lives";[41] "[T]he Church **is** Christ".[42]

Certainly we are "of" his flesh – i.e. we belong to Him and ought to abide in Him as closely as His own flesh, but we are *not His actual flesh*. We are really only Christ's body in the sense that a bride's body *belongs to* her husband (1 Cor. 7:4). Christ Jesus is perfectly capable of making things happen in the world without using our physical bodies.

20:6 THE ROMISH CONNECTION   At the age of two, Benny Hinn was enrolled into a Catholic school and was trained by nuns, and later, by monks for fourteen years. Given Hinn's very long and deep association with Rome, it is notable that Catholicism teaches that the church is Christ too:

> "Let us rejoice then and give thanks that we have become not **only** Christians, but **Christ Himself** ... Marvel and rejoice: **we have become Christ...**".[43] (Romanists like Origen and Clement also taught the divinity of man; and Alpha legitimizes both.)

The 'Faith' movement is a bridge to Rome. The writings of 'Faith' teachers are frequently sympathetic to Rome, and 'Faith' leaders are happy to cooperate with Romanists.[44] Hinn and the other 'Faith' teachers often support Rome. Hinn maintains particularly intimate links to Rome and often endorses that institution.[45] In fact, Rome is very similar in all sorts of ways to the 'Faith' movement...

As we proved in Part 2 of this book with respect to Rome, both are heavily money-oriented 'ministries' exploiting ignorance, guilt and fear to exact as much money as they can from their followers. Both employ human

---

itself Christ. This would make us God!

[41] Talk 14, Edn 2.1.

42 Talk 14.

[43] *Catechism of the Catholic Church*, 2nd edition, English Translation, 1997 (official Latin text promulgated by John Paul II on same date), para #795.

[44] For instance, Kenneth Hagin shared a platform with 'Fr.' Ralph DiOrio, and Copeland has spoken alongside 'Fr.' Tom Forrest.

[45] The title sequence for Hinn's television show includes a photo of him shaking hands with 'Pope' John Paul II. Hinn had meetings with JPII in 1987 and 1995, but clearly he had a closer relationship than even this implies, for his website admits that Hinn was invited by a "liaison to the Vatican" to participate in a private Catholic mass at St. Peter's Basilica "for members of Vatican staff who worked **closely** with the Pontiff" [www.bennyhinn.org/resources/pope.cfm as cited by Roger Oakland].

bodyguards. Both demand total allegiance, insisting that their followers must never question what they say, and both teach that anyone who leaves their insititution will lose his or her salvation. Both also delight in making the Word of God "of none effect" by "the tradition of men". For example, both idolise objects; both subtly attack the doctrine of the Trinity; both take the focus off Christ and undermine His Deity (and His humanity); and both alter what Scripture says about, among other things, the atonement and the resurrection.

Like Rome, various 'streams' that teach part, or all, of the 'Faith' message claim to be true churches but have actually perverted the gospel. They have replaced true holiness and true doctrine with things that impress and entertain and subjugate so as to hide the fact that they have a flawed gospel. Fascinating the people keeps those souls from questioning the true nature of the 'church'…

Despite the repeated cry in Holy Writ *not* to look on the outward appearance, both groups manage to transport and deceive us with expensive buildings set off with smart décor. The 'leaders', as well as their 'choirs', wear attractive outfits. (Where do we see *any* of this in the early church described in Scripture?) They both use well-choreographed ceremonies and processions, and beguiling images. They arrange enchanting singing to very pleasing music, albeit often with trite and unscriptural words. (Do *we* check the lyrics of the songs *we* are singing?)…

Many use "holy" objects like crosses or banners, intricately made. There is a great deal of careful organisation behind the scenes enabling these churches to put on a dazzling, theatrical, show that bears no resemblance to the simplicity and humility and *inner* beauty of the New Testament church gatherings. The whole experience serves to take the congregation's mind off of the strange, confused, gnostic teachings they are being fed. (How do our own Fellowships compare? Do we care about an impressive image and not enough about God's truth?)

Like most cults, these churches depend more on humour than on the Bible. They rely more on emotive tunes than on godliness, more on threats than patience, more on charming, well-dressed "leaders" than on humble, God-fearing servants, more on clever speeches than honest teaching. Yet Alpha would have us accept all these groups blindly. Nicky has written the following. Remember the teachings of the Word-of-Faith churches as you read it:

> "I feel **particularly** strongly ... we need to **unite**. We need to encourage ... **whatever** God is doing in different places, not try to put our experience onto **any** other church [i.e. not expect the Bible to apply?!] ... Locally we have always worked with **all** the denominations, and all the Alpha conferences go **right across the board**. ... [This 'board' includes] **Roman Catholics** ... **Nobody** is suspicious of **anybody** else. **Everyone** is working together and **I believe that is what the Spirit achieves**".[46]

How can we know that it *is* "the Sprit" who is operating in all these "different places"? Nicky doesn't say. Does God not care about false things, i.e. lies, being taught about Him? And when did Christ Jesus or the apostles indicate that different churches would have disparate experiences of the *same* Spirit? Where are the scriptures warning of deception? What spirit is it that causes confusion of belief and practice? Nicky has his own view of what the Holy Spirit achieves, but the Spirit of *God* achieves *separation* from heresy and unrighteousness, not unity with the 'Faith' movement and its siblings.

---

[46] *Renewal*, May 1995, pp14-16 (also in *The Impact of Toronto*, pp82-83).

CHAPTER **21**

$\mathscr{T}$HE TELL-TALE EXAMPLE OF PAUL

21:1 WHAT ELSE DOES SCRIPTURE SAY?   It is beyond the scope of this book to look at *every* false teaching and *every* argument that the 'Faith' movement gives. Hopefully we have shown that, in order to determine the veracity of such pronouncements, it is vital to check the *full context* of any verse used - and also to test all "revelations" against the *whole* Word. When we do so we will find that many other teachings are similarly built on sand.

So much for the 'Faith' movement's *doctrines*. It is now time to take a closer look at what God's Word says about the 'Faith' movement's *teachers*.

Paul, in his second letter to the Corinthians, begged the church to compare the behaviour of the "so-called" apostles who were around in his day with his own behaviour, so that the sharp contrast would expose these "super-apostles" for what they really were. Any 'leader' who claims to be filled with the same spirit as Paul should obviously *exhibit* that same spirit, i.e. by having similar traits. So, starting at Corinthians Chapter 10...

Paul taught with "meekness" (v1).

Paul didn't make a big fuss about the extraordinary things the Lord did through him. And he made sure that it was the Lord, rather than he, who received the glory. Compare this with the self-congratulation of Kenneth Hagin's **"I've been able** to live for nearly sixty years without having a headache".[1] (Hagin was obliged to admit that he suffered all the *symptoms* of a headache, but tried to claim that this was somehow totally different from having a *real* headache.) Similarly he said, "**I** have not had **one** sick day in 45 years" –despite suffering "alarming heart symptoms ... for **six weeks**" on one occasion. Note that the Lord didn't get the praise for these "miracles"; Hagin did.[2]

God saves the **meek** of the earth (Psa. 76:9, Zeph. 2:3). Can the 'Faith' teachers be described as *meek*? In fact most are supremely proud and boastful of their 'knowledge', of their possessions, and of their "anointed" walks. They love to praise themselves, but the Lord says "Let **another** man praise thee, and **not** thine own mouth; a stranger, and **not** thine own lips" (Prov. 27:2). They prefer to glorify themselves rather than the Lord, but "He that glorieth, let him **glory in the Lord.** For **not** he that commendeth himself is approved, but whom the **Lord** commendeth" (2 Cor. 10:17-18; see also Prov. 15:33b).

Paul taught with "gentleness" (v1).

Paul's gentleness contrasts starkly with the style of many teachers today who shout and scream and express little patience or charity for those who question them. For example, although Benny Hinn claims he regrets saying he wished God would give him a "Holy Ghost machine gun" so he could blow off the heads of his critics,[3] he has actually moved on to *cursing* his detractors...

Despite telling his camera crew to stop recording on one occasion, he was inadvertently taped saying: "With the mighty power of God on me ... **You hear this**: There are men and women ... attacking me [i.e. criticising my teachings]. I will tell you under the anointing now, you'll reap it in your **children** unless you stop ... [Y]our **children will suffer**. You're attacking me ... **you'll pay** and your **children will** [**too**] ... 'Touch not my

---

[1] *C in C*, p401 fn4.

[2] *C in C*, p401 fn4.

[3] *C in C*, p336.

anointed"".[4] On a later occasion, far from repenting of these horrible words, Hinn again promised: "You have attacked me, **your children will pay for it**".[5] But Paul said no such thing to the "super-apostles" who opposed, or spoke against, him.

Paul did not walk "according to the flesh" (vv2-3).

Paul's un-fleshly walk could hardly be more different from those who champion the prosperity 'gospel'. The latter encourage covetousness, and then lure people into accepting false doctrines by appealing to their flesh with statements like: "If the **Mafia** can ride around in Lincoln Continental town cars, why can't the **King's Kids**?".[6] Does that comment agree with Paul's teaching? It certainly doesn't agree with Christ's:

> "[Jesus] said unto them ... that which is **highly esteemed** among **men** is **abomination** in the sight of **God**" (Luke 16:15).

Copeland states that there is "**no** reason for you to live in poverty of **any** kind".[7] Did Paul teach this? No. Nor does the Word teach Hinn's doctrine that "the Lord giveth and **never** taketh away".[8] (See Job 9:12 and Job 12:23). However, the Bible *does* tell us what will happen to those who, like Hinn, add to God's Word (see, for example, Prov. 30:5-9 and section 18:3 of this book).

> "If we live in the Spirit, let us also **walk** in the **Spirit**. Let us **not** be desirous of vain glory, provoking one another, **envying** one another" (Gal. 5:25-26). See also Titus 2:11-13.

> "They that trust in their **wealth**, and **boast themselves** in the multitude of their **riches**; None of them can by **any** means redeem his brother, nor give to God a ransom for him" (Psa. 49:6-7). See also Gal. 5:24, Prov. 28:19-20 and Rev. 3:16-18.

(The worldliness of the 'Faith' teachers also manifests itself in, for instance, the way they often employ bodyguards - but see Jer. 17:5 and Psa. 118 - and in the way they are so litigious, in spite of the clear teaching in 1 Cor. 6:1-8. How can they claim to walk so intimately with the Lord and yet

---

[4] *C in C*, p344.
[5] *C in C*, p345.
[6] *C in C*, p191.
[7] *C in C*, p214.
[8] *C in C*, p98.

have to rely on the world's methods of protection? Again, how can they tell others to have more faith while showing such little faith in God themselves?)

Paul's "bodily presence [was] weak" (v10).

Paul did not want God's people to "look on things after the outward appearance" so he did not take trouble over his appearance. He didn't want the church to be dazzled by presentation or the *impression* of righteousness but rather to concentrate on his *spirit* and his *teaching* so that they could determine if he, and it, were true. Compare this with the expensive, highly tailored silk suits and the costly coiffeurs of many of the 'Faith' teachers. Paul's emotions were sincere, but the 'Faith' teachers have to rely on false humility and crocodile tears.

Just as there were hypocritical leaders in *Christ's* day, so there have been throughout history and are today. If they give offerings, it is done very openly; if they pray it is long and very public; if they are fasting they make sure people know about it. But Holy Scripture tells us to "beware" of those 'leaders' and teachers who seek to be noticed (e.g. in Luke 20:45-47, 11:43).

> "**Woe** unto you ... **hypocrites**! for ye ... **appear beautiful outward**, but are within full of ... all uncleanness. Even so ye also outwardly **appear** righteous unto men, but within ye are full of hypocrisy and iniquity" (Matt. 23:23-28), and "[T]he LORD seeth **not** as man seeth; for **man** looketh on the **outward appearance**, but the LORD looketh on the **heart**" (1 Sam. 16:7).

Paul's "speech [was] contemptible" (v10).

Just like the 'Faith' teachers today who have to undermine Paul in order to convince people of their doctrine, so there were "super-apostles" in Paul's day who sought to undermine him. One way they tried to do this was by claiming that his unimpressive style of speaking meant he was beneath them. Paul himself admitted he "was rude [i.e. plain] in speech"; he didn't rely on seductive words but on the authority of the truth and the power of the pure gospel. He knew the Word, and he taught it accurately.

In contrast, Hagin, Copeland, Hinn and their like are very smooth and charming talkers. But they rely on their "fair speeches" to disguise the ambiguities and half-truths they preach.

> "For they ... by **good [i.e. impressive] words** and **fair** speeches **deceive** the hearts of the simple" (Rom. 16:18), "I **beseech** you, brethren, **mark** ... and **avoid** them" (v17).

"Better is the poor that walketh in his integrity, than he that is perverse in his lips and is a fool" (Prov. 19:1).

"Be no more children, tossed to and fro, and carried about with every wind of doctrine, by the **sleight** of men, and **cunning craftiness**, whereby they lie in wait to **deceive**" (Eph. 4:14-15).

We must take care not to be like those in Isaiah 30:9-15 who chose nice words rather than the (potentially less convenient, but always much more important) truth.

Paul's teaching was "weighty and powerful" (v10).

Despite his apparent lack of eloquence, Paul's words were godly, sound, edifying and effective. How different from the shallow and confused utterances produced by those in the 'Faith' movement. We've already heard Copeland's bizarre description of God and His "Mother Planet"; perhaps now it is time for a description of Adam from Hinn: "Adam ... used to **fly** ... Adam **not only flew**, he flew to **space** ... [W]ith one thought he would be **on the moon**".[9] Hinn also informs us that: "God's **original** plan was that the woman was to bring forth children out of her **side**".[10] (Hinn bases this notion on the way that Eve was created – except, of course that Adam didn't *give birth to* Eve, he merely gave up a rib to God). How edifying is this sort of material? Not at all, we would venture. Such statements are just fables and pointless – i.e. vain - babblings:

"Neither give heed to **fables** ... which minister questions, rather than godly edifying which is in faith ... some having swerved have turned aside unto **vain** jangling" (1 Tim. 1:4-6). See also 2 Tim. 2:16.

Like Hinn, Copeland is another seemingly endless fount of fables. For example, he says that "the Spirit of God spoke to me and said ... 'if you'd had the knowledge of the Word of God [that Christ did] **you** could've done the same thing [i.e. redeemed mankind]'".[11] Note that, in contrast to such self-exalting blasphemy, Paul was in the business of "casting **down** imaginations, and every high thing that **exalteth itself** against the knowledge of God" (v5).

---

[9] *C in C*, p119.
[10] *C in C*, p380 fn22.
[11] *C in C*, pp172-3. See Psa. 49:6-7 as quoted a few pages ago.

Paul did not "boast" of his "authority" (vv8-16).

Paul had a unique calling, yet he did not dwell on it, nor use it to cow his audience. Neither did he try to impress his hearers by comparing his giftedness to anyone else's. Such statements must seem totally alien to the world of the 'Faith' movement where the 'leaders' all proudly claim special revelation and unique knowledge.

> "And if any man **think** that he knoweth any thing, **he knoweth nothing yet** as he ought to know" (1 Cor. 8:2); "Be **not** wise in thine own eyes: **fear the LORD, and depart from evil**" (Prov. 3:7), and "**Woe** unto them that are wise in their own eyes, and prudent in their own sight!" (Isa. 5:21).

Christ warned us of those who would come 'in His Name' claiming to be specially anointed. He also told us very plainly that such people are deceivers (Matt. 24:4-5).

Paul wanted to present the church "as a chaste virgin to Christ" (11:2).

Paul knew that Christ Jesus is not the means to an end: He *is* the end. Compare this view with the "prosperity" teachers who would have us prostitute our faith for the sake of worldly satisfaction of the flesh:

> "Beguiling unstable souls: an heart they have exercised with **covetous** practices; … For when they speak **great swelling words of vanity**, they **allure** through the **lusts** of the **flesh**, through much **wantonness**, those that were clean **escaped** from them who live in error" (11:14-18).

Paul encouraged purity of behaviour, yet the examples set by many Faith teachers are a world away from this. For example, Hagin shamelessly plagiarized the work of others – and then lied about it.[12] Similarly, Hinn is on film saying "I was in Ghana just recently. We had half a million people show up. And a man was raised from the dead **on the platform**. That's a **fact** people. **We** have it on video". His spokesman, Jeff Pitman, was obliged to confess that this was simply not true. They did NOT have it on video, and had never even seen it happen, despite it supposedly taking place "on the platform".[13]

---

[12] Dan McConnell, *The Promise of Health and Wealth*, (Hodder and Stoughton, 1990), pp6-12.
[13] *The Many Faces of Benny Hinn*, video, (The Door, 2000).

Paul feared people's minds being "corrupted from the simplicity which is in Christ" (v3).

Paul was also desperately concerned for *doctrinal* purity and that the church stick rigidly to the true gospel. Compare this with the view of one of the most powerful and influential supporters of the 'Faith' movement, who called the issue "doctrinal doo-doo" about which nobody should care.[14]

As we have seen, Copeland and Co. have complicated the gospel and confused their followers. Unnecessary and unhelpful statements include Hinn's "Had the Holy Spirit not been with Jesus, He **would** have **sinned**."[15] This is vain babbling which belittles Christ. As other observers have pointed out, even when Hinn (under pressure and unannounced) changed his book to read instead that "Jesus ... **might** have sinned" he was still being heretical since he denied Him "the sinlessness that is an essential attribute of God".[16]

Hinn caused more complication and confusion when he famously prophesied:

> "Man, I feel **revelation knowledge** already coming on **me** here ... **Holy Spirit, take over** in the Name of Jesus ... God the Father ... is a triune being by Himself ... Each one of them is a triune being by Himself ... **there's nine of them**".[17]

After being challenged over this statement, Hinn's repentance was, as usual, minimal. He maintained that each member of the Trinity has His own spirit body – making *three* Gods, whereas Scripture proves that there is *one* God, revealed in three Persons. (We will only see one Divine Being in Heaven, not three!) Given the number of times Hinn has had to 'repent' of his deceptive teachings, he seems to have huge difficulty bridling his tongue:

> "If any man among you seem to be religious, and **bridleth not his tongue**, but deceiveth his own heart, this man's religion is **vain**" (James 1:26).

Paul "preached ... the gospel of God freely" (v7).

Paul didn't ask for a *penny* from the Corinthians, even for his living expenses, despite his very obvious need. How totally this contrasts with the

---

[14] Paul Crouch, *C in C*, p219.

[15] *C in C*, p139.

[16] *C in C*, p394 fn6.

[17] *C in C*, pp123-4.

extortion and emotional blackmail so frequently used by so many of the 'Faith' teachers.

> "**Woe** unto you ... hypocrites! for ye ... are full of **extortion** and **excess**" (Matt. 23:23, see also 1 Cor. 5:11), "Neither ... thieves, **nor covetous**, ... nor revilers, nor extortioners, shall inherit the Kingdom of God" (1 Cor. 6:10).

21:2 PAUL'S CONCLUSIONS   As well as these two Bible Chapters we have studied, there are other entire Chapters of the Bible which pertain to the sort of people and the sort of teachings given to us by the 'Faith' movement. These include 1 Tim. 6 and the Book of Jude. The entirety of 2 Peter 2 also directly relates to them...

For example, we have already seen how these people have brought in "damnable heresies" (v1) and how they "through covetousness ... make merchandise" of their many followers (v3). They also "walk after the flesh", are "self-willed" and rail at the powers of darkness (v10, plus see Jude 1:8-11). (Note that Satan can do nothing God does not allow him to, so Faith teachers should be crying out to God, not railing at the Devil.) While they promise men liberty, they are actually entangling their followers into corrupt ways, thus bringing them back into bondage (vv19-20).

So, what was Paul's conclusion? Those 'apostles' who show the opposite spirit to Paul's, and/or claim to be better than he was, "are **false** apostles, **deceitful workers**, transforming themselves into the apostles of Christ. And no marvel; for **Satan himself** is transformed into an angel of light. Therefore it is no great thing if his ministers also be transformed as the **ministers of righteousness**; whose end shall be according to their works" (2 Cor. 11:13-15). Paul was absolutely unequivocal here. There is no room for compromise. He concludes that such people are bogus spiritual leaders, sent by the enemy.

One particularly major implication of Paul's conclusion is that we ought to *expect* spiritual 'achievements' - and even spiritual 'outpourings' - from such a movement - all of which will be counterfeit: "For false Christs and false prophets shall rise, and **shall** shew **signs and wonders, to seduce**" (Mark 13:22a) and "a corrupt tree **bringeth forth** evil **fruit**" (Matt. 7:17b). Satan can produce counterfeit healings, and we have surely proved that no spiritual outpouring which has emanated from Hagin, Copeland and Hinn can possibly be of God. We will revisit this point later in the book, but in the meantime we should bear in mind that rotten fruit can often look fine on the surface.

(Note: We need to look out for these same ungodly characteristics developing in those whom we allow to teach us. Do those men who claim to be apostles compare with the behaviour of the *true* apostles (e.g. as per Acts 20:17-38 or 2 Cor. 6:1-10)? Do our 'anointed' leaders remind us of Christ? For, if they truly have the spirit of Christ then they should exhibit a similar character. Or do some of them manifest *another* spirit?)

21:3 SO WHAT DO WE DO?   Given all this information, we need to ask what God's Word tells us to *do* about it.

Firstly, we must not fear these false teachers (Psa. 118:6) - despite their threats of damnation towards those who would escape their clutches. These men seek to stop those who want to search for God for themselves (see Matt. 23:13-15).

Once we realise that these people, although they claim to dispense revelation direct from God, are *not* speaking the Lord's words of truth, we need to stop listening to them:

> "He that followeth vain persons is void of understanding" (Prov. 12:11b), and "Go from the presence of a foolish man, when thou perceivest not in him the lips of knowledge" (Prov. 14:7). See also Jer. 23:16 & 29:8-9, e.g. regarding Benny Hinn's numerous false prophetic statements.

We are not to respect these prideful teachers: "Blessed is that man that maketh **the LORD** his trust, and **respecteth not** the proud, nor such as turn aside to lies" (Psa. 40:4). Nor are we to envy them, but rather choose the fear of the Lord (Prov. 23:17). We will be incomparably better off that way (Prov. 15:16).

Note that we are not merely commanded to *depart* from all such teachings, but actually to *flee* them:

> "Perverse disputings of men of corrupt minds, and destitute of the truth, ... But thou, O man of God, **flee** these things; and follow after righteousness, godliness, ... meekness" (1 Tim. 6:5-12). See also Psa. 26:4-5.

And beyond this, we need to recognise that these teachers are, in truth, *enemies* of the cross:

> "**Many** walk, of whom I have told you often, and now tell you even weeping, that they are the **enemies** of the cross of Christ: Whose end is destruction, whose God is their **belly**, and whose glory is in their shame, who mind **earthly things**" (Php. 3:17-19).

We are required to love our enemies, but apart from feeling grieved how should we think of these "enemies of the cross of Christ"? God hates seeing His sheep led away from Him, hence King David's very strong words below:

> "Thou hast redeemed me, O LORD God of **truth**. I have **hated** them that regard lying vanities: but I trust in the LORD" (Psa. 31:5-6). See also Psa. 26:5.

Indeed, in 2 Kings 13:16-22 Elisha was rightly furious at the king of Israel for not being *angry enough* about those who were trying to destroy God's People. (Naturally, we must direct our anger purely into spiritual, not physical, warfare today, but that does not mean we should have less feeling. The problem here is not the *feeling*; the problem is what you actually do as a result. Christians must never physically hurt people in order to spread the gospel or to reduce apostasy. Indeed, it is the *Word-Faith* movement which promotes the use of force for the sake of the Kingdom.)

We need to study the Word and learn what the Christian faith really is, and endeavour to live by it. Finally, we ought (prayerfully) to do our bit to expose false teachers (Eph. 5:5-11), not fearing the causeless curses that some of them have spoken against their detractors.

Alpha basically says nothing about any of this, fundamental though these issues plainly are. People hide behind the excuse that "Alpha is only an *introduction* to the Christian faith". But why doesn't Alpha even bother to recommend any books on church history or material exposing such groups so that guests can make up for what the Course doesn't cover (and doesn't even *hint* at)? The closest Nicky Gumbel appears to get to criticising the Faith movement (although he notably avoids using this term) is

> "[W]hen [an **American** preacher] arrived here, there was, I think it true to say, a **certain** level of suspicion, because we **all** know about **tele-evangelists** and all that kind of thing, and there's always, I suppose, the British being what we are, there's a

suspicion of anything that is too, kind of, extrovert and too open and all that kind of thing" [Talk 13, 1st. Edn.] (Even this very mild comment was removed from the 2nd edition videos.)

Note the way in which Nicky fails to identify *any* of the problems with "tele-evangelists", but actually goes on to imply that the true fault lies with the British outlook rather than with the Word-Faith people themselves. And if we "ALL" know about "tele-evangelists", why do they have so many millions of followers? In fact, there is a major gulf between what God's Word says and what Nicky tries to teach, for he says:

"When Christians quarrel they say to God 'choose between us and them'".[18]

But true Christians are saying no such thing. They are simply obeying God's Word and seeking to save brothers from false ways that will otherwise destroy them. When Paul 'quarrelled' with a church he wasn't saying to God "choose between me and them": he was standing up for the truth of the gospel. And once a Fellowship has tried unsuccessfully to bring correction to another, in line with Scripture, it must look after its own flock and ensure they are not led into error themselves. Ultimately, it must do this by distancing itself from unbiblical teachings and those who espouse them.

"Beloved ... it was needful for me to write unto you, and **exhort** you that ye should **earnestly contend** for the faith" (Jude 1:3).

This verse needs to be meditated upon. We should also stop and ask ourselves why this verse is almost never mentioned in many churches today. Those who do "contend for the faith" are frequently despised rather than praised. And those who *earnestly* contend are often thrown out of their churches altogether. Yet these are the very ones who are trying to obey God's life-giving commands.

Nicky is in danger of calling 'righteous' those disobedient people who are happy to rebel against God and who promote a superficial unity at the expense of right behaviour and right teaching about the Lord. At the same time, Nicky seems to condemn (as "very bigoted") those folks who refuse to sell out on the truth - even at the expense of their popularity. But which category did Christ fall into? Which of the prophets or apostles was commended for *compromising* on the truth rather than contending for it? Nicky needs to take care in this, because:

---

[18] Talk 14.

> "He that justifieth the wicked, and he that condemneth the just, even they both are **abomination** to the LORD" (Prov. 17:15). See also Isa. 5:20 and Prov. 24:24-25.

As Paul said so heart-rendingly, in Galatians 4:16, to those who had allowed false teachings to prevail:

> "Am I therefore become your **enemy**, because I tell you the **truth**?"

21:4 ALPHA AND ADVENTISM   As we noted earlier, the Alpha organisation has no apparent problem at all with the Seventh-day Adventist Church despite its denial of justification by faith alone. HTB confirms that "Alpha is … uniting different **denominations**" and then happily relates that, in Perth for example, "six churches including the Roman Catholic church, the church of Scotland, and the **Seventh Day Adventist**, are joining together to run an interdenominational Alpha".[19]

Regardless of the devious arguments woven by Adventists from a few scriptures, their insistence on Sabbath observance as a requirement for salvation is an attack on the very centre of the gospel: "For by **grace** are ye saved through **faith** … **Not** of **works**" (Eph. 2:8-9, see also Gal. 4:10-11, Rom. 5:1 and Titus 3:5-7). The Sabbath is *symbolic* of the rest which Christ brings. It is a personal matter, not a current legal requirement:

> "Let **no** man therefore judge you in meat, or in drink, **or** in respect of an holyday, or of the new moon, **or of the sabbath days**: Which are a **shadow**" (Col. 2:16).

A non-negligible proportion of America's professing Christians are Adventists, and the church is growing elsewhere too. It may thus be helpful, at this point, to mention a few of the other subtle, but heretical, dogmas of Adventism so that readers are forewarned:

1. Adventism's guru, Ellen G. White, declared Satan to be joint sin-bearer! She wrote that "The scapegoat typified **Satan**, the author of sin, upon **whom** the sins of the truly penitent will finally be placed". To believe that Satan is substitute in any way for the finished work on Calvary is a dreadful heresy (see 1 Pet. 2:24, 1 John 1:7, Lev. 17:11 etc). It was *Christ* who was made the scapegoat for us – i.e. was punished for *our*

---

[19] *Alpha News*, Jul - Oct 1998, p10.

sin. (Satan will be punished for his own sins.) It was *Christ* who was 'made sin' for us – i.e. had our sin placed on His shoulders. It was *Christ* who was led out of the city. It is *Christ* who "**taketh away** the sin of the world". Adventism has turned all this on its head.

2. The Adventist 'denomination' states that Christ Jesus inherited a nature tainted by the Original sin. It insists that "Christ partook of our **sinful**, fallen **nature**... On His human side, Christ **inherited** just what **every child of Adam inherits** - a **sinful nature**."[20] However, according to the Word, Jesus was "holy, harmless, **undefiled** and **separate** from sinners" (Heb. 7:26). He inherited *nothing* at His incarnation, not least because He had no human father. He did take on "flesh and blood" (Heb. 2:14) and He did share the "**likeness**" of us sinful men (Rom. 8:3) – in other words he "took on" the same *body* as us (i.e. He was just as prone to tiredness and temptation as we are), but if He truly partook of our sinful, fallen ***nature*** then He would have required His own Saviour, because men are "by **nature**, the children of **wrath**" (Eph. 2:3).

3. Adventism goes on to teach that, "On the divine side, ... He [Jesus] was begotten and born of the Spirit ... [I]n the **same** way **everyone** who is 'born of the spirit' may gain victories over **sin in his own sinful flesh**. Thus **each** one is to overcome **as Christ overcame**".[21] This is just as dangerous, for the clear implication is that everyone who is 'born of the spirit' is the *same* as the Lord Jesus. We will never fully overcome sin in this life, but to teach that Christ "overcame" sin is to imply that He suffered from it at some stage and had some sin to overcome. Christ overcame "the **world**" (John 16:33), defeating the god of this world, but He was born free from sin and always remained so.

4. After Adventism's progenitor, a man called William Miller, prophesied falsely that the Lord would return in 1844, one of Adventism's most revered books claims instead that, in this year, Christ actually entered "the holy of holies [in heaven] ... to make an **atonement** for all who are shown to be entitled to its benefits".[22] This denies the finished work of Christ *on the cross* (see John 19:30, Heb. 9:26,28; 10:14). Christ, our High Priest, makes *intercession* for us (Heb. 7:25, Rom. 8:34), but He has no need to make further *atonement*.

---

[20] *Bible Readings for the Home Circle*, 1915 Edition, p115.
[21] *Ibid*.
[22] Ellen White, *The Great Controversy*, pp479-91.

5. Needless to say, Seventh-day Adventism denies the verbal inspiration of the holy Scriptures.[23] This despite verses like Matt. 5:18, 2 Pet. 1:21 and 2 Tim. 3:16. (Note that Adventism frequently uses very clever and subtle – not to say confusing – wording in order to lead its devotees into error while appearing to be orthodox to the outside world. The very way in which Adventism consistently avoids supplying unambiguous doctrinal statements is proof that all is far from well.)

There are other fundamental problems with Adventism.[24] What are 'evangelicals' doing endorsing such a church and encouraging folk into it with no warnings? HTB legitimizes the Seventh-day Adventist church as one which is suitable for Alpha participants to join – but see the Epistle to the Galatians for the *correct* attitude to have towards this institution.

---

[23] White wrote that "It is NOT the **words** of the Bible that are inspired but the MEN that were inspired ... who, under the influence of the Holy Ghost, [were] imbued with **thoughts**" [quoted by Harold J. Berry, *Seventh-Day Adventists*, p8]. An additional problem is that Seventh-day Adventists appear to attach this very same degree of inspiration to the writings of White herself!

[24] See for example the booklet *Seventh-Day Adventists*, by Harold J. Berry. Ellen White also taught that Satan and the rest of the damned, far from suffering the full horrors of Hell, will merely "be blotted from existence". She needs to explain Mark 9:42-48, Isa. 66:24, Matt. 25:46 & Rev. 14:11. What unbeliever is going to cry out desperately to God for mercy if they are taught that, at the end of their fleshly lives, they will simply be "blotted out"? It is similar to the folly of preaching that Hell is only unpleasant because of its absence of God (besides, see Rev. 14:10 and Psa. 139:7-8 in this regard). This world, which already rejects God, will hardly beg for His forgiveness on such a basis – which is one reason why Christ never taught it.

CHAPTER **22**

*T*RUE LOVE

22:1 WHAT ABOUT LOVE?   Some people will accuse this material of being 'hard' and 'unloving'. After all, Christ said "By this shall all men know that ye are My disciples, if ye have love one to another" (John 13:35). But let us, as always, examine this charge in the light of Scripture.

A Christian's *first* commitment is to the Lord and the glory of His Name: "Thou shalt **love** the **LORD thy God** with **all** thine heart, and with **all** thy soul, and with **all** thy might" (Deut. 6:5). The Lord is jealous for His holy Name (Ezek. 39:25). We are justified by His Name (1 Cor. 6:11), and as such we must love it and seek its honour. God will not forget "your **work and labour of love**, which ye have shewed toward His **Name**" (Heb. 6:10). The Psalmist said "I will **bless** Thy Name **for ever and ever**" and "I will **glorify** Thy Name **for evermore**" (Psa. 145:1-2, Psa. 86:12).

However, in Part One we discovered that we should love God's Word, the truth, because God honours His Word even more highly than His own wonderful Name (Psa. 138:2). Besides, we are saved through truth:

"[We obtain] **salvation** through ... **belief** of **the truth** ... **Therefore**, brethren, **stand fast**" (2 Thess. 2:13-15).

If the Lord's Name is being profaned, if His honour is threatened by false teachings then we are constrained, by God's Word, to act. The 'Faith' teachers have brought utter disgrace to the word "Christian" and brought God's Name into disrepute. It would be unloving to our *first* love, the Lord, not to stand up for His Truth and expose the real spirit behind such false apostles.

Next in our priorities, we are to love Christ's betrothed, i.e. God's obedient people, *as a whole.* If anyone is leading the Lord's Bride astray, even from 'within', then it is not hard to imagine the Bridegroom's hot anger and indignation. Scripture even says it is a *righteous* thing for the Lord to recompense tribulation on anyone who causes trouble to His beloved Bride (2 Thess. 1:6). As we see God's People being led away from the truth about their Saviour, and as we watch others lose their health, their faith, and even their lives because of these teachings, is it *really* 'unloving' to attempt to diminish the influence of the 'Faith' gurus and to warn Christ's body of what the Word says about such people? Accusations that this is 'unloving' only serve the *enemy's* purposes.

Elijah had no qualms about exposing the false prophets who were leading the People of God astray in *his* day. Was John the Baptist being 'out of order' when he called the apostate leaders of God's People a "generation of vipers"? Was Christ Jesus Himself being unloving when he called the same "hypocrites", "vipers", "whited sepulchres" and "fools"?

We should certainly love the brethren. We should be prepared to *lay down our lives* for them. But this assumes that we are dealing with *true* brethren. If people do not demonstrate the new life they profess, if they do not show the character of Christ, if they adamantly follow a different gospel from that recorded in Scripture, then we have no choice but to treat them as false brethren. We are doing no-one any favours by acting otherwise. The Christian life is not a game; it is a deadly (spiritual) *war* against a powerful and cunning foe. We in the West often treat the Church like a social club - but its true purpose is infinitely more serious. We must not deal negligently with such a responsibility.

Assuming we are actually dealing with a *true* brother, this brings us onto the question of what love really means. A strange statement? What we are asking is, does God's view of love (as shown by His actions in Scripture) line up with our modern, Western idea? If not, then we need to get back in line with our Father.

For example, does loving our brother mean never rebuking him? The Lord rebuked Peter, and Paul rebuked Elymas. (See also Titus 1:10.) Does loving our brother mean never confronting his falsehoods? Paul did with Peter, and Jude taught that we should. Does loving our brother mean never distancing one's self from him - *for his own sake*? Paul taught the church at Thessalonica to do this very thing. In extremis, does loving our brother mean never putting him out of the church for a time? Paul did, and he also taught the Corinthians to.

To gain a truly *biblical* view of love - and a biblical idea of God's priorities - consider the following:

- God *is* love, yet there were several occasions during the journey to the Promised Land when people who disobeyed God's commandments and followed other ways were destroyed by the Lord (e.g. Num. 11:31-34, 16:19-35 and 21:5-7).

- God *is* love, yet when two men tried to worship Him in a way which brought attention to themselves rather than to God, He immediately sent down fire which killed them both (Lev. 10:1-3).

- God *is* love, yet when He was not being treated in a properly fearful way by Uzza, He instantly killed him (1 Chr. 13:7-12; 2 Sam. 6:1-11).

Some will cry "But these are all in the **Old** Testament"! True, we are currently enjoying the "year of favour" of our Lord, but the point about the Lord's character is hopefully made. God does not change. God was "love" in the Old Testament days too. And we should remember that, when Ananias and Sapphira tried to lie, just once, to the Holy Spirit in the early *New* Testament church, God destroyed them very swiftly. (Note: the effect Ananias and Sapphira being purged from His Church was that "**multitudes**" of believers were "added to the Lord" - Acts 5:1-11.) Similarly, Herod was "immediately" killed by God for not giving God the glory when he received praise (Acts 12:21-24). Scripture also prophesies that the Lord will not deal lightly with unbelievers nor apostasy when He returns:

> "I will tread them in Mine **anger**, and trample them in My **fury**; and **their blood** shall be sprinkled upon My garments, and **I** will stain **all** My raiment. For the day of **vengeance** is in Mine heart ... And I will tread down the people in Mine anger, and make them drunk in My fury, and I will bring down their strength to the earth" (Isa. 63:3-6).

Do we still have a treacly view of love? Love is not some soppy, fuzzy feeling. It is not about compromise, and it does not equal unity. We are not *biblical*ly loving our brothers by being slack about error and false ways for the sake of *so-called* love. Love is not compatible with turning a blind eye to false beliefs among those in our Fellowships.[1] Rather, true love seeks the protection and welfare and maturing of each other - something we achieve by adhering to the Word of God:

> "And now I beseech thee ... that we love one another. And **this** is **love**, that we **walk after His commandments**. This is the commandment, That, as ye have heard **from the beginning**, ye should walk in it" (2 John 1:5-6). See also 1 John 2:5.

Hence Paul's encouragement that each believer, by "speaking **the truth** in love, may grow up into Him in all things, which is the head, even Christ" (Eph. 4:15). The truth must come first. Indeed, if we are to *truly* love people then we need the Spirit of Christ, and *this* is given to those who do not deny the power of godliness (2 Tim. 3:5) but who obey God's Word, the truth. Compare this with Nicky's rather naïve and impoverished idea of love:

> "We are **not** to criticise one another ... we are to ... **love**" [Talk 14].

22:2 OUR RESPONSE TO FALSE WAYS AMONG THE 'LAITY'

We've looked in detail at how God instructs us to deal with false / heretical *teachers*, but what does the Bible have to say about falsehood *among the 'rank and file'*? What are the effects? How are we to handle them?

Although we must draw a distinction between *false* brethren and those who are merely *deceived*, nevertheless heresy is heresy regardless of the source, and will, if not faced up to, spread like leaven to hinder the whole Fellowship:

> "Ye **did** run well; who did **hinder you** that ye should not obey the **truth**? This persuasion cometh **not** of Him that calleth you. A **little** leaven leaveneth **the whole lump**" (Gal. 5:7-9).

---

[1] Ironically, Nicky agrees with regard to sinful *behaviour*, for he states "[W]e **must** speak out against the sin. Indeed it is part of **loving** people" [*Searching Issues*, p46]. How tragic that he fails to teach the same thing about *doctrinal* error.

One could perhaps liken the leavening effect of error to a thimble full of black paint stirred into a tin of brilliant white. It would discolour the lot, and the tin could no longer be used for its designated purpose. We could also liken the leaven of error to a small amount of a strong poison placed in a vat of wine. It will work its way through until the whole vat is poisonous (and thus useless). We could never again drink from the vat. To be able to use *any* of the wine would require small amounts to be filtered and cleaned until they were free of the toxin.

These metaphors attempt to illustrate how the enemy will try to inject leaven through every unguarded avenue (even through pretty worship songs and pleasant visiting speakers). However, while these analogies may communicate the danger posed to a church and its members by unimpeded error, neither analogy is adequate to express the *subtlety and perniciousness* of it. Error *grows*, like a living thing. Paul likened this to a "canker" – an 'eating sore' comparable to cancer (2 Tim. 2:17). If people do not take swift and firm action to protect the infected body – i.e. by expelling the error - then it will replicate, turning good cells cancerous until a complete organ transplant is needed.

This may sound melodramatic, but we have already observed Paul's three years of warnings to the church in Ephesus about the poisonous blight of false ways. We must see error as a self-perpetuating foe against whom we need always to be doing battle. We are all susceptible to false ways. Allowing those who encourage error to continue among us brings dishonour - rather than blessing - on the People. (See, for example, the story of Achan in Joshua 8, or the words of the Lord in Jude 1:8-13).

*It is worth noting that "leaven" in Scripture is <u>always</u> a picture of <u>false</u> ways or <u>sinful</u> man: "Ye shall eat **nothing** leavened" (Exod. 12:20), "**Beware** ye of the **leaven** of the Pharisees, which is **hypocrisy**" (Luke 12:1), "Take heed, beware of ... the **leaven** of Herod" (Mark 8:15). See also Exod. 12:15&19 and Gal. 5:4-12.*

*Our point is that, when the Christian Church is likened to "leaven, which a woman took and hid in three measures of meal, till the whole was **leavened**" (Matt. 13:33), it does not mean what many think, else it would undermine the other references to 'leaven' - and would introduce further major problems.[2] As the following passages confirm, this parable actually means that falsehood and sin are contagious:[3]*

---

[2] The usual interpretation certainly does not fit with verses like Luke 18:8 or Rev. 12:9, or the many similar verses referred to in chapter 24 of our book! God is not a God of confusion. He

> *"Ye [disciples] should beware of the **leaven** of the Pharisees and of the Sadducees ... Then understood they how that He [Jesus] bade them ... beware ... of the **doctrine** of the Pharisees and of the Sadducees" (Matt. 16:11-12).*

> *"Your glorying is not good. Know ye not that a **little** leaven **leaveneth the whole** lump? **Purge out** therefore the old leaven, that ye may be a **new** lump, as ye are **unleavened** ... Therefore let us keep the feast, not with old leaven, neither with the leaven of malice and wickedness; but with the **un**leavened bread of sincerity and **truth**" (1 Cor. 5:6-8).*

---

is therefore unlikely to use 'leaven' to represent error or sinful man in every other passage in which it appears and then employ it in a solitary place to mean the opposite. As can be seen from the rest of the chapter, the 'Kingdom of Heaven' is a reference to those who make God their King. The argument that the 'Kingdom of heaven' cannot include evil denies the fact that even believers are sinful – and that vv40-1 *and* vv47-8 of Matthew 13 prove that this kingdom can indeed contain "things that offend" and "bad" things respectively (see also vv24-25). Furthermore, if the leaven is good then why is it "**hid**" in the meal, when the apostles etc were very *open* about their presence in marketplaces and in other public spaces - and when the Lord said what He did in Mark 4:21-23? Falsehood, on the other hand, is always introduced *secretly* into a church. And what is the identity of the woman in the leaven parable if she is not the false church (*frequently* likened in Scripture to a woman – e.g. throughout Jer. 50 and 51 and Rev. 17 and 18)? Does God commonly liken Himself to a human female elsewhere in the Bible? We can't just ignore her. The Lord would not have mentioned *any person at all* here if it were not necessary to get across a relevant point. (See the next footnote for more on this parable.)

[3] All four of the parables in Matthew 13 which deal with the *Church as a whole*, rather than with individual hearts, refer time and again to the *intermingling of evil* through it: i.e. the spread of (evil) tares among the wheat; the intermingling of evil fish among the good; the gathering of (evil) fowls among the branches of professing Christendom (see below); and *thus the spread of (evil) leaven among the (good) meal*. The remaining parables deal with individual hearts and show just how committed we must be to God *in order to minimize the impact of the evil around us*. (Regarding the parable of the mustard seed, which immediately precedes the leaven parable, this again does not mean what many people suppose. The "birds of the air" (in Matthew) or "fowls of the air" (in Luke and Mark) are both references throughout Scripture to devils and evil – as per vv4,19 of the passage in Matthew. For evidence that "the birds" (or "fowls") "**of the air**" (or "of Heaven") are pictures *throughout* the Bible of *devils and of evil*, see Ezek. 31:13; 1 Ki. 14:11; Psa. 79:1-2; Jer. 7:32-34; 15:3; 34:20 etc. Thus the mustard seed parable means that the visible, professing Church will grow very large but will become so leavened with error that devils can actually *lodge* in parts of it. The suggestion that the tree represents only the *true* Church means it must grow to a vast size, but this does not explain the reference to the 'birds of the air' and is completely at odds with the biblical data we present in chapter 24 as well.)

(The misinterpretation of the woman-and-leaven passage is a great example of precisely what we have discussed in earlier chapters – i.e. that people interpret a scripture without reference to the other relevant passages. We must love, and look at, the Bible as a whole. Indeed, even a brief look at the verses preceding and following the Luke 13:21 version of this parable show that the Lord is talking about increasing corruption not holiness, hence the reference to the Lord's mourning over Jerusalem's apostasy.[4])

The purpose of Satan's false brethren and false ways is to destroy a church - but not necessarily to destroy it *physically*. If the church can be made to accept a corrupt version of the gospel and thus be brought back under Satan's bondage then it will have been destroyed spiritually - which is what counts. In fact, Paul reports to the Galatians his experience with "false brethren" whom Satan had "unawares brought in ... that they might **bring us into bondage**" (Gal. 2:4). Note that if *Paul* was "in perils among false brethren" (2 Cor. 11:26) then it would be extremely foolish to believe that *our* Fellowships are ever immune from their presence and threat.

If a false brother cannot get an entire Fellowship to backslide on the gospel then he will try such things as sowing gossip or attempting to draw people into sin so as to cause rifts. Note that it is crucial to recognise the difference between division caused by people standing up for true teaching and division caused any other way. The following verses help distinguish between those who rightly refuse to compromise on true doctrine and those who, through scorn or lies or other methods, cause unnecessary splits:

"He that **speaketh truth** showeth forth **righteousness**: but a false witness **deceit**" (Prov. 12:17).

"Now we **command** you, brethren, in the name of our Lord Jesus Christ, that ye **withdraw** yourselves from **every brother** that walketh disorderly, and **not** after **the tradition which he received of us**" (2 Thess. 3:6).

Failing to hold to the teachings of the Apostles (i.e. the Canon of Scripture) is to have a disorderly walk. This represents a threat to the rest of the Body because the person is going in the wrong spiritual direction. For the good of the church *and of the individual concerned* (see 1 Cor. 5:1-6), we must be prepared to retreat from those who endanger the Fellowship's position before God.

---

[4] See especially verses 25ff but see also the hypocrisy exposed in vv14-16.

Compare this with Nicky's line: "The Father loves all His children ... We should say 'we accept as our brothers **all** those you receive'".[5] Nicky avoids defining what he means by the word "accept" here. We should certainly acknowledge as a brother anyone who fulfils the descriptions that God has given us in His Word of a brother, but the Bible says that there *can* be circumstances when we need to separate even from a true brother.

(We will investigate the relative importance of unity and truth in a short while. But we need to be aware that, by *false* brothers quietly sowing error among the *genuine* brothers, disagreement and division is encouraged. Congregants can be set at odds with each other, or even with the leadership, and a church can be thoroughly undermined. This is obviously something for which to be on the look out.)

False brethren are not necessarily easy to spot. But as we saw in section 18:2, Scripture tells us what to be alert for. For instance,

> "I have written unto you **not to keep company**, if any man that is **called** a brother be a fornicator, or covetous, ... or a railer; ... **with such an one** no not to **eat**" (1 Cor. 5:11).

Similarly, there will be people who put on a show of godliness, but who, outside of meetings, are actually:

> "Covetous, boasters, proud, ... unthankful, ... Having a **form** of **godliness**, ... from such **turn away**" (2 Tim. 3:2-5).

If someone truly has the Spirit of Christ, then it should show. They will display the fruit, singular: "The fruit of the Spirit **is** [not 'are'] love, joy, peace, longsuffering, gentleness, goodness, faith, meekness, temperance" (Gal. 5:22-23). "The fruit of the Spirit **is** in all goodness and righteousness **and truth**" (Eph. 5:9). Regarding the issue of determining who is, and who is not, of God, beware of those who say "Let's just leave it to Jesus to decide on Judgment Day". Such an attitude will maximise the harm that heresy is able to do in the Church. Their suggestion is unbiblical and very dangerous.

So, what about *true* brothers who persist in holding to unscriptural views? Perhaps the first point is that, if they really have the Spirit of Christ and have received the love of the truth then they will be open to correction. They will also accept God's Word when they hear it, and they will seek to

---

[5] Talk 14.

live by the teachings they have so far received – even if they have not yet been taught to test those teachings.

If we love our brothers and sisters then we will want them to put right any false beliefs and to understand the truth about the Kingdom of God. Far from accepting "diversity" of belief, we are responsible to each other to ensure that we all find, and stick to, the truth:

> "Brethren, if any of you do **err** from the **truth**, and one convert him; Let him know, that **he which converteth** the sinner from the **error** of his way shall **save** a soul from **death**" (James 5:19-20).

> "Wherefore I take you to record this day, that I am pure **from the blood** of all men. **For** I have **not shunned** to declare unto you all the counsel of God" (Acts 20:26-27).

The correction of error is certainly one of the duties of the elders, who ought "in meekness [to be] instructing those that oppose themselves; if God peradventure will give them repentance to the acknowledging of **the truth**" (2 Tim. 2:25). Nevertheless, we should *all* be on the alert and able to bring warning just as each sheep in a fold keeps an eye out for problems and warns the others of danger.[6]

22:3 UNCORRECTABLE?   But what if someone refuses to submit to the Bible and won't be corrected? The Word says: "He that refuseth instruction **despiseth his own soul**: but he that heareth reproof getteth understanding" (Prov. 15:32; see also Prov. 10:17 & 29:1). (We should always be checking and re-checking our own beliefs. It will be no excuse before the judgment seat of God that "I didn't agree to re-examine my doctrines when challenged because I was brought up with those doctrines" or "I have never bothered listening to anyone who has questioned my views because they weren't as anointed as me" or "I have stuck with my beliefs because they are what I

---

[6] Note that, just as a field of sheep might have men stationed to watch out for dangerous things coming into the field (as in 1 Sam. 25:16), so the Lord may give a Fellowship one or two souls with a 'watchman' calling (as per Ezek. 3:17-21, Ezek. 33:1-20, Isa. 62:6 and Jer. 6:16,17). In fact, we should *all* be watchmen (Mark 13:37), but among immature sheep God may supply one or two folks to whom He has given a strong gift for discerning error, who are knowledgeable of church history and God's Word, and who have a record of rightly identifying falsehood. This is a heavy responsibility, and such people ought to be listened to – but still tested!

have always been taught from the pulpit". Proverbs 15:10 says that anyone who hates reproof will end up destroying themselves.)

It seems that Scripture calls us to associate with such a person at a degree of closeness which reflects their degree of inexcusable error. (There *are* excuses for a believer to be in error at times. If, for example, the person is a new Christian, then we can obviously let them worship with us. Or if someone has been rescued from deception and is demonstrating that they are going in the right direction, but still have some blindspots not yet dealt with, again we would still allow them to pray with us. Both have an excuse.)

But of those who have had years of access to God's Word, yet are still in error, Scripture warns us that we may have to separate from them to reduce the danger of *us* being deceived. Let's look at this point. The Bible tells us, over a variety of issues, "let no man deceive you" - e.g. see 1 John 3:7 and Eph. 5:5-6. Another example revolves around the Lord's return:

> "We **beseech** you, brethren, by [i.e. regarding] the coming of our Lord Jesus Christ, and by our gathering together unto Him [i.e. the 'Rapture'] ... **Let no** man deceive you **by any means**: for that day shall not come, except there come a falling away first, **and** that **man of sin be revealed**, the son of perdition Who opposeth and exalteth himself above all that is called God, [and, pretending to be God] sitteth in the temple of God" (2 Thess. 2:1,3).

Over such matters, a Fellowship is clearly instructed to avoid being deceived by someone, however godly, who holds a different view. In this particular case – despite the fact that a person's view about the end-times is often said to be a secondary issue about which we should never 'quarrel' - where someone's unyielding position about the end-times does not fit with that described in the epistle quoted above, the church is told:

> "If **any** man obey not our **word** by **this epistle**, note that man, and have **no** company with him, that he may be ashamed. **Yet** count him not as an enemy, but admonish him as a brother" (2 Thess. 3:14-15).

(As we shall see later, Nicky regrettably mocks a desire for purity of doctrine over the crucial matter of the end-times.[7] Nevertheless it is actually *very* dangerous to have an erroneous understanding of this issue.)

---

[7] Talk 14.

The above passage unambiguously tells us that anyone who refuses to accept 'this epistle' must be kept from corporate meetings until he yields to what the Scripture teaches. Note that, harsh though this treatment may seem, it is not only a safeguard for the rest of the Body but is also done for the man's own good - "that he may be ashamed" and thus encouraged to repent. (See 1 Tim. 1:19 for another example.) Our meetings must be pure, especially where worship is involved:

> "But the hour cometh, **and now is,** when the **true** worshippers shall worship the Father in spirit **and in truth**: for the Father **seeketh such** to worship Him" (John 4:23-24).

There is an important distinction to re-emphasise at this point. The understanding about God that we need in order to be *saved* is not nearly as great as that which we need in order to be a complete, trusted, member of a Fellowship. A new baby requires constant nursing and education and cannot work. Likewise, until a person ceases to be a *doctrinally immature* baby, they cannot sensibly be a *full* working member of the 'adult' Church. How else can they go on to disciple others and teach new babes the many things that the early Church were taught, if they themselves are not mature?

(If an individual claims to be mature in the Faith then they should certainly be full of truth – i.e. doctrinally sound - since God promises this in Php. 3:15. If they are *not* doctrinally sound then their maturity must be questioned.)

These exhortations from Scripture apply to fellow *brethren*. Note that, as we have already seen, the instructions on what to do about *teachers* who hold false doctrines are even more robust (e.g. as in 2 John 1:9-11 and Gal. 1:8). Note also that unrepentant *sinfulness* requires similar discipline to that for unrepentant *error*. (See, for example, 1 Cor. 5:11-13). It all sounds very draconian, particularly in these liberal days, but God has given us His commands and they are there for everyone's safety. We ignore these divine safeguards at our peril.

We must all put truth *first*, walking in the truth that we have so far received (Php. 3:16). We must be wise and must emulate the example of the godly, wise people around us (v17, see also Psa. 37:37), for that is how a church will stay spiritually healthy and strong.

(Some readers may still think we are being unrealistic in what we are saying in these chapters. However, since we are simply reporting God's Word, that view logically implies that God is unrealistic. We cannot agree.

We recommend the Church take God's instructions to the Church seriously rather than just paying lip-service to them. Even if the Bible <u>were</u> idealistic – though Christ said the opposite - it would still not justify us failing to do our best to <u>try</u> to be obedient to God's Word.)

CHAPTER 23

𝒯RUE UNITY

23:1 WHAT ABOUT UNITY?!   Despite the very transparent scriptural statements above, many will reject them for the sake of unity – which is part of our witness after all (John 17:21). We are indeed told to seek unity with, and between, true brethren. We must each, for example, be very forgiving of those who trespass against us. Many Christians today understandably put overriding emphasis on unity. But is unity the Lord's *top* priority for us, as Nicky seems to imply, or is there something else that needs to be put before it – something which will make unity more attainable and more effective? Some prerequisite which will enable us to experience a deeper, God-given - and thus "good and pleasant" - unity rather than a contrived version? Let's see what the Word says…

From other material in this book, e.g. the opening sections of Part One, it will be realised that the Lord attaches staggering importance to His Word, the *truth*. For example:

- He Himself is called the "God of **truth**".
- He commands us to "**love** the truth" (Zech. 8:19) and He declares that He is close to those who are committed to the truth: "The LORD is **nigh unto** all them … that call upon Him in **truth**" (Psa. 145:18).

- We are kept safe by God's truth. For example: "His **truth** shall be thy shield and buckler" (Psa. 91:4, see also Psa. 40:11).
- We shall even be judged by the truth, and saved by abiding in it, for only those "which **keepeth the truth** may **enter in**" (Isa. 26:2, see also Psa. 96:13 and 2 Thess. 2:13).

So, which is the priority? Unity or truth? We need the answer, for there are times when they may be in conflict.

Those who believe that *unity* is the priority regularly point to John 17:11, which quotes Christ praying "Holy Father, keep through Thine own Name those whom Thou hast given Me, **that they may be one**, as We are". But does this *really* teach that we are to put unity before truth?…

(1) To begin with, we should note that this was a *prayer to the Father*, not a *command* to us. Like all the Lord's other supplications it will have been heard and fulfilled. Contrary to what we are frequently taught, Christ's prayer for unity has *already been answered*. It's not something *we* have to work up artificially to satisfy. *God the Father*, not we ourselves, makes us one. The Lord engendered an eternal unity *in the spirit* which can never be broken whether we are able to have *physical* unity or not.

(2) Secondly, we must look at the context. It was a prayer regarding those who truly know and follow the Lord. Look at the description of those to whom this prayer pertains: "I have given unto them the **words** which Thou gavest Me; and **they have received them**", "I am **glorified in them** … I have given them **Thy Word**; and the world hath **hated** them", but "they have **kept Thy Word**". Those who receive and keep the *truth* even in the face of persecution will know this God-given unity.

(3) The Lord prayed "that they may be one, **as We are**". This suffix must not be forgotten. The Godhead is not divided doctrinally! All three Persons of the Trinity are utterly committed to the truth. The Son spoke *only* what the Father gave Him; the Spirit does the same. If we want to be part of the body, then we too must love the *truth* first. Remember that Christ said "If a man love Me, he will **keep My words**: and My Father will love him, and We will **come unto him**, and **make Our abode** with him" (John 14:23-24, see also John 15:10).

(4) The Lord Jesus Christ prayed that the Father would "Keep them through Thine own Name". As we have seen, the "Name" of the Lord refers to His character – which is one of pure truthfulness. Hence the Father is called the "Lord God of **truth**" (Psalm 31:5b); the Son is described as

"full of **truth**"; the Holy Ghost is the "Spirit of **truth**". For those folks who imagine that God thinks *unity* is the more important thing, Christ said "Suppose ye that I am come to give peace on earth? I tell you, Nay; but rather **division**. For from henceforth there shall be five in one house divided, three against two, and two against three" (Luke 12:51-52, see also Matt. 10:34-39). In other words, the Lord Himself sometimes has to lead those who love His truth to divide from those, *even in their own household*, who do not.

(5)   In the selfsame prayer, the Lord made plain how absolutely *crucial* truth is: "They are not of the world, even as I am not of the world. **Sanctify them** through Thy **truth**: Thy **Word** is **truth** … And for their sakes I sanctify Myself, that they also might be **sanctified through the truth**" (John 17:16-19). Elsewhere, of course, the Lord had *much* more to say about how *fundamental* the matter of truth and error is.

As so often happens, people have chosen to place excessive weight on one verse rather than to keep it in balance with everything else that God's Word says on a matter. And this is only to be expected, for it appeals to the soul to have unity. No-one likes to separate from friends. It's much nicer when we all forget our differences for the sake of being part of one happy group. The trouble is that this is the *world's* way; not *God's* way. It allows error and compromise to run rife, and hence is playing straight into Satan's hands. Besides, this isn't *true* unity since the group is not unified in its view about the Lord and His Kingdom.

"But", some retort, "Jesus says we must be one 'that the world may believe'!". Well, let's check *this* against the *whole* Word too…

To start with, the full Scripture is "Neither pray I for these alone, but for them also which shall **believe on** Me through their word; That they all may be one; as Thou, Father, art in Me, and I in Thee, that they also may be one in Us: **that the world may believe** that Thou hast sent Me" (John 17:20-21).

Again it is not a command to us, but a prayer to God. Again, it has therefore already been answered. Those who truly "believe on" Christ (i.e. who rightly trust in, cling to, and rely on the *true* Jesus Christ) experience a God-given unity of the spirit regardless of their physical circumstances. The passage does not give us 'carte blanche' to ignore all the other commands in the Bible as to how the Church should operate.

Secondly, Christ did *not* pray that they "may be one that the world may believe", but that they "may be one **in Us** that the world may believe". It is true spiritual unity *with* - and *about* - the Lord, not just man-made unity with each other, which will testify that Christ is who He claimed to be. Do we honestly think the world will be impressed by a group of people who manufacture some superficial unity while actually harbouring all manner of differing beliefs about God? The world is crying out for the *truth* - not some huge amalgamation of confused Christians. They will be drawn to our *light* (i.e. the truth lived out in our lives) not to a collection of people who don't know the truth and therefore *can't* live it. The Lord confirmed this when He taught, in verse 20, that other men shall be led to believe on Him through the "**word**" of His disciples more than "through their **unity**".

On a national radio show, Nicky was asked about the main things which turn people off of Christianity. He was asked to explain the unbiblical *titles*, the expensive *buildings*, the corruption (and hence hypocrisy) and the greed. He was questioned on these things because *these* are the principal things which keep the unsaved from seeking God. These types of issues are much more troublesome for unbelievers than disunity.[1] What really attracts and impresses an unbeliever is a Fellowship which seriously lives by the scriptures – and therefore hears God, as per 1 Cor. 14:24-26.

A Fellowship's effectiveness derives not from its size, but from its purity. And the fact is that God will honour and use the Fellowships which put His Word first and which seek to be true to - i.e. live by - the whole of it. We must be committed to the Lord's ways, not our own ideas or preferences. God will be close to truth-loving Fellowships, blessing them spiritually, and *that* is what will attract those in the world who want to find the true God. How can we hope to explain God's Word to such people if we do not know and understand it ourselves? The world needs God's Word, the Bible, rather than yet another uncertain version of the truth.

Even if our desire for unity springs from a longing to bring truth to those who lack it, we may *still* not be in line with God's Word, for He calls us to separate from those who will not endure sound doctrine - and He calls us to protect ourselves from those who do not respect His Word. God's way is to avoid mixture and instead keep a Fellowship comprising those who love the truth. The Lord God will then spiritually bless and *use* that group. As a result, others - both the world and also believers who are in error - will see that it has something they are missing and will be encouraged to repent and

---

[1] *Johnny Walker Show* Interview, BBC Radio 2, UK, 20th July 2000.

join. The faces and lives of real disciples will shine Christ rather than show compromise.

23:2 UNITY 3, TRUTH 300   We *must* get the respective importance between unity and truth right. The word "unity" appears just *three* times in Scripture, whereas the word "truth" appears nearly three *HUNDRED* times. Which one do we think God calls us to pursue first? Despite what this ratio should tell us, let's concentrate for a while on those few verses that do refer to "unity":

- One of the 3 is: "With all lowliness and meekness, with longsuffering, forbearing one another **in love**; endeavouring to keep the unity **of the Spirit** in the bond of peace" (Eph. 4:2-3). We have already seen that *true* love acts to help our brethren find, and live by, the truth. Beyond this, we are to seek the "unity of ... [God's] **Spirit**" – which will plainly be broken if we all have differing beliefs about God!

- "Till we all come in the unity **of the faith**, and of the knowledge of the Son of God, unto a perfect man, unto the measure of the stature of the fulness of Christ" (Eph. 4:13). Here too, the unity is not of any old type; it is unity "of **the faith**". It is unity in the *whole truth* about the Son of God that we should be seeking. We will never reach "the measure of the stature" of Christ if we don't share the same overriding commitment to the truth that He displayed.

- Finally, "Behold, how good and how pleasant it is for **brethren** to dwell together in unity!" (Psa. 133:1). There is no argument here; it is indeed very good. But nowhere does this Psalm – or *any* Psalm - teach that truth is secondary. The spiritually pleasant unity being referred to is the *God-given* variety, not a feigned one. A *real* unity can only derive from truth. And, from personal experience, we can assure our readers that fellowship with even a *handful* of other believers who fear God and trust His Word and genuinely love the truth and are open to correction is infinitely more "good and pleasant" and precious and blessed than being in the company of a hundred people who possess divergent doctrines. Any beneficial conversation about the Lord God is all but impossible among the latter group because they all believe different things.

Yes, the Bible does call for unity - but *very* few times compared to its call for truth. We must attach the respective weight to unity and truth that Scripture does - otherwise we are not being balanced, and God says that a false balance is an "abomination" (Prov. 11:1). We must not disregard either matter but we must recognise that Scripture consistently gives *first* place to truth.

(Note: The truth, i.e. the Bible, commands those who love the truth to live in unity. So if we love the truth then we must seek such unity. Is it not far better to seek unity because the truth tells us to than to do so for any less stable reasons? The same principle applies to brotherly love.)

Yes, unity is important, but truth more so. We are commanded to "Love the **truth**" and "Rejoice in the **truth**". We are called to be "valiant for the **truth**". Does Scripture say that the fruit of the spirit is "in all unity"? No. It is "in all **truth**". Will unity "make us free"? Despite what some try to teach, Scripture says it is "the **truth**" that makes us free.

We have always found that true love and deep unity will flow, with little effort, between people who share a genuine devotion to the truth. The contrived, or "feigned", love which Alpha espouses is just not biblical. The following scripture proves that sincerely *obeying the truth* is what will help engender sincere - "unfeigned" - love:

> "Ye have **purified** your souls in obeying **the truth** through the Spirit unto **un**feigned love of the brethren" (1 Pet. 1:22). See also 2 Cor. 6:6.

This is completely turned around in Alpha. Nicky says, with no qualification, "We are to seek **unity** at **every level**".[2] In the same talk he also states that "It's amazing the issues about which churches divide", but he gives no examples, nor any scriptures to reveal what the Word says about these issues. Alpha leaders must stand up for truth.

23:3 ON JOHN   Since Nicky's central verse on this topic comes from the prayer recorded in the Gospel of the apostle John, why don't we get a more complete picture by looking at some of what John wrote on the subject of *truth*?

> "And **hereby** we do know that we know Him, **if we keep His commandments** ... [W]hoso keepeth **His Word**, in him verily is the **love** of God **perfected**: hereby know we that we are in Him" (1 John 2:3-5).

---

[2] Talk 14.

"I rejoiced **greatly** that I found of thy children walking in **truth,** as we have received a commandment from the Father" (2 John 1:4).

"He that **keepeth His [God's] commandments** dwelleth in Him, and He in him" (1 John 3:23). See also 2 John 1:9.

And perhaps the clearest proof imaginable that we need to walk in truth before unity:

"I **rejoiced greatly,** when the brethren came and testified of **the truth** that is in thee, even as thou walkest in **the truth.** I have **no greater joy** than to hear that my children **walk** in **truth**" (3 John 1:3-4). See also 2 John 1:4.

Yet Nicky actually *admonishes* those who put truth first, and claims that the Spirit of God, far from seeking this, actually promotes compromise!

"There has been some comment which is not altogether helpful to **unity.** [But the required test should always be whether the comment was helpful to **truth.**] Let us **drop** that and **get on.** ["Get on" with opening the floodgates to error?] It is wonderful that the movement of the Spirit will **always** bring churches together. **He is doing that right across** the denominations and within the traditions".³

We don't know which 'Spirit' Nicky is talking about here, but it can't be the "Spirit of **Truth**" that leads people into *truth* before He leads them into unity (John 16:13-15). The unity we often see in today's visible church, is *man*-made - engineered to embrace all and sundry at the cost of purity of teaching. (Note that concessions on truth for the sake of popularity have also taken place in the creation of many modern Bible versions - which have been translated to appeal to as many different doctrinal positions as possible, in order to maximise sales rather than maximise availability of the truth.)

Here is some more background regarding Nicky's view of unity. Notice that he avoids (a) any mention of truth, (b) any scriptural support for his statement, and (c) any distinction between the visible church - with all its "false brethren" and "deceitful workers" etc - and the *true* church:

"The Spirit brings unity to the church. People are no longer 'labelling' themselves or others ... A disunited church,

---

³ The Spirit and Evangelism, in Wallace Boulton, ed., *The Impact of Toronto,* pp82-83.

squabbling and criticising makes it very hard for the world to believe…".[4]

Of course, if each church was properly committed to the truth as it is supposed to be, then any "squabbling", as Nicky puts it - or "contending for the faith" as Scripture terms it - would quickly yield correction and thus true unity. The truth is that regardless of how "united" a church may appear *physically*, if it is full of people who all have differing views about God and His Word and His Kingdom then it is actually very *dis*united *spiritually* and is therefore effectively divided. Added to which, every member who holds to a false doctrine is divided from *God* too. In fact, even if the person does have accurate teaching they are *still* divided from God to some extent if they are disobeying His call to be separate from heresy. It is not the Fellowships which are *doing* the criticising that are the problem; it is those which refuse to *listen* to the criticism which cause the problem - and which perpetuate the "squabbling".

(Important: Alpha is meant to be encouraging participants to learn God's Word. But if Nicky Gumbel implies, as he does, that doctrine isn't important then however much the Course might *appear* to be advocating that people read and understand their Bible, guests are simply not going to be encouraged to, since they will not be able to see any point.)

Nicky thinks that unity is the main thing that will attract the world, but his version of attractiveness is actually the world's version:

> "Some churches are not very **attractive**. Imagine the Church as it was intended to be – the body of **Christ**. But everyone must play their part – **unity** – **then** we become attractive. [You] cannot get anything more attractive to the world but the body of **Christ**".[5]

Christ's attraction was *not* that He brought unity – for He didn't! It was that He brought the unadulterated *truth*. It was *apostates*, the Pharisees and Sadducees for instance, who put their differences aside for the sake of public unity. Their veneer of unity may have held some attraction, but their teachings were inconsistent and confused, and thus deeply *un*attractive. In contrast, Christ's attraction was that He was bold enough to stand against the compromised leaders and their falsehoods – of which many of God's People had become so sick.

---

[4] *Renewal*, May 1995, pp14-16.
[5] Talk 14, 1st Edn.

Here is a little analogy. A professional choir may look fabulous on the outside, but what one really cares about is the quality of the *singing*. It doesn't matter how 'together' and organised they look on the outside, what their listeners want most of all is good music. If each chorister is allowed to sing whatever he wants, or to interpret the music in an inconsistent way at odds with the others, then the result will be dischordant and repulsive. If the singers are able to get away with not even *looking at* the music score – or not even sharing the same choirmaster – then the ensuing cacophony will only interest superficial people who like the outfits. It will hold no attraction for those hungry for heavenly music.

Nicky is wrong to suggest that the Lord Jesus Christ was attractive to the world. As we noted earlier, He was *not* attractive to the world at large - and He warned us not to expect to be:

"If the world hate you, ye know that it **hated Me**" (John 15:18).

"Because ye are **not** of the **world** … therefore the world **hateth you** … If **they have persecuted Me**, they will also persecute you … They **hated** Me" (John 15:19-20,25).

23:4 RIGHTLY DIVIDING DIVISIVENESS   As we saw previously, the enemy seeks to divide each Christian Fellowship. Again, it is vital to distinguish between those individuals who cause division for the sake of the truth and those who do it for any other reason. The two are not the same! The former are, for the purity of the body, rightly "standing fast and holding to" the Word. They are refusing to sell out on the truth no matter what – hence the command in Prov. 23:23 to "Buy the truth, and **sell it not**, also wisdom, and instruction, and understanding". No church is perfect, but it should at least be going in the right *direction* - i.e. towards God's Word. If a church is going *away* from the Bible then people within it need to 'Stand fast for **the gospel'**.

False brethren don't care that God is pure; they don't care about His truth. They spread lies about Him and lead people *away* from His Word so as to destroy churches. According to Scripture, such people must be spotted and rejected for the sake of everyone.

On the question of dividing from people, it would be very easy to misrepresent Scripture and quote only the verses or part-verses which seem to prohibit *any* divisiveness - for example, where Paul says: "Now I beseech you ... that there be no divisions among you". But that would be to miss out the crucial preconditions:

> "Now I beseech you, brethren, by the name of our Lord Jesus Christ, that ye **all** speak the **same** thing, and that there be no divisions among you; but that ye be **perfectly** joined together in the **same** mind and in the **same judgment**" (1 Cor. 1:10).

Here are two further scriptures about being divisive or contentious which, when *honestly* quoted, similarly prove that *truth* comes before unity:

> "[God] will render to every man according to his deeds ... [U]nto them that are contentious, and do not **obey the truth**, but obey unrighteousness, **indignation and wrath**" (Rom. 2:6-8).

> "[M]ark them which cause divisions and offences **contrary to the doctrine** which ye have learned; and avoid them" (Rom. 16:17). Note that the command to "avoid them" *requires* us to "divide"!

(Note: The passage in 1 Cor. 1:12-15, which commands us not to cause division by saying things like "I follow **Apollos**" or "I follow **Paul**", is an indictment not of dividing for the sake of *truth* but of dividing for the sake of a name or a particular ministry. We are never told to compromise on truth in this, or in any other, part of Scripture.)

23:5 WHAT UNITES US   The following is another worying statement from Nicky:

> "Father Raniero Cantalamessa[6] – the preacher to the papal household - I heard him once give the most wonderful talk about unity. He said this 'What unites us is infinitely greater than what divides us'".[7]

Aside from the fact that Cantalamessa is a Romanist – and that we are not supposed to keep company with idolaters (1 Cor. 5:10) - there are various other problems with this statement. The most obvious one is that many people today, including Catholics, believe in a different 'Jesus' from the true Saviour. What unites many people is not Christ but compromise...

---

[6] One of Cantalamessa's seven post-Alpha talks, promoted by HTB, is entitled 'The Eucharist makes us **holy**'!

[7] Talk 14.

As we have surely proved beyond any doubt, Scripture says that, under certain circumstances, we are simply not permitted to mix with certain believers or with those who hold to certain teachings. Ultimately, if they consistently refuse to listen to scriptural correction then we must separate ourselves and leave them to the Lord (e.g. see 1 Tim. 1:19-20; 2 Tim. 3:2-5; & 2 Thess. 3:14). If a sheep was determined, after clear warnings, to wander 'doctrinally' into a minefield, what thinking sheep would stay with him for the sake of "unity"? We have actually now seen that the true Christ brings *division* rather than unity where truth is threatened.

If Cantalamessa is right, why does the underground church in China have nothing whatsoever to do with the State-accredited churches there? Members of the underground church would rather suffer imprisonment or death than join a compromised church where truth is sacrificed. We repeat: Scripture *never* allows us to dilute the truth for the sake of unity - or indeed for any other reason. (Nicky is obliged to admit that the underground church "by all accounts, is **very strong indeed**",[8] but he doesn't hypothesise as to why this might be!)

We may be "united" with others in the sense of having things in common with them, but that does not mean we should *physically* unite with them. Two people can share the same name or same hobbies or same school or same anything else, but unless they share the *same teachings about God* then Scripture tells us not to unite with them. David and Saul were united by the fact they were both part of God's chosen People, yet David was right not to have unity with Saul (the Lord even killed a man who looked down on David for "breaking away" from his king – see 1 Sam. 25:10,38).

If we look at the seven churches listed in Revelation 2 and 3, *none* of them is congratulated for their unity, but rather for (a) testing 'apostles', (b) holding fast to God's Name and not denying the faith, (c) not allowing false prophets to operate, and (d) keeping God's Word. Similarly, none is chided for separating for the sake of truth - but rather for *not* doing so and for thus allowing false ways to creep in (e.g. see Rev. 2:14-15, 20-25 and 3:17-18).

Our 'vertical' unity with the Lord must always come before our 'horizontal' relationships. The former is seriously jeopardised if we disobey God's commands. Isaiah 8:9-22 shows the danger of putting our links with

---

[8] Talk 14.

people before our walk with God. To follow Cantalamessa's teaching would actually lead to us being disunited from *God*.[9]

23:6   GOD'S DIRECTION   Nicky says "The Bible is a kind of compass".[10]   And, sure enough, God's Word does indeed show us where inaccurate teachings "go wrong", as Nicky puts it. The problem is that God *demands* that our doctrines point accurately in the right direction. Even a few degrees off the true will lead a church to the wrong destination (Matt. 7:13-14), whereas Nicky seems to feel that churches are free to go off at wide tangents to each other - provided a few "absolute essentials"[11] are in place. For example, he calls for "**liberty** in non-essentials". Unfortunately, Nicky doesn't list which are the "essentials" that apply to churches. Perhaps this is because the Bible gives no such latitude.

Nicky only supplies one example of an "absolute essential"; and his choice is very telling. He doesn't select 'belief that the Bible is the final authority for all matters of faith and practice'. Instead he picks: "the life, death, and resurrection of Jesus". However, many cults accept that Jesus lived, died and rose again – including Mormonism and the Faith movement. Indeed, Satan himself believes in the life, death and resurrection of Jesus. Even our *salvation* depends on more than this, let alone a fully functioning church.

For example, salvation requires that we believe in the Deity of the Lord Jesus Christ – and hence the Trinity. We are also required to believe that salvation is through faith alone. But *churches* need to have *many* more truths if they are to operate rightly and know God's blessing and protection. Indeed, which teachings does the Bible say are *not* essential for a church to have correct? Where does Scripture say that churches have the liberty to believe differently from the apostles' teaching?

In fact, Paul warned that very few of us should 'presume' to give authoritative teaching because it is such a grave responsibility and thus those

---

[9] Incidentally, the book *Biblical Separation* as cited in our Recommended Reading section provides much valuable background on the issue of unity and truth. While not perfect, it does supply strong rebuttals for twenty common arguments used to denounce putting truth first. It also cogently explains why infant baptism is so very dangerous to the biblical unity of a Fellowship.

[10] Talk 5.

[11] Talk 14.

giving it "shall receive the greater condemnation [i.e. stricter judgment]" (James 3:1). Why would God say this, if teaching was unimportant?

Surely one "essential" for a church is to love Jesus Christ. How can we *tell* that that someone loves Him? Well, Christ gave this clear indicator:

> "He that hath My commandments, **and keepeth them**, he it is that loveth Me" (John 14:21).

In other words, commitment to God's Word is the sign that we truly love Him. *This* is the God-given, and only, basis for unity. Compatibility can only exist if we are on the same heading of the Divine "compass". It is ironic that the teaching Nicky gives about *marriage* unions does not extend to *church* unions in his economy:

> "...Are we spiritually compatible? ... [i.e. is the other party] going in **the same direction** as us in our faith?"

Indeed, in Amos 3:3, the Word *mocks* the idea that there can be true unity between people who have divergent bearings:

> "**Can** two walk together, **except** they be **agreed**?"

23:7 SMALL BUT BRIGHT   Unity for its own sake is the world's way. God is not impressed by numbers but by those who have "received the love of the truth", who fear Him and live by His Word. These are the people He will use. Gideon showed that God can do huge things with just a handful of true followers (see Judges 7) - Jonathan and his armour-bearer likewise (1 Sam. 14).

Christ confirmed this. He could easily have 'given ground' on the hard message He gave in John 6:53-66. He had built up a big following, but rather than say "don't go away, mine is a broad church – just accept *some* of My sayings and that will suffice" He knew that only those who were utterly committed to Him would be of real use. The Lord Jesus knew that He could do far more with twelve men who were totally devoted to the Word of God than with twelve *thousand* who were prepared to compromise on it.

Nicky seems desperate to convince us that "The unity of the people of God was a **high** priority on Jesus' agenda and it should be so on ours",[12] yet Nicky was only able to quote a solitary scripture to defend this idea. But

---

[12] Gumbel, *Telling Others*, p114.

there can be no question that Christ's *top* priority was *truth*. Even if it meant rejection by His own nation, by His own town and even by His own family, the Lord Jesus was prepared to stand alone for the truth - just like Elijah and Isaiah and Jeremiah and the other prophets right up to, and including, John the Baptist. They all realised it is incomparably wiser to stand alone for the truth than compromise on it for the sake of outward unity. (For an idea of the value of truth in God's eyes, see Jer. 5:1-5).

While fellowship is of great importance, it is better to be right and on one's own (because we are never on our own with God) than to be among apostate believers who might lure us away from the true God.

We are not to follow the sheep - we are to follow the Shepherd. At the time Christ came, the People of God almost all seemed simply to follow the crowd. They possessed all the external trappings of faith but they had allowed the Word of God to be misused and replaced by man's ideas. They finally ended up in a terrible situation where they were so confused and so incapable of thinking for themselves, and so misled and closed to correction, that the whole generation was cursed (Matt. 12:39). They were often taught in *parables* rather than in clear terms because God was so angry with them that He demanded they be *desperate* for the truth in order to grasp it (see Isa. 6:10, Matt. 13:10-15, John 9:39 etc). Satan's tactics today for the People of God are the same. Get them confused. Limit their knowledge of the Word. But tell them they are saved and to blindly trust their leaders.

> "Enter ye in at the strait [i.e. narrow] gate: for **wide** is the gate, and **broad** is the way, that leadeth to **destruction**, and **many** there be which go in thereat" (Matt. 7:13). See also 1 Cor. 16:13.

112

CHAPTER **24**

"*Ri*GHTLY DIVIDING THE WORD"

24:1 REVIVAL REQUIREMENT?   Every true believer should love true revival. But the real key to revival is not 'having a unified face'; it isn't 'all churches co-operating'; it isn't even prayer. The key to revival is individual repentance and individual, unadulterated, walks with the Lord. If Wesley could achieve it in Britain without manufacturing unity with churches – and even being rejected by many Fellowships for his overriding commitment to God's Word - then it does not require huge numbers and a unity-at-all-costs attitude today.

The Western church has been promised revival for decades by most of its 'leaders'. Revival has been prophesied, but with little or no result. It has been hyped-up without materialising, and people have been brought to such a fever pitch of expectation and desperation that they are prepared to do or try anything, no matter how unbiblical, to make it happen. But this is all based on a presupposition which is not truly scriptural.

We will explain this controversial comment in stages, but please note that the following material may be hard to accept for people who **(a)** aren't open to correction, **(b)** aren't committed to seeking out the truth, or **(c)** aren't prepared to be "Berean" and check what is being said against God's Word. We urge our readers to be prepared to consider even those teachings which threaten views they've held for a long time, because the following material will demand humility and an overriding determination to seek the truth no matter what the cost or how uncomfortable the conclusion. We must be single-minded for the truth if we are to see The Lord Jesus Christ. (Please just jump to Part Five at any stage if necessary.)

24:2 RIGHTLY DIVIDING THE WORD   Numerous false doctrines are based on a close approximation to the truth. How else could the enemy draw believers away? These doctrines don't need to deny the Deity of Christ to be fatal. For example, people can teach us that it doesn't matter if a believer commits certain unrighteous acts – whereas Scripture says we should not let anyone dupe us, for "**All** unrighteousness is sin" (1 John 5:17, 1 John 3:7-8) - and we know what the payback for sin is. Alternatively, teachers can keep us from being spiritually prepared for the sacrifices and sufferings which go along with following Christ, so that we are rendered incapable of enduring. (This particular topic is dealt with more fully elsewhere in this book.)

False teachers could claim it is permissible to deny Christ - where our lives depend on doing so - whereas God's Word says:

> "**If** we **suffer**, we **shall** also reign with Him: if we **deny** Him, He also **will** deny **us**" (2 Tim. 2:12). See also Matt. 10:33 and Heb. 3:12-14.

> "For **whosoever** will **save** his life **shall lose** it: and whosoever will lose his life for My sake shall **find** it" (Matt. 16:25). See also Matt. 10:39 and Heb. 10:26-27.

> "Ye shall have tribulation … be thou **faithful** unto **death**, and I will give thee a crown of life" (Rev. 2:10). See also Luke 9:23-26 and 2 Cor. 1:13.

They could even teach us that the final antichrist is the true Christ. After all, this man is bound to quote lots of scripture and appear loving and humble and outwardly godly – he is, remember, the person that "deceiveth the **whole world**" (Rev. 12:9).

But God has given us His complete Word so that we can determine whether these doctrines are in line with the *whole* truth or whether they are unrepresentative, unbalanced deceptions. The *whole* of the Word is true, so our doctrines must be in equilibrium with it in its entirety. We must weigh

114

all teachings, based on an honest view of the complete Word. That God's People are supposed to have respect for ALL of God's Word, is made plain in verses like Exo. 24:3; Lev. 19:37, 20:22, 26:15; Deu. 5:31, 11:32; 2 Sam. 22:23; 1 Ki. 6:12, 8:58, 9:4; 2 Chr. 7:17; Neh. 10:29; Psa. 18:22 and 119:13. The following verse is very apt here:

> "A false balance is **abomination** to the LORD" (Prov. 11:1a). See also Prov. 20:23.

The basic rules of Bible interpretation appear to be relatively well known. We would suggest that the fundamental one is to read it prayerfully, respectfully, regularly, and with no bias other than an overriding desire to discover the pure truth. Two quotes give further helpful guidance:

> "A good working rule to follow is that the literal interpretation ... is to be accepted unless (a) the passages contain obviously figurative language, or (b) unless the New Testament gives authority for interpreting them in other than a literal sense, or (c) unless a literal interpretation would produce a contradiction with truths, principles or factual statements contained in non-symbolic ... [passages] of the New Testament".[1]

> "The infallible rule of interpretation of Scripture is the Scripture itself; and therefore, when there is a question about the true ... sense of any Scripture, ... it must be searched and known by other places that speak more clearly".[2]

Another principle is to beware of conclusions which delight the *soul* rather than the spirit. According to 1 John 2:16 and Eccl. 1:18 doctrines that appeal to the flesh are highly unlikely to be correct.

There is another crucial guiding principle. Many verses offer *part* of a given doctrine rather than the whole. The enemy loves to have us 'pick and choose' which verses to respect when deciding what is true. Only the doctrine which fits *all* the biblical data can be right, even if it requires a bit of thought. Here are some examples of both principles in action:

- One set of Bible passages indicates that we are saved through faith plus works (e.g. 1 Pet. 4:18-19). Another set points in the opposite direction

---

[1] Floyd Hamilton, cited by Cox, *Amillennialism*, p24, quoted by Dr. Jeffrey Khoo, *Dispensationalism & Covenant Theology*, p1.
[2] *Westminster Confession of Faith*, Chapter 1, para 9.

(e.g. Gal. 3:11). The midpoint - i.e. that genuine, saving faith inevitably results in works - is the one which reconciles both sets.

• Some scriptures imply that the Trinity comprises multiple gods (e.g. Gen. 1:26). Others seem to suggest that there is one God and no Trinity (e.g. Mark 12:29-32). The balanced doctrine, albeit mysterious, which explains all references to the Godhead, is that there is one God 'made up of' three Persons.

More Dishonesty

One particularly *inappropriate* - and dangerous - method of Bible interpretation is to selectively take literal prophecies that were not fulfilled during Bible times and then to spiritualise, or allegorise, them. Everything that happened to the physical nation of Israel throughout Scripture is written down as ensamples for us. Those literal prophecies made about her which were completely fulfilled *while the Bible was being written* certainly have spiritual applications for the church today. But there remain many other prophecies (especially in the Books of the Prophets – like Jeremiah and Zechariah) which were still awaiting complete fulfilment when the canon of Scripture was finished. Like all other literal prophecies that God has made, these too will all come *literally* true and there is no precedent whatsoever in Scripture for allegorising such prophecies.

So, what are the effects of using the manner of interpretation we castigate above? There are several, and some are absolutely deadly:

1) The first thing is that, alongside those prophecies which just require lots of imagination to spiritualise, we end up with a lot of others that are *meaningless* unless taken literally. For instance, Isaiah 17:1 prophesies that "Damascus ... [will cease] being a city, and it shall be a ruinous heap". How can this be applied to the Church? It can't. (Note that Damascus has never yet ceased to be a city, far less ever been made a "ruinous heap", although nuclear warheads are now capable of bringing this about.) We could give many scores of other examples, of which Isa. 11:11-16, Ezek. 36:8-15 and Zeph. 2:4-15 are just a fraction. But the moment we decide to trust God's Word and accept that the literal prophecies He has given *are to be taken literally*, they make much more sense.

2) A side-effect of point 1) above is that anyone can come along to our Fellowships and, while claiming to have 'special anointing', make these prophecies out to mean *whatever* he (or the enemy) wants them to mean.

116

There are many texts which can be violently twisted and manipulated - or "wrested" as Scripture puts it.

3) Another side-effect of point 1) - and equally serious - is that believers are put off reading the Books of the Prophets in the Bible. They believe them to be incomprehensible, and such folks lose out on the other highly valuable material in those books. These individuals end up relying on "more illumined" people to explain what, they conclude, the Holy Spirit seemingly won't.

4) Inappropriate interpretation of the Books of the Prophets has the effect of making other portions of Scripture (e.g. Rom. 9-11) and even *whole books* of the Bible (e.g. Revelation) much more difficult to understand. And we risk getting back into the situation in point 2) where people are able to pick out a few verses from these *other* books, link them together however they choose, and thus knit some new, but *'biblical'*, doctrine. Scripture explains Scripture: "In Thy light shall we see light" (Psalm 36:9), but if we twist *one* part it throws the other parts out and leads to confusion and further error. (The figurative references in Revelation can be explained by looking them up elsewhere in Scripture – including the Books of Prophets such as Daniel.)

5) Since these prophecies revolve around the "day of the Lord" – i.e. that period leading up to His return – misinterpretation means that we lose sight of God's timing regarding the very last days and are rendered less able to prepare for them. (See later for more details about this.)

24:3 THE LAST DAYS There are even more unfortunate implications of this dishonest method of Bible interpretation. For, by using this inconsistent and confusing method where unfulfilled literal prophecy is spiritualised, it is commonly taught that, leading up to the return of the Lord, the Church will inevitably "take the nations" and bring the whole world under its authority. Tremendously appealing as this sounds, it does not seem to agree with the Lord's own description of the last days - for, when asked by His disciples, in Matt 24:3, "What shall be the **sign** of Thy coming, and of **the end of the world**?" Jesus did not say "The Church will have taken authority over the world and made it ready for Me". In fact He answered:

> "[People shall] deliver you up to be **afflicted** ... and ye shall be **hated** of **all** nations for My name's sake ... And because iniquity shall abound, the love of **many** shall wax cold. But he that shall **endure** unto the end, the same shall be saved" (vv5-13); "[T]hey

shall lay their hands on you and **persecute** you ... And ye shall be hated of **all** men for My name's sake" (Luke 21:12,17).

God's Word further states, regarding this period:

"[T]ake **heed** to yourselves: for they shall deliver you up to councils; and ... ye shall be **beaten**: and ye shall be brought before rulers and kings for My sake, for a testimony **against** them" (Mark 13:9).

This doesn't sound too much like the nations of the world coming under the authority of Christ's followers. Rather, it seems to suggest a time of *adversity* for believers. (Consider also Matt. 24:21-24.) Similarly, the Lord warned, regarding the period just before His return:

"**Beware** of men: for they will **deliver you up** to the councils, **and** they will **scourge** you ... And ye shall be **hated** of **all** men for My name's sake: but he that **endureth** to the end shall be saved" (Matt 10:16-23a).

Ah, but surely the Bible says that the gospel will be preached to all nations! Yes it does. But it does *not* say that the nations will listen to and *accept* the gospel. In fact, Scripture indicates that it will be preached partly to purify us - through the persecution which results from their rejection of our message and Lord - and partly as a testimony *against them*, so that they will be without excuse:

"Take heed to yourselves: ... ye shall be **beaten**: and ye shall be brought before rulers and kings for My sake, **for a testimony against them**" (Mark 13:9). See also Matt. 24:14!

"They shall **lay their hands on you, and persecute you**, delivering you up ... into prisons, being brought before kings and rulers for My Name's sake. And **it shall turn to you for a testimony** ... And ye shall be **betrayed** both by parents, and **brethren**, and kinsfolks, and friends; and some of you shall they cause to be **put to death**" (Luke 21:12-16).

24:4 IT GETS WORSE The Lord's return will actually be preceded by a *falling away* - and one so widespread that it makes possible the rise and acceptance of the ultimate manifestation of the Antichrist:

"Now we **beseech** you, brethren, by [i.e. regarding] the coming of our Lord Jesus Christ, ... [T]hat day shall not come except there come a **falling away** first, and that Man of Sin [the final Antichrist] be revealed, the son of perdition" (2 Thess. 2:1-3).

This Antichrist will be able to "make war with the saints, and to **overcome** them" (Rev. 13:7; Dan. 7:21,25). In fact, far from us enjoying dominion, Christ Jesus went on to say that Christians shall suffer "great **tribulation** ... And except those days should be shortened, there would no flesh be saved" (vv21-24). This is somewhat at odds with Nicky's assurance that we have cause for "great **optimism**" about a huge future harvest.[3]

The scriptures actually indicate that only a "remnant" (a very small minority) will remain faithful to biblical truth and will therefore avoid this "falling away". These are the ones which the last Antichrist will attack. He will "make war with the remnant ... which keep the commandments of God, and have the testimony of Jesus Christ" (Rev. 12:17; see also Dan. 8:24).

According to Holy Scripture, the visible church will contain many apostates in the last days. These are people who put on a mask of piety but who are actually far from truly Christian. They will threaten not just the good Name of the Lord Jesus but His People too, making it a perilous time for Christ's real disciples:

> "This know also, that in the **last** days **perilous** times shall come. For men shall be lovers of their own selves, **covetous**, ... Without natural affection, trucebreakers, **false** accusers, incontinent [i.e. unable to control themselves], fierce, despisers of those that are good, Traitors, heady, highminded, lovers of pleasures more than lovers of God; **Having a form of godliness** but denying the power thereof [i.e. maintaining a 'Christian' exterior, but rejecting the idea that true spiritual strength and God's *genuine* anointing stem from deep, biblical godliness]" (2 Tim. 3:1-5).

Paul goes on to warn us further of these people who:

> "Resist the **truth**: men of **corrupt** minds, **reprobate** concerning **the faith** ... But thou hast fully known my **doctrine**, manner of life, purpose, faith, longsuffering, charity, patience, persecutions ..." (2 Tim. 3:8-13).

Going back to our original passage; below are the words the Lord uttered straight after being asked "What shall be the **sign** of Thy coming?"

---

[3] Gumbel, *Searching Issues*, p33.

The reader may wish to compare them with the claims and promises of some in the church about how its influence will spread like leaven and make all nations bow the knee:

> "[People shall] **deliver you up** to be **afflicted**, and **shall kill you**: and ye **shall be hated** of **all** nations for My Name's sake. And **then** shall **many** be offended, and shall **betray** one another, and shall **hate** one another. And **many** false prophets shall rise, and **shall deceive many**. And because iniquity shall abound, the **love of many shall wax cold**. But he that shall endure unto the end, the same shall be saved" (Matt. 24:3-13).

24:5 REVIVAL IS COMING   Although we are boldly to preach the gospel, let us not fool ourselves into believing that we will 'win the world [or even just our nation] for Christ' before He returns. Scripture strongly indicates that, at least in the vast majority of nations, relatively few will actually be saved in the end times. Seemingly it will be just as it was, for example, in Elijah's day when only a remnant were saved. Likewise on Israel's return from Babylon.

> "As it was in the days of Noah, **so shall it be also** in the days of **the Son of man.**" (Luke 17:26), "In the days of Noah ... **few**, that is, **eight** souls were saved" (1 Pet. 3:20); "**Likewise also** as it was in the days of **Lot**" (Luke 17:28) - when only *one* household was saved (Gen. 19:14-16).

> "Because strait is the gate, and narrow is the way, which leadeth unto life, and **few** there be that find it" (Matt. 7:14). See also Rev. 10:18-21.

> "[M]any are called, but **few** are chosen" (Matt. 22:14).

Many in the church are due to be killed or lured into apostasy, or led, through persecution and threat of death, to deny Christ. According to Scripture, many others will give up their faith because of the temptations of the world. It is thus a dreadful falsehood to teach that the church is going to take the nations for Christ. (What we have written in these sections is often dismissed as being pessimistic, but the only proper test is whether or not it is biblical. Indeed, the Lord was under no illusion as to how terrible the very last days would be, and how few would "continue in the faith" and be saved. He even asked, in Luke 18:8, "When the Son of man cometh [i.e. when He returns], **shall He find faith** [i.e. anyone left who has a really serious faith in the true God] **on the earth?**".)

We *hope* there will be revival – but the word actually implies the reinvigoration of something *already alive*. All of us weak, carnal, believers need to be revived if we are to endure that which is coming. We need the separation and purification which will surely result from the unique time of tribulation approaching:

> "What are these which are arrayed in white robes? ... These are they which came out of **great tribulation**, and have **washed their robes**, and made them **white in the blood of the Lamb** ... They shall hunger no more, neither thirst any more; neither shall the sun light on them, nor any heat ... [A]nd God shall wipe away all tears from their eyes" (Rev. 7:13-17). See also Rom. 5:3-4, 2 Cor. 4:17 and Jas. 1:2-4.

24:6 SIGN OF THE TIMES   So what *is* the "restoration" of which the scriptures speak, e.g. in Isaiah 49? If we take the unbiased method of Bible interpretation that says "God's literal prophecies will all come true **literally**" (i.e. before they have any allegorical meaning), then we would expect to see a restoration of *physical* Israel shortly before the Lord's return...

This is confirmed several times in the New Testament including: (a) where Christ says that we shall not see Him "til ye [i.e. Israel] shall say, Blessed is He that cometh in the name of the Lord" (Matt. 23:39),[4] (b) where Paul reveals that Israel's restoration is bound up with the resurrection to come (Rom. 11:15), and (c) where Christ uses the 'shooting forth' of the *fig tree*, an allusion to physical Israel, to be a portent of the end-times (Mark 13:28-29, c.f. Hos. 9:10). God will bring Jews back to their original home for at least one very good reason:

> "I had pity for **Mine holy Name**, which the house of Israel had profaned among the heathen, ... Thus saith the Lord GOD; I do not this for your sakes, O house of Israel, but for **Mine holy Name's** sake, ... **I will sanctify** My great Name, ... For I will take you from among the heathen, and gather you out of **all countries**, and will bring you into your own land" (Ezek. 36:22-24).

(Jehovah is also known the world over as "the God of Israel". The Israeli people thus affect God's reputation. Furthermore, the nation of 'Isra-

---

[4] Israelites now routinely say this phrase as part of their culture. And 99% of them also observe the Feast of Passover.

el' actually bears God's name - "EL" - which the Lord will vindicate before the world – see Ezek. 20:44 and Isa. 48:11-12. As 1 Sam. 12:22 says: "The LORD will **not** forsake His people **for** His **great Name's** sake".)

A restoration, in many forms, of physical Israel is *precisely* what we have seen going on over the last century. The following is only a *partial* list to prove the point, and numerous other scriptures could be quoted to support many of the aspects mentioned below. The reader is strongly encouraged to look up the more important references quoted. It will incontestably be seen how absolutely literal, rather than figurative, the passages are.

Restoration of the language – Despite Hebrew, like Latin, being a dead language for many centuries, it was restored in the 19th century. We now have not just the limited range of Hebrew words that appear in Scripture but the *complete* tongue to enable everyday use - just as prophesied in Zeph. 3:9 and Isa. 19:18.

Restoration of the people – Despite all the unspeakable and widespread persecutions committed against the Jewish people by the enemy over the last two thousand years, the Lord has kept them from being totally destroyed, as prophesied in places like Lev. 26:44-46 and Ezek. 11:16. He is regathering them from *numerous* (well over one hundred) nations - just as predicted in several passages including Ezek. 36:24, Jer. 29:14 and Isa. 49:12-13.[5]

> "He ... shall assemble the outcasts of Israel, and gather together the dispersed of Judah from the **four corners of the earth**" (Isa. 11:12). See also v11.

Restoration of the land – Despite the huge improbability of such an event, the people have returned back, nearly 2000 years later, to the *original* land they were given, as prophesied in Ezek. 20:41-42, 37:12; Jer. 3:18 and Isa. 14:1. Note that this is a land which *God* has given them *forever* (Gen. 13:14-17 and Psa. 105:7-11). If they have no right to the land now, why did they have a right to it in Jesus' day? (Incidentally, the return and re-settlement has been greatly helped by non-Jews who care about the Jewish people, as per Isa. 14:1, 49:22 and 61:5.)

> "Thus saith the Lord GOD; I will even gather you from the people, and assemble you out of the countries where ye have been scattered, and I will give you the land of Israel" (Ezek. 11:17).

---

[5] The return which followed WWII often involved only one or two people from an entire village, just as prophesied in Jer. 3:14.

The reader is urged to be careful of the various 'ten lost tribes' arguments. Whenever parts of Israel were exiled, lowly remnants of each tribe were always left to look after the land - see, for example, 2 Ki. 24:14b, 2 Ki. 25:12, 2 Chr. 30:11 and 2 Chr. 34:9. This is proved beyond doubt in Luke 2:36-38 because Anna is identified as coming from the 'lost' tribe of Asher. (Note that those Jews who have assimilated with other peoples are no longer considered Jews by the Lord.) The issue of who is, or is not, a physical Jew is easy to answer. Whoever truly believes they are Jewish, and identifies with God's People, is a Jew (as per Rom. 2:28-29). This deals with various arguments about the physical composition of modern Israel.)

Restoration of the nation – Despite all the pressures on them to assimilate, God has kept the Jewish people identifiable - and not just through genetic testing! This was promised in Psa. 94:14 and Jer. 31:35-37. God has also restored them as one Kingdom instead of two - as specifically prophesied in Ezek. 37:21-22 and Jer. 3:18. The restored nation was born in a single day as foretold in Isaiah 66:8, and, despite overwhelming odds faced during each military attack she has suffered, has been protected so that she can never be uprooted again, just as promised in Amos 9:15, Jer. 24:6 & 31:38-40.

> "The God of **Jacob** ... will **not** cast off His people, neither will He forsake His inheritance" (Psa. 94:7&14).

(See the Recommended Reading section later for astounding details of Israel's many Divine deliverances.)

Restoration of the capital – Despite the world's great efforts to avoid it, another huge miracle has been the return of the Old City of Jerusalem to the nation of Israel, as literally prophesied in Zech. 8:7-8 and Luke 21:20-24. The Lord also foretold that, despite Arabs controlling the two places most sacred to Islam, there would be an immense fuss over Israel having control over *her* foremost, indeed her only, holy spot (see Zech. 12 & 14). Note: (a) The Temple Mount site is not even *referred to* in the Koran, and (b) When journalists deceptively talk about "Arab East Jerusalem" they are actually referring to the Old City, the City of *David*.

Restoration of the environment – Despite the incredible desolation of the land of Israel right up until the last century, as prophesied in Ezek. 33:28, it has now been transformed. The Lord promised that the "waste cities" and historic settlements would be rebuilt after *many* generations - and *never to be uprooted again* (this *cannot* therefore refer to any previous return). See Isa. 61:4 and Ezek. 36:37-38 for proof.

God further promised that the land, which barely had *any* trees on it as recently as the 19th Century, would become fertile and blessed, just as we have witnessed (Ezek. 36:8-12, 34:13-14 and Amos 9:13-14). Unbelievably, Israel is now a huge exporter of fruit just as prophesied in Isa. 27:6 and Ezek. 36:30. In fact, the land has returned to such high quality as to even support restoration of the vine culture as prophesied in Jer. 31:4-5,10-12 and Zech. 8:12. Many restorations are ongoing, but they are also irrefutable.

> "And I will bring again [i.e. undo] the captivity of my people of Israel, and they shall build the waste cities, and inhabit them; and they shall plant vineyards, and drink the wine thereof; they shall also make gardens, and eat the fruit of them" (Amos 9:14).

Restoration of the faith – We could go on and on about Israel's miraculous *physical* restoration. But the most exciting thing is to see the beginnings of her *spiritual* restoration - particularly now that she has regained her spiritual home, Jerusalem. Despite being tormented by Rome and its horrible version of Christianity for centuries, the Jewish people are beginning to want to find out about their countryman, Jesus Christ. (They have been utterly put off Christianity because they have been told that Catholicism – whose adherents have massacred so many Jews 'in the Name of Jesus' – is Christian.) The restoration of Israel's heart is promised in passages like Ezek. 11:19-20, 36:25-26 and Jer. 31:33.

A few arguments, based on ambiguous verses pulled out of context, have been invented to deny that God's original purposes for physical Israel are still intact. The reader is encouraged to read the whole of Jeremiah 30 and 31 before deciding what is true. (Please also see Ezek. 36-39 and Zech. 8.) Additionally, the reader is encouraged to consider the dozens of parallels between the story of Joseph, the son of Jacob who ultimately revealed Himself to – and then saved - his brothers, the other sons of Jacob, and the two comings of Christ Jesus (who will, according to Zechariah, ultimately reveal Himself to – and then save – his brothers according to the flesh).

Now, we should categorically state here that, *all* must have faith in the Messiah, the Word of God, to be saved (hence Rom. 10:11-13). And if a person is "in Christ" then they have equal value and standing regardless of their circumstances - hence Gal. 3:8 which says "there is neither Jew nor Greek … **in Christ Jesus**". But to take such a verse to mean that God sees His ancient People, the physical nation of Israel, as being just like any other nation, is to fly in the face of Scripture. Even a simple reading of Romans 9-

11 should be enough to dispel such a view, for those who put the truth first and have no axe to grind.

Suffice it to say that, although God has indeed forsaken *individual generations* of Jews, He has neverthless promised never to forsake physical Israel in perpetuity:

> "I will **not** cast them away, neither will I abhor them, to destroy them **utterly**, and to **break My Covenant with them**: for I am the LORD **their** God. But I will for their sakes remember the Covenant **of their ancestors**" (Lev. 26:44-45).

> "Zion said, The LORD hath forsaken me, and my Lord hath forgotten me. **Can** a woman forget her sucking child, that she should not have compassion on the son of her womb? yea, they may forget, yet will I **not** forget thee. **Behold**, I have **graven thee upon the palms of My hands**" (Isa. 49:14-16).

> "For a small moment have I forsaken thee; but with great mercies will I gather thee. In a little wrath I hid My face from thee for a **moment**; but with **everlasting** kindness will I have mercy on thee, saith the LORD thy Redeemer" (Isa. 54:8). See also Isa. 62:4 and Ezek. 39:33ff.

Note that the Bible still identifies the Lord as the "God of Abraham, Isaac and Jacob" *after* the cross (Acts 3:13; Matt. 22:31-32).

24:7 AN OLD OBJECTION   It certainly appeals to the flesh to believe that the Church has replaced Israel and has inherited all the promises made to her. However, the test is not how *appealing* the idea is, but how *biblical*. Under the circumstances it is no surprise that some people hunt for reasons to avoid the truth. "The Jews killed Jesus" is the most common cry, especially among Romanists.[6]

(a) While many of the *deceived* Jewish people of Christ's day *rejected* Him, it would be unrighteous to blame the entire nation for His death. For a start, it was not Jews, but Roman soldiers who nailed Him to the cross. And this was done at the insistence of the false *leaders* of God's People: "The **chief priests and elders** persuaded the multitude that they should

---

[6] Although Nicky does not say this on Alpha, neither does he distinguish between the "Jews" who wanted to 'kill Jesus' and the "Jews" comprising the rest of the nation. The impression Nicky gives is that the great majority of the Jewish people wanted the Lord dead, whereas the Bible refers to "Jews" in two very distinct contexts (i.e. leaders and people).

ask [for] Barabbas" (Matt. 27:20, see also Luke 24:20; Mark 11:27-12:12 or Matt. 21:37-39,45).

But in truth it was *all* our sins that put Him there. (And just because the portion of Israel that was present said "His blood be on us and on our children" does *not* mean that *every* generation of the *entire* People are cursed – especially since Christ said "Father, **forgive** them; for they know not what they do".[7])

(b) We Gentiles were given the gospel to *provoke Israel to jealousy* - and thus to repentance (Rom. 10:19, Rom. 11:11, Deut. 32:21) - not to reject them and slaughter them in their millions. They only rejected the Lord because they had been led away from God's Word by false shepherds (Jer. 50:6, Jer. 23:1-2, Matt. 23:13, Luke 11:52).

(c) Satan hates Israel and has always sought her destruction. Initially this was in order to prevent Christ's first coming; now it is to try and prevent His *second* coming (Matt. 23:37-39). As "god of this world", Satan has encouraged the world throughout history to reject Israel and to persecute her. We must be careful not to assist him - e.g. by rejecting the "apple of God's eye" (Zech. 2:6-8) just because of a minority of bad apples.

Satan continues to turn mankind against Israel to this day. He uses disgraceful deceptions and highly biased 'news' reports about her – freely propagated through the media. (See our Recommended Reading section on Israel for proof of this.) The truth is that she is the *only* true democracy in the region (the arrangement forced on Iraq by America aside); unlike many countries in the region she has freedom of speech and a free press; she has, despite facing fanatical terrorist threats, a vastly better human rights record than her neighbours – including the Palestinians; she shows a much greater religious tolerance than other nations (no Jew is allowed to live in Jordan for example); and she has *far* less government corruption than her Middle East counterparts. (She has also made big concession after big concession in the 'peace' process with the Palestinians, only receiving tiny salami slices back from the other side.)

Israel is simply trying to defend her tiny country (which is only a fraction of the size promised by Britain in 1917) from nations committed to "driving Israel into the sea". These are nations who had no sympathy for her

---

[7] Note the way in which the Person who was killed forgave them straight away, and compare this with His so-called followers who still refuse to forgive them nearly 2000 years later. (Many of these people purport to emulate Christ, if not to actually BE Christ.)

unimaginable sufferings during the holocaust, but who instead attacked this terribly battered and under-equipped people as soon as the United Nations gave her a home. (It is true that a tiny handful of 'terrorist' acts have been committed by Israelis in the last sixty years, but if one compares the quantity and type of acts committed on both sides, and even more so if one compares the justifications and provocations that lay behind the acts on both sides, the Israelis are *infinitely* more decent in this regard.)

It is important to realise that, in 1948, Palestinians left the land for a variety of reasons – but very few were expelled. In 1967, Palestinians fled Israel to get out of the way *of the attacking forces of their Arab brothers.* Again, Israel did *not* throw them out.[8] Palestinian and Jew had co-habited peacefully for decades previously. Israel's enemies claim that Palestine is a sovereign state. But it has *never* been one:

> "Early Arab nationalists **never** referred to the Palestinians as such or to their rights. In May 1947 their argument at the U.N. General Assembly was that 'Palestine was part of the province of **Syria**' and that 'politically, the Arabs of Palestine were **not** independent in the sense of forming a separate political entity'. As late as May 31st, **1956**, [8 years *after* the Arab 'refugees' left] Ahmed Shukairy, the **Saudi Arabian** delegate to the U.N. (and later the leader of the Palestinian Liberation Organization) told the Security Council 'It is **common** knowledge that Palestine is **nothing but Southern Syria**'".[9] (See the rest of the Appendix of that book for many other facts which put the whole matter in a fundamentally different light from the one usually publicised.)

The tragic Palestinians who left the land could so easily have been absorbed by Israel's many anti-semitic neighbours. They have instead been cynically exploited as political pawns, and held unnecessarily in miserable camps for decades. (Please see the superb book *From Time Immemorial: The Origins of the Arab-Jewish Conflict Over Palestine* by Joan Peters for much more information on this subject. And see the article 'Alpha on Israel' available from the 'Better Than Rubies' section of our website, bayith.org, for numerous problems with Alpha's treatment of the Jewish people.)

Regrettably, the world's press has been duped. As the fine website HonestReporting.com proves, the media have allowed in the worldly spirit

---

[8] An event at a place in Israel called Deir Yassin has been grossly exaggerated and used very dishonestly as a stick with which to beat Israel. Be sure to read reports from ALL sides about this incident before drawing any conclusions!

[9] Lance Lambert, *Battle for Israel*, Appx, Section 2.

of anti-Semitism. The world's press use every lever possible to denounce Israel. They even make international news items about trivial problems in the Prime Minister's homelife - while barely finding a single column inch for the frequent vicious conflicts within, and between, the nearby Arab nations – or indeed the grotesque bruatlity and corruption of the Palenstinian Authority (which is so great that most Palestinians prefer to live under Israeli rule). We strongly recommend readers check the history of modern Israel. They will discover that the media have given us a totally misleading picture – something God is greatly angered by, according to Jer. 50:7,11-13 and Jer. 30:20.

*Note: Because the Jewish people are not yet spiritually restored, some commentators feel that the ongoing restoration of the modern state of Israel is a **satanic counterfeit** of a future restoration. However, we should remember a few things:*

Firstly, the Jewish people have suffered appallingly through the centuries and yet have shown a serious degree of godliness by withstanding unbelievable pressures to assimilate into the world. Many survivors of this 'sifting' have tried to remain faithful to their veiled understanding of God's laws, and they are now displaying a real, if rudimentary, faith in the God of Israel by returning to the land He gave them.

*Secondly, a physical restoration in the Bible sometimes precedes spiritual restoration (e.g. Ezek. 37:11-14; Gen. 42:25) and Israel's promised spiritual restoration will apparently be fulfilled when Christ reveals Himself to His physical brethren - just as Joseph made himself known to the sons of Israel who originally rejected Him. See Gen. 45:1-8 & Zech. 12:10, 13:1-2,6. Only after this will the physical restoration be **completed**.*

If any readers reject our comments, then we would beseech them at least to look inside their hearts and ask themselves if they love the Jewish people to begin with. The spirit of anti-Semitism is very powerful and will certainly colour one's attitude to Israel. If we do not care for them then we are badly out of step with our merciful God who has loved the nation of Israel with an "**everlasting** love" (Jer. 31:1-3) and His mercy towards her "endureth **for ever**" (Ezra 3:11). See also 1 Ki. 10:9!

As an aside...

As we have seen, the Church has not replaced physical Israel. So what is the true relationship between them? Two remaining possibilities exist, and the reader must decide which one is most in harmony with God's eternal Word. (This decision is crucial because the two positions lead to *very* different doctrines - and to radically disparate interpretations as to what proportion of the *spiritual* principles and *non*-symbolic instructions listed in the Bible have relevance to believers today.)

Either the Church and Israel are completely distinct (the much more popular view), or there is a middle position where God's spiritual nation and His physical nation are different *but related* (akin, in some sense, to the way in which believing Jews were obviously related to unbelieving Jews before the New Covenant was made) - as is indicated by Rom. 11:18-24; Gal. 3:6-9,29; 6:16; Eph. 2:11-22 and Rom. 4:11-18. But, either way, the Church certainly cannot afford to spiritualize, or appropriate for herself, any physical promises to physical Israel that have yet to be completely fulfilled.

In fact, we owe Israel an unrepayable debt. Moses, David, Elijah: all were produced by Israel. As were all the other Patriarchs after Jacob. Israel gave birth to John the Baptist, to all the apostles, plus the writers of the scriptures. It was Israelites who gave safe transmission of the Word to us too. Amazingly, for the first fourteen years of its existence, *all* members of the early church were Jewish. Most of all, it was Israel which physically gave us Jesus Christ Himself ("the glory of Thy People Israel"). In view of all this, we should seek to comfort her (Isa. 40:1-2, Rom 15:27) and should pursue her good (Psa. 122:6-9, Isa. 62:1-7).

Most of all, we should pray regularly for her spiritual restoration (Jer. 31:7, 1 Sam. 14:23). As noted earlier, Queen Esther is a picture of the Lord's Bride.[10] Intercession for Israel was not optional for her (Esther 4:14).

God promised Abraham, Isaac and Jacob, on separate occasions: "I will ... **curse** those that curse you". This promise has never been revoked. Christians need to think carefully about this before turning against God's ancient People or stealing His promises from them. Indeed, I can vouch - from personal experience - that if we take God's literal prophecies literally and obey His command to pray for Israel, it will not only transform our understanding of Scripture, but will revolutionise our whole walk with the God, for He also repeatedly said of Israel: "I will bless those that **bless** you".

24:8 WHAT DOES THIS MEAN?   The biblical prophecies regarding the world coming under the Lord's subjection refer to the period *after* Christ's return to Jerusalem (when He will set up His promised Kingdom). Christ's

---

[10] Esther was adopted into a Jewish family just as we have been.

earthly Kingdom will only start when He comes back. But Nicky Gumbel talks of "the Kingdom which Jesus **inaugurated**".[11] According to the Oxford English Dictionary, the word "inaugurate" means: "Admit **formally** to office; Initiate **public** use of; Introduce with ceremony", but Christ's Kingdom has *not* begun in that sense yet. Nicky further states:

> "There is also a **present** aspect of the Kingdom ... the **dawning** ... of the Kingdom ... Jesus said 'the Kingdom ... is among you' [Except He didn't!]. The Kingdom is something which can be discovered and experienced *now*, in *this* age ... [T]he 'age to come' has **begun**. The 'old age' goes on but the **powers** of the **new age** [sic] have erupted into this age. The future **Kingdom** has broken into history".[12]

If we follow, to its logical conclusion, Nicky's claim that Christ is already reigning (and there is a lot more evidence we could offer here), then we face some bizarre problems, a few of the more obvious being:

- Christ, when questioned about the setting up of His earthly Kingdom, confirmed that it *would* take place (Acts 1:6-7), but not immediately. He illustrated this with the parable of the nobleman who "goes away to a **far** country for a **long** time" while his servants are left behind to "do business" *until he returns* (Luke 19:11-15, 20:9, Mark 13:34). The Lord clearly expected to receive His Kingdom at His Second Coming, *not* at Pentecost. (The spiritual 'Kingdom of God' or 'Kingdom of heaven' is not the same as the physical, millennial reign of Christ. The Lord Jesus is King *of His disciples* but has not yet been crowned King *of the nations* - though many believers are taught that He has. See below for proof.)

- Christ's reign on this earth is supposed to last for a thousand years. The "thousand year" duration is unequivocally stated SIX times in the highly literal passage in Rev 20:2-7. But it has been more than a thousand years since Pentecost, so either Scripture is being unimaginably misleading or Christ's Kingdom did not start when people claim. The future earthly reign of Christ from Jerusalem is described clearly and thoroughly in the Books of the Prophets: "Thus saith the LORD; I ... **will** dwell in the midst of Jerusalem" (Zech. 8:2-8,20-23; 2:10-11). "And the LORD **shall be** king over all the **earth**" (Zech. 14:4, 9-11, 16-17). See also Isa. 2:1-4; 11:1-10; 33:17-24; 65:19-25, Psa. 2:6-12 and Psa. 48:1-8.

---

[11] E.g. in Talk 13.
[12] Talk 13.

If God likens a thousand years to a day (Psa. 90:4-5), then, just as the final day of the week was holy unto the Lord, so the final thousand years of world history will be holy - sanctified by being ruled by Christ Jesus. Hence Peter's very urgent command, written in the context of the Lord's second coming, "Beloved, be **not** ignorant of this **one** thing, that one day is with the Lord as a thousand years, and a thousand years as one day" (2 Pet. 3:8). Note his emphasis "be not ignorant of THIS **ONE** THING" – demonstrating the great importance of getting this matter correct. Also note that this interpretation means Hosea's apparent prophecy of Israel's restoration is therefore accurate, since it has happened about 2000 years after Christ's day (Hos. 6:1-2).

This is another matter which demonstrates the importance of finding the position which encompasses *all* scriptural references. Some passages can be read as supporting the 'amillennial' view - which flatly denies any millennium. There are also a few verses which can be used to support the 'postmillennial' view that we are already in the millennial reign. The balanced position is that Christ Jesus will usher in His Kingdom when He comes - and that we are not to try and pre-empt it in any way.

- Christ's reign is to see the Jewish feasts reinstated (Zech. 14:16, Zech. 8:19), the Levitical priesthood restored (Isa. 66:20, Ezek. 44:11), and, as a lasting commemoration of His own sacrifice on the cross, the offering of sacrifices renewed in a rebuilt temple (Jer. 33:14-18, Isa. 60:7, Ezek. 40-46). None of these things can be done by the Church but only by a physical Israel. (And Israel is, indeed, unwittingly preparing herself for these things – although the *final* temple will be as per the prophecies in Ezek. 40-48.)

Readers may be tempted to ask what *difference* is made by Nicky's 'post-millennial' stance. The fact is that it causes his hearers to have a rose-tinted view of every development in the Church (and in the world). The idea, fostered by Post-Millennialism, that things in this world will inevitably get better and better as time goes on, discourages folks from checking weak conversion testimonies, or questioning 'unorthodox' preachers, or testing spiritual occurrences, or mourning (and staying apart from) the increasingly depraved state of the nations... because post-millennialists are convinced that everything is going to work out beautifully *before* Christ Jesus comes back. As we have already seen, this is the very *opposite* of what God's Word says will happen. See also Dan. 7:21-22; Rev. 13:8; Mark 13:9, 13:12-23 etc.

24:9 FINALLY...   In closing, many folks have heard arguments and seen individual Bible verses which appear to oppose the material in this chapter, and we have not had space to discuss them all explicitly. But if any of our readers are tempted to dismiss the points we made here, please be certain to triple-check that those 'arguments' *really* stand up to the *whole* Bible rather than being rooted in just one or two inconclusive scriptures. Hopefully we have already exposed a number of examples where people have "made the commandment of God to none effect" by their own traditions. If our readers look a little deeper at other ideas they've been taught, they should find that these too prove to be chaff that just blows away. We end with this sober, *biblical*, advice:

> "Evil men and seducers shall wax **worse and worse**, deceiving, and being deceived. But ... the holy **Scriptures**, ... are able to make thee wise unto **salvation** through faith which is in Christ Jesus" (2 Tim. 3:13-15).

RECOMMENDED READING

Note: We consider all the books and websites we have recommended in this - and the following - Part to be sound and very helpful, but please test them against Scripture. If any teaching does not line up with the Bible then that teaching *must* be rejected (see 2 John 1:9-11, 1 Tim. 6:3, Gal. 1:8 etc). We ought to remember that the Bereans were commended as being "more noble" because "they received the Word with all readiness of mind, and **searched the Scriptures daily,** [to find out] **whether those things** [that Paul taught them] **were so**" (Acts 17:11). Note also that, just because we recommend a particular book or website here does not necessarily imply that we endorse *every* aspect of the writer's ministry.

False Ways

Albert James Dager, Vengeance is Ours: The Church in Dominion, (Sword Publishers, Redmond, Washington, USA, 1990)
The author looks at the growth of 'Kingdom-Now' and 'Reconstructionist' teachings within the Church. One of the best analyses of the subject.

W. Phillip Keller, Predators in our Pulpits (Nova Publishing Limited, 29 Milber Industrial Estate, Newton Abbot, TQ12 4SG, UK, 1988)
A truly superb little book on the marks of true (and false) Christian leaders. Brilliantly written.

Replacement Theology
David Hocking, Replacement Theology, (HFT Publications, 2005)
A very helpful booklet on this pivotal matter.

Ecumenism

Martin Lloyd Jones, Unity in Truth, (Evangelical Press, 12 Wooler St., Darlington, County Durham, DL1 1RQ, UK, 1991)
This is a collection of some of the author's best sermons and addresses on the subject of the unity of churches. It includes: 'Luther and his Message for Today', 'Wrong Divisions and True Unity', and 'True and False Religion'. It is a "must read".

J.C. Ryle, Warnings to the Churches, (The Banner Of Truth Trust, 1967)
"As a pastor of the flock of God, ... Ryle recognised he had a responsibility to guard Christ's sheep and to warn them whenever he saw approaching dangers... His comments in this collection of essays are as wise and relevant today as they were when he first wrote them." A really excellent book.

The Word-Faith Movement

Reachout Trust, The Faith Movement may be Prospering but is it Healthy? (24 Ormond Rd., Richmond, Surrey, TW10 6TH , UK, 1995)
"This short booklet examines some of the roots of the deadly teachings which are currently sweeping through the Church ... [P]rovides a resource for anyone who has come into contact with the so-called Faith movement."

G.R. Fisher and M.K. Goedelman, The Confusing World of Benny Hinn, (Personal Freedom Outreach, P.O. Box 26062, St. Louis, Missouri 63136, USA, 1996)
"A collection of several popular articles investigating the best-selling author and healing evangelist."

D. R. McConnell, A Different Gospel, *(Hendrikson Publishers, 1988)*
A very important treatment of the Word-Faith 'gospel'. (Note that we have not recommended Hanegraaff's work on this subject here because (a) it is inferior to McConnell's, (b) it contains significant falsehoods of its own, (c) Hanegraaff's organisation (CRI) harbours Romish sympathies and other

hazardous views, and (d) Hanegraaff has been found guilty of plagiarism and other ungodly practices. Therefore we cannot endorse his ministry)

Rome

Loraine Boettner, Roman Catholicism, (Presbyterian and Reformed Publishing Company, 1962)
A scholarly work, but very readable. The author "contrasts evangelical Protestantism and Roman Catholic doctrines, as well as the practical effects these two systems have had in people's lives."

Alexander Hislop, The Two Babylons, (Loizeaux Brothers, Inc., 1959)
This really and truly is "One of the great books in the Christian literature of apologetics. The author brilliantly demonstrates that almost all of the practices of the Roman cult have been brought over from paganism." An indispensable book for anyone wishing to understand the actual nature of Rome's worship.

Charles Chiniquy, Fifty Years in the Church of Rome, (Abridged version, Chick Publications)
"The thrilling life story of Pastor Chiniquy who was, for twenty-five years, a priest in the Roman Catholic Church." A tremendous book from an insider.

Israel

Please see the 'Better Than Rubies' section of our website (bayith.org) for a regularly augmented selection of the best articles we have ever read about this crucial topic, plus other recommendations.

Joan Peters, From Time Immemorial: The Origins of the Arab-Jewish Conflict Over Palestine, (JKAP Publications, 1000 N. Lake Shore Drive, #801, Chicago, IL, USA, 1984).
"Scrupulously researched" and truly "monumental". We consider this book to be essential. An extraordinary example of those times when "the children of this world are in their generation wiser than the children of light".

Reginald Oduor, To the Jew First, (Berean Publications Ltd P.O. Box 41693, Nairobi, Kenya, 1996).
A superb book on the believer's responsibility towards Israel. Grounded in Scripture and full of wisdom.

Norma Parrish Archbold, The Mountains of Israel – The Bible and the West Bank, (Publisher Unknown, 4th Edition 2003).
This study "addresses many of the issues that are being ignored by today's ... media commentators". *"God's purposes for the land of Israel, and in particular, the hill country of Judea and Samaria, as outlined in the Biblical prophets, are clearly and concisely presented"*

Bible Versions

See the 'Better Than Rubies' section of our website (bayith.org) for our own articles on this topic.

In the light of the many Bible passages we have quoted in this book, some readers may, by now, be surprised at how easy the King James (Authorised) Version is to follow – especially compared to what they have been told. We can thoroughly recommend the purchase of the following to assist your devotional times:
Alexander Scourby, Holy Bible, King James Version, (World Audio).

Helpful Websites
Well researched articles on 'Unity', Word of Faith, Restorationist and Kingdom-Now teachings, Israel, and events surrounding the Lord's return can be found here.

Bayith Ministries (i.e. us!) - **//www.bayith.org**

CROSS + WORD - **//www.banner.org.uk**

Deception in the Church - **//www.deceptioninthechurch.com**

Eastern Regional Watch - **//www.erwm.com**

Zion's Hope - **//www.zionshope.org**

Ministries

Up to date information and news / prayerletters on the subjects discussed in this Part can be obtained from the following two organisations. However, we cannot endorse *all* the views held by them.

Intercessors For Britain, 14 Orchard Road, Moreton, Wirral, Merseyside, CH46 8TS, UK

Light For The Last Days, Box BM – 4226, London, WC1N 3XX, UK

PART FIVE
SPIRIT MATTERS

CHAPTER **25**

*T*HE SPIRIT OF GOD

25:1 INTRODUCTION   Before we explore the remarkable testimonies of manifestations reported by Alpha participants, we need to take a swift look at the subject of the 'end-times'. The reason for doing so will be made clear shortly.

As we saw in the previous Part, Scripture has a lot to say about the very last days. The Bible gives an extensive list of "signs" to indicate when the world has reached those final years before Christ Himself returns for His People. HTB's Sandy Millar often states that we are in the "end-times"[1] and, sure enough, for the first time in history, ALL these biblical indicators are with us…

---

[1] For instance, Sandy has stated: "I have **often** referred to the marks of the _end-time_ church as…" [Mark Elsdon-Dew, Ed., *The Collection*, (HTB Publications, 1996), p39]. See also Ruth Gledhill's article about Millar's "apocalyptic warning" in *The London Times* 12/JUN/2000.

For example, in the last few decades the world has known many "wars and rumours of wars". Indeed the Greek wording behind the phrase "nation shall rise against nation, and Kingdom against Kingdom" actually refers to *ethnic* clashes (just like those we have seen over recent years in, for instance, Eastern Europe and Africa). So terribly frequent are the "famines, and pestilences, and earthquakes, in divers places" that we are sometimes in danger of becoming blasé about them. (Of course, famines and pestilences can occur as a result of many of the natural disasters we are seeing now.)

Just as the Lord used a sign in the heavens to herald His Son's *First* Coming, so the world has seen a notable increase in "fearful sights and great signs ... from heaven" portending His Son's *Second* Coming. For instance, not so long ago we were treated to the appearance, for the first time in four *thousand* years, of the huge comet Hale-Bopp. We have also experienced rare, blood-red, moons over Israel (as predicted in Joel 2) and Shoemaker-Levi 9, which comprised twenty-one *mountain*-sized rocks, colliding with Jupiter - each occurring at highly significant points on the Jewish calendar. Since the start of manned flight and thence the space race, man has himself been responsible for some "fearful sights" in the heavens!

The book of Revelation tells us that "sorceries" will be a feature of the end-times. The Greek word used here is "pharmakeia" from which we get "pharmacy" and "pharmaceutical" and the unavoidable inference of drug-taking. This is a practice which has seen an explosive increase in use in the last few decades. (Abuse of hallucinogens, and other drugs, involves giving up control of one's mind / soul - albeit temporarily - and thus has a *spiritual* dimension... as LSD users will testify.)

Also in the end-times, "iniquity will abound" and, sure enough, the ungodliness - e.g. of many Western nations - has increased dramatically in recent years, with truly horrible crimes being perpetrated, abortions at a staggering level and materialism and lasciviousness abounding. If, as Christ said in Luke 17:28-33, the 'end-times' will be just "as in the days of Lot" in Sodom, then the enormous growth in homosexual persuasion and activity is a 'give-away' too.

The colossal increase in travel, and the remarkable multiplication of knowledge which the world has seen in the last century or so are prophesied in Daniel 12:4. And the 'progress' towards a biometric identification system for humans - along the lines of the ID chips being implanted into dogs, cats, horses and so on - is predicted in Revelation 13:16-17.[2]

It seems, even if we ignore the miraculous restoration of Israel to her original land, that we must assume we are indeed living in the 'last days of the last days'. The significance of this fact with regard to Alpha will become plain below.

25:2 WHAT DO THE LAST DAYS HOLD FOR *US*?   In the closing sections of Part Four we saw that the true Church will suffer persecution during the very last days. But what *else* is prophesied about the Church in the 'end-times'?

The one feature about which we are warned more than any other is *deception*. Believers in *any* age should be on their guard against deception, but Christ's warnings about the deception to which His followers would be exposed *in the last days* are considered so important that they are repeated explicitly in *each* of the Synoptic gospels. Matthew 24 is devoted to the end-times. It refers frequently to deception, saying, for example, "**Take heed** that no man deceive you. For **many** shall come **in My [i.e. Christ's] Name** ... and **shall** deceive **many**", and "**many false prophets** shall rise, and shall deceive **many**." Beyond this, "There shall arise **false** Christs, and **false** prophets, and shall show **great** signs and wonders". Mark 13 and Luke 21 are the equivalent passages and are equally urgent in their alerts regarding powerful deception.

Luke 21 exhorts us, in the face of all the pressures we will suffer, to stand firm in our Faith. "In your patience possess ye your souls" (Luke 21:19). Those days will, by all accounts, be an exceedingly difficult time. But as long as we stay close to God and His truth, He promises that "he that endureth to the end shall be saved". We will have many things to overcome, but if we faithfully abide in Christ Jesus we will surely do so. And the Lord makes some beautiful promises to those who keep standing, including that in Revelation 3:5 – "He that overcometh, the same shall be clothed in white raiment; and I will **not** blot out his name out of the book of life".

Mark 13 refers to false christs (and also false prophets) "seducing" people. As we saw in Part Four, we believers are *not* inherently immune to deception. Some folks choose to cling to the *solitary* verse that says it is not

---

[2] This system is damned in Rev. 14:11 because, although its purpose is supposedly to stop crime, it will bring people under subjection to the god of this world rather than to the true God.

possible for the "elect" to be deceived, and they ignore the *many* other verses showing that we Christians are indeed deceivable. The Lord was drawing attention, in the "elect" passage, to the greatness of the deception that will be present, not to our immunity. (God lives outside of time and thus already knows who will 'make it' – but we don't.) The point is that the deception will be so compelling that *no-one* should consider themselves safe from it.

We will only be safe from deception when we reach heaven, just as we will only be safe from sin's snare (and the "**deceitfulness** of sin") when we meet our Lord. But such will be the power of the beguiling spirits that we must firmly resist them until then...

If Christ's followers were automatically safe, why would He bother to say to them "**take heed** that no man deceive **you**"? And why would Paul write: "Now the Spirit speaketh expressly, that in the latter times some shall **depart** from **the faith**, giving heed to **seducing** spirits" (1 Tim. 4:1, see also 1 Cor. 15:33, Eph. 5:6, 2 Thess. 2:3 etc). Why would Peter warn that there will be "false teachers" among *us*, and warn too that "**many** will follow their pernicious ways" (2 Pet. 2:1-2)? Why would John write "let no man deceive **you**" (1 John 3:7), and alert the church to antichrists "who seduce **you**" (1 John 2:18,26)? Clearly the Lord is calling us all to be wise, to keep our eyes open and to be watching for the enemy's subtle deceptions as he attempts to outflank us.

25:3 HOW SHOULD WE RESPOND?   We obviously need to do as Christ commanded us, and "take heed" - i.e. be *very* careful. We must not be *fearful* of the enemy, but we must be alert at all times. To believe that Satan's minions cannot be present at any given meeting of Christians is naïve and unbiblical. Both Christ and His apostles warned of false teachers, false brethren, false doctrines *and deceiving spirits*. Any or all of these can be expected to be among us. Indeed, the more 'sound' a group is, the more effort the enemy will put into craftily secreting falsehood and false believers into it.

We must test everything we see, hear, and do, against Scripture – including all activity within the spiritual realm. After all, the *Spirit* of God will never contradict the *Word of God*. The Lord wants us to be safe and He has given us the safeguard we need - His Word. We will be preserved if we hold fast to His truth (Psa. 61:7 & 91:4b) and if we keep all of our spiritual armour on. However, we certainly cannot count on God's protection if we compromise on His truth - indeed we can expect quite the reverse (see, for example, Rom. 2:8).

We need to be obedient to our Lord's commands - including the instruction given in 1 Peter 5:8 to "be **vigilant**; because your adversary the devil, ... walketh about, seeking whom he may devour." When dealing with the spirit realm, we need to be on our guard and right with God so that we receive *His* Spirit only.

A.W.Tozer once said that, even if the most impressive angel from heaven appeared to him with teachings *but without Scriptural proof*, then Tozer would be forced to tell him to leave - because the angel had "come without his references". Isn't this what the scripture above is telling us to do? But is this what is presently being done on Alpha Courses?

> "But though we, **or an angel from heaven**, preach any other gospel unto you than that which we have preached unto you, let him be accursed" (Gal. 1:8).

It is astonishing these crucial warnings are not being spelled out in the Alpha material - even to Course leaders. For, while Nicky admits that evil forces are "cunning", he encourages complacency by emphasizing that "Satan is relatively **powerless**" and that "Satan is defeated. The **mopping up** operations are underway".[3] Without balancing statements, such comments leave attendees at risk of erroneous dabbling with things of which they have precious little understanding.

25:4 HOLY TELL-TALES   How can we tell whether it is God's Spirit or *another* spirit that is active at a particular church meeting?

To begin with, is it enough that miracles occur? This is indeed the only test that many in the Church seem to use nowadays. The answer is an unqualified "NO" and we have already looked at a number of scriptures to demonstrate this. Here is another: "And I saw ... **unclean** spirits ... they are the spirits of devils, **working miracles**" (Rev. 16:13-14), and another: "And then shall that **Wicked** be revealed, ... Even him, whose coming is after the working of Satan with all **power** and **signs** and **lying wonders**" (2 Thess. 2:8-9). Here's yet another: "And the beast was taken, and with him the **false** prophet that wrought **miracles**" (Rev. 19:20).

So how can we know that it is the Spirit of *God* doing something? What *is* the character of God's Spirit? To begin with, His ministry is to

---

[3] Talk 11.

testify to, and glorify, the Son (John 16:14). So if a spiritual experience does not glorify the Lord Jesus Christ then we can know the Spirit of God is not causing it.

The Holy Spirit has the same character as the Lord showed. We know this because the Spirit of God rested on Christ:

> "The spirit of the LORD shall **rest upon Him**, the spirit of wisdom and understanding, the spirit of counsel and might, the spirit of knowledge and of the fear of the LORD" (Isa. 11:2).

So when we look at Christ's earthly life we have a helpful idea of the Spirit's personality. The Lord was meek and humble, reverent before His Father, committed to the truth, very prayerful, giving, and so on. If any spiritual manifestations don't line up with Christ's character then we can be sure it is not the Spirit of Christ generating them. Nicky helpfully states that "God can't act in a way that is inconsistent with His character".[4]

The Spirit of God is described as the "spirit of grace" and the "spirit of holiness". If a spiritual experience is not graceful and holy then there must be a different spirit behind it. More than once the Holy Spirit is also called the "spirit of truth", so truth will be valued by those who experience the genuine Holy Spirit. (Finally, the Spirit of God gave us the Scriptures - including those parts of the Bible where we are warned of deception. He is hardly going to do things in our lives which can't be checked against those scriptures.)

25:5 COMPARING THE SPIRITS   What, then, are the signs that it is "*another* spirit" at work in a given situation? One obvious point to make is that a demonic spirit will appeal to the *flesh* - to our carnal nature. This is not true of the Holy Spirit:

> "For the flesh lusteth **against** [i.e. is forcefully inclined against] the Spirit, and the Spirit **against** the flesh: and these are **contrary** the one to the other" (Gal. 5:17a).

> "For they that are after the **flesh** do mind the things of the flesh; but they that are after the **Spirit** the things of the Spirit. For to be carnally minded is death; but to be spiritually minded is life and peace. Because the carnal mind is enmity [i.e. hostility] against

---

[4] Talk 6.

God ... So then they that are in the **flesh** cannot please God"
(Rom. 8:5-8).

Seducing, counterfeit spirits will produce feelings and experiences
which are the carnal counterpart of the spiritual. It is therefore not enough
for someone to claim feelings of "love", "joy", or "peace" - particularly if
they cannot state the reason for feeling those things - since the enemy is
perfectly capable of supplying his version of these...

Love

The enemy is easily subtle enough to be able to generate a strong
sense of "love" - although it is a soulish version. For example, the *New
Ager* Ken Vincent writes of his antichristian spiritual experience: "The
white light was wonderful! It was just **love**. I knew I had done things that I
was not proud of, but there was total acceptance".[5] Of *course* there was
total acceptance; Satan is very happy to give people a feeling of acceptance
if it will make them accept his ways. Note the vague remorse in place of
true repentance. A person may not just feel *loved* but may also feel they
love everyone else - hence the "love-in" effect of the sixties' drug use and
spiritualism:

> "Most of those who awaken this [New Age] connection with the
> ecstatic inner Self will ... [live] their lives with more contentment
> or a gentler perspective, perhaps more involved and committed
> in service to others, perhaps more energised and expressive ...
> **loving** unconditionally."[6]

Joy

Where the *Holy* Spirit of God brings a deep sense of joy, even in
adversity, for those who live godly lives (Eccl 2:26), an *un*holy spirit may, in
contrast, bring shallow or short-term happiness that demands no godly
behaviour.

Peace

Similarly, where the *Holy* Spirit brings the peace which requires
true faith to know (see Rom. 15:13), an unholy spirit may bring a false
feeling of peace which requires no discipline to obtain and retain. Indeed,

---

[5] Quoted in Dave Hunt, *Occult Invasion*, pp376-378.
[6] Bonnie Greenwell, *Energies of Transformation, a Guide to the Kundalini Process*, quoted in
El Collie, *Kundalini and the Awakening of Spirit.*

New Agers *often* experience "Ecstasy, bliss and intervals of **tremendous** joy, love, peace and compassion".[7]

This comparison between the true and the counterfeit can be made with *all* the different blessings that the Spirit of God bestows. The following illustrates the difference. Contrast:

> "But the fruit of the Spirit is love, joy, peace, longsuffering, gentleness, goodness, faith, Meekness, temperance ... And they that are Christ's have **crucified the flesh** with the affections and lusts" (Gal. 5:22-24).
>
> *with*:
>
> "In the last days ... men shall be lovers of their own selves, covetous, boasters, proud, ... unthankful, unholy, ... heady, highminded, lovers of pleasures more than lovers of God; Having a **form of godliness**, but **denying** the power thereof" (2 Tim. 3:1-5).

Note that Scripture here gives a prophecy that people will deny the "power" of living a truly godly life. They will seemingly teach that, because it is a gift, God will happily bestow His Holy Spirit on anyone, regardless of whether they have been living obediently to Him or not. But they err, for God only gives the Holy Ghost "to them that **obey** Him" (Acts 5:32, John 14:15-16). These erring teachers themselves do not appear to know the *true* "power of God", for everyone in Scripture who received a gift of the Holy Spirit was living an *obedient* life. Thus we have to conclude that any power these teachers possess is from another source.

Sadly, the following Alpha testimony does not show the sort of discernment that we are called to have regarding spiritual encounters:

> "During the Holy Spirit weekend on Skye I was tingling and I **knew** that I'd met Jesus".[8]

Note that this contrasts acutely with this *non*-Alpha conversion testimony from an ex-New Ager:

> "My New Age background made me think I had been in the 'presence of God' all my life ... Neither Denny nor I had ever heard explanations like this [the gospel preached to them] ...

---

[7] El Collie, *Kundalini Signs and Symptoms*.

[8] *The Good News*, Advertisement, *Aberdeen Evening Express*, Summer 1998, p5.

Richard invited us to admit we were sinners and thank the Lord Jesus for dying in our place on the cross...

"Tears fell to the ground as I was overcome by a sense of shame … I was a wretched sinner. I believed that Christ died in my place on the cross – for my sins. I was overwhelmed by His unwarranted love for me through this act. There [was] … only remorse mingled with gratefulness, a sense of peace in reconciliation and assurance of security for eternity. I had confidence in a joy and safety I'd never known before".[9]

This woman was able to explain, in *each* case, *why* she felt love, joy and peace. Again, contrast this with:

"Nicky invited us all to say a prayer which we could say with him. It was one to welcome Jesus into our lives and to say sorry for all the things that we had done. As I said the prayer, I had this feeling like a gold Catherine wheel[10] hitting me in the chest and then shooting all down my arms and legs".[11]

From the ex-New Ager's testimony (and, more importantly, from Scripture) one surmises that if someone is going to yield to God and hand their lives over to Him, this event would occur when confronted by Christ and His cross, rather than at a 'Holy Spirit' retreat. Strangely, this is not usually the case with Alpha:

"On the **Holy Spirit** Day, I prayed a prayer to **accept** Jesus as my Saviour. It was so **easy** to say…" [*Alpha News*].[12]

"On the **weekend away**, … Nicky Gumbel was asking if anyone would like to pray the prayer of commitment and receive Jesus. I prayed the prayer and **something** very profound happened to me. I **know** I was filled with the Holy Spirit" [*Alpha News*].[13]

Should not the "something" in the second testimony above have been describable? A feeling of conviction and grief? A sense of forgiveness and joy? A love for one's Saviour? But no, the focus here is not on Christ at all even though that is precisely the ministry of the true Holy Spirit. We

---

[9] Caryl Matriciana, Outer Beauty, Inner Despair, *Dawn Of The New Age: 5 New Agers Relate Their Search For The Truth*, pp48-49.

[10] A 'Catherine Wheel' is the name given to a type of rotating firework.

[11] *UK Focus*, Jan 1999, pp4-5.

[12] *Alpha News*, Jul – Oct 1998, p4.

[13] *Alpha News*, Nov 1998 – Feb 1999, p7.

must try to be wiser and more discerning, for the sake of biblically-unaware participants.

25:6 THE FRUIT OF THE SPIRIT IS SELF-CONTROL   Another important test of a spiritual experience is whether or not it is *forced* upon the recipient. According to Galatians 5, a fruit of the *Holy* Spirit is self-control (or "temperance"). Another scriptural proof is given in 1 Cor. 14:32 where we are taught that "the spirits of the prophets **are subject to** the prophets". If God wants one of His servants to do something, He may well exhort them to do it, encourage them, command them or even threaten them, but He will never *force* them. Yet many Alpha participants speak of *compulsion* to do certain things, so that we come across such statements as:

> "I just **couldn't** move from the chair. I sat there until the group leader realised I had been affected and came over" [HTB's *UK Focus* newspaper][14]

> "Then **suddenly** ... I began to laugh **uncontrollably**... " [*Alpha News*];[15] "I felt the Spirit ... and began laughing **uncontrollably**".[16]

The only examples in Holy Scripture of God *forcing* people to do anything is in *judgment*. (Some instances are given later in this book.[17]) We must question whether the above phenomena came from the Holy Spirit. Unfortunately, Nicky refers to the Holy Spirit as a "controlling" Spirit.[18] But while the scriptures speak of the *convicting* work of the Holy Spirit, to the end that the sinner sees his sin as God does, the Holy Spirit is not shown as *compelling* a sinner to repent or forcing a disciple to do something.

Writing on this subject, one researcher says:

> "[Teresa of Avila] describes the experience as '**irresistible**' – that is another indication of its origin in the **occult** realm. God ... woos, but He will not *compel* us into His presence. That is the act of a dictator, not a loving father. Whenever an experience leaves no room for reason or choice, it is not of God".[19]

---

[14] *UK Focus*, Mar 1999, p2.
[15] *Alpha News*, Jun – Oct 1997, p9.
[16] *Telling Others*, (2001), pp123-4.
[17] For now, though, consider Nebuchadnezzar being forced to eat grass (Dan. 7:28-33). See also the case in Jer. 23:12.
[18] *Questions of Life*, p113.
[19] Tricia Tillin, *Mainstream* magazine, Spring 1994, p2.

While a satanic spirit controls the actions of initiates into the New Age, the *Holy* Spirit does not control the believer or compel him to perform actions against his will. (Worryingly, God *does* sometimes force his will on those who are going *against* the truth. See, for instance, Exod. 9:12. See also 1 Sam. 19:20-24 and 1 Sam. 18:10 where God *forced* his opponents to prophesy.)

Even if someone experienced a deeply amazing revelation of the type that is translated "trance" in the Bible (and the only three examples in Scripture - involving Balaam, Peter and Paul - were all for *extremely* special reasons), a true believer will *always* be able to exercise self-control. The final situation of one who hands over control of himself to an outside force is surely demonic possession:[20]

> "When the energy has been awakened and the first stormy years are over, the energy (or the Tao) **takes over**. With the higher level of energy the person is more and more **forced** (from the inside – not from the outside) to live a life as the Tao wants her or him to live. This is necessarily *not* what we think we want ... until we are finally just 'a white cloud' in the hands of the winds (that is, in the hands of the Tao)".[21] Note: wind is related to spirit in the Bible. These poor souls are being blown about by evil spirits.

25:7 THE ECSTATIC   Furthermore, there are Alpha testimonies that refer to uncontrollable *feelings*. This is similarly unbiblical. People in Scripture not only know *why* they feel joyous or sorrowful, *why* they laugh or cry, but they can also stop if they so wish. "If the Son therefore shall make you **free**, ye shall be **free indeed**" (John 8:36). They are not being controlled by someone, or something, else. Yet:

> "I felt this **amazing pull** towards [the minister] and a sense that I **had** to ask him something" [*Alpha News*];[22] "I felt myself drawn forward, almost **compelled** to come forward..." [*Alpha News*][23]

---

[20] Nicky does not help this situation when he teaches that "the Lord is totally in control now" [Hand, *op. cit.*, p88].
[21] *Zenhouse.com.*
[22] *Alpha News*, Mar – Jun 1998, p12.
[23] *Alpha News*, Nov 1998 – Feb 1999, p15.

"During the worship I broke down into tears ... I **couldn't work out** what was going on ... I **couldn't** stop it..." [Elsdon-Dew, Ed.].[24]

25:8 FAITH AND PRACTICE   One important way of helping to make sure we are dealing with the *Holy* Spirit is by approaching God only in ways He has told us we can. We will investigate this more closely when we look at further Alpha testimonies, but it is worth spending a moment considering the relationship between Word and Spirit:

The Word

As we saw in Part One, those folks who are devoted to the Bible are today often labelled "Pharisees". But, as also noted in the first volume, the Pharisees were far from committed to the whole Word. They introduced men's traditions and gave them more weight than Scripture. And that is exactly what some in the Church are now doing too. For example, Scripture gives clear instructions in the Epistles as to how to run Fellowships. These directions are from God for our *safety* and our *good* and our *effectiveness* yet they are regularly ignored and replaced by traditions of men. Little wonder that Fellowships today do not have the same effect on the world as the Acts Church did. They are picking and choosing which verses to accept.

The Spirit

We must NEVER compromise on God's Word, rightly divided - i.e. interpreted honestly and consistently. We have been given His Word for a reason. These days it is popular to dispraise the Bible and to only pay lip-service to it (especially when its content doesn't line up with what people want to teach or hear). Many feel that we need to "move on" from Scripture and "into the Spirit" and they frequently quote the part verse, "the letter killeth, but the spirit giveth life" (2 Cor. 3:6b) in support. (Oddly, these people are prepared to rely on *that* part of the scriptures, but not the rest!) However, Paul is not rejecting the Word here. Indeed, he elsewhere says:

> "**All scripture** is given by inspiration of **God**, and is profitable for doctrine, for reproof, for correction, for instruction in righteousness: That the man of God may be ... **thoroughly furnished**" (2 Tim. 3:16-17). See also Rom. 15:4.

---

[24] Elsdon-Dew, Ed., *The God Who Changes Lives*, Vol 2, pp222-3.

Paul actually *expected* the Church to be devoted to the scriptures (as demonstrated in Rom. 4:3, Rom. 11:2 and Gal. 4:30) and he pointed out that the Bible is "the sword of the **Spirit**" (Eph. 6:17).

A look at the context of the "letter killeth" statement will prove that Paul is referring to "the letter" *of the law*. He is comparing the law *of Moses* (v13) which was written on "tables of stone" (v7) and has been "done away" with (v11) to life in Christ. Trying to live by the Old Covenant, now that the New Covenant has been given, is fatal. The fuller sense of the verse is that the law points people to the cross and shows them that they need to die to their old selves – hence Gal. 2:19.

(For proof that the term "**Old** Testament" actually refers only to the *Mosaic* portion of the Hebrew Canon see vv14-15 of 2 Cor. 3. Only this *Mosaic* part has been "abolished" - v13.) And anyway, living in the Spirit should be perfectly compatible with revering the Word – as the apostles demonstrated. Indeed, if the spirit that is guiding someone leads them into contention with *the scriptures that the Holy Spirit Himself gave us*, then that person can be certain he is dealing with a false spirit.

Furthermore, as we saw in Part One, Jesus lived by the Word but was fully in the Spirit. Of all those in the Bible who were "led by the spirit", Christ was obviously the most anointed. Yet this did not stop Him from both knowing and promoting the scriptures *and living by them*. He told His followers: "**If** ye **continue** in **My** [logos] **Word**, **then** are ye My disciples indeed" - and He said of such instructions "they are **spirit**, and they are **life**". This is the *opposite* of the common interpretation of Paul's words above.

Paul's *true* concern about Scripture, as he showed later on in the very same epistle, was with its *mis*-use by those not devoted to prayerfully seeking out and learning the truth, but who were instead guilty of "handling the Word of God **deceitfully**". Such behaviour will certainly kill. Those who feign a commitment to God's Word, but who actually twist it and teach man's traditions instead of it, are the Pharisees of today. Those who claim to love God's Word but also claim that only they and their "specially anointed" colleagues can actually interpret it, *they* are what we should be avoiding, not the Word itself.

Is this idea – i.e. that we should not be fully committed to the Bible and that we need not be under its authority - a view expressed by God in the rest of the New Testament? Or is it another case of people interpreting the unambiguous weight of Scripture in the light of one ambiguous part-verse? No-one would call David, the man after God's own heart, a Pharisee -

especially in view of Mark 2:24-26, yet look at what he had to say in Psalm 19:7-11. The Psalmist also wrote the following remarkable verses. (Note that terms like "precepts", "testimonies", "commandments" and "statutes" are all aspects of the scriptures, as confirmed in places like 1 Ki. 2:3 and 2 Ki. 23:3, cf 2 Ki. 22:13)...

> "**Thy testimonies** ... are **righteous** and **very** faithful. My zeal hath **consumed** me, because mine enemies have **forgotten Thy words**. Thy Word is **very pure**: therefore Thy servant **loveth** it. ... **Thy law** is **the truth**. ... **Thy commandments** are **my delights**. The **righteousness** of Thy testimonies is **everlasting**" (Psa. 119:138-144).

> "Wherewithal shall a young man cleanse his way? by taking heed thereto **according to Thy Word**. ... **O let me not wander from Thy commandments**. Thy **word** have I **hid in mine heart**, that I might not sin against Thee" (Psa. 119:9-11).

According to David, we should love God's pure Word. We should not forget it. We should believe it and delight in it in *all* ages. (Far from the Bible prophesying of itself that it will become obsolete or redundant before Christ's return, it says it applies "for ever and ever". See, for example, Psa. 119 especially verses 44, 89, 144, 152 and 160.) It helps to cleanse us (Eph. 5:26), and keeps us from sin and close to God.

We must not imagine that God's Word kills! Indeed if we sincerely ask the Lord to speak to us through it by His Holy Spirit then it will bring us light and *life* (Psa. 119:105; Php. 2:16; Prov. 3:1,2; & 22:17-21). A bride-to-be who was given a love-letter from her Betrothed would read it frequently and carefully and avidly. In a sense this is very much our condition. We should be extremely suspicious of anyone who would discourage us from loving and studying the Bible.

The Holy Spirit brings the Word alive - giving us the right meaning of it, enabling us to understand it and highlighting what the Lord is saying to us at a particular moment in our lives. Equally though, a counterfeit spirit may imitate this. Hence an "increased interest in" or "better understanding of" God's Word is not, in itself, proof that the Holy Spirit has been involved. Many unbelievers and pagans have a real "interest in" God's Word. The true test is whether the person *lives* by it (John 8:31).

In the next Chapter we will consider how well the experiences of Alpha participants line up with the Word of God - and with the Spirit of God revealed in His Word.

CHAPTER 26

$\mathscr{A}$LPHA'S EXPERIENCES

26:1 FEELINGS OF HEAT AND WARMTH When someone truly repents and knows the forgiveness of God, they could well be expected to feel warm-*hearted* towards their Saviour. Instead, and despite the lack of scriptural precedent, quite a few Alpha participants speak of feeling *physical* warmth or even 'burning sensations' when someone lays hands on them to pray with them.

> "[O]n the weekend away ... He [Nicky] put his hand on my back ... It felt like there was a bar heater against my back" [*Alpha News*].[1]

> "As the prayer over me continued, I became hotter and hotter to such a degree my clothes were wringing wet. My thoughts were, 'Please hurry up and finish. I cannot take any more'" [*Alpha News*].[2]

---

[1] *Alpha News*, Nov 1997 – Feb 1998, p7.
[2] *Alpha News*, Jul - Oct 2000, p36.

Prayed for at a mothers and toddlers group, one woman says:

> "As [the lady] prayed, I felt an **enormous heat** flowing through every part of my body" [*Alpha News*].[3]

Though the above did not happen as part of an Alpha Course, it did lead to this woman and her husband attending one. And, on the Holy Spirit day, her husband had a similar experience:

> "When I received the Spirit, it felt like my feet were **burning**. I feel that I'm changing gradually, becoming more peaceful all the time" [*Alpha News*].[4] (Note this peacefulness. We will return to this aspect in a moment.)

One person was disappointed that he didn't feel anything when he "went through the words" of the prayer "where you confess your sins, say sorry and ask the Holy Spirit to come". His motivation was to get rid of all the "baggage" in his life. Early the next morning...

> "I just felt this **huge heat** coming out from the centre of my chest, just radiating out. **Massive**. Absolutely massive" [Elsdon-Dew, Ed.].[5]

Another 'hot' testimony, but one where saving faith again seems lacking, follows:

> "[O]n the Alpha weekend, ... I was still doubtful and couldn't shake off my feelings of scepticism. The Saturday sessions were enlightening but I still wasn't certain God, Jesus and the Holy Spirit really **existed**. The evening session ended with a song but instead of leaving, people started to pray. I decided to **give it a try**, so while standing I raised my hands and ... felt a **warmth** start to spread through me until it had completely filled me – through each deep **breath** [Trying to breathe something in?] it was getting **stronger** and **then** there was an overwhelming sense of relief..." [*UK Focus*].[6] (Remember, this person's experience took place *before* making any commitment to Christ.)

While *Scripture* does not provide us with any examples of this kind of thing amongst the early church, there *are* similarities to be found in, for

---

[3] *Alpha News*, Nov 1997 – Feb 1998, p7.

[4] *Ibid*, p7.

[5] Elsdon-Dew, Ed., *The God Who Changes Lives*, Vol 2, p78.

[6] *UK Focus*, Jan 1999, p6.

example, the 'healing techniques' used by practitioners of paganism's *Reiki Therapy*. 'Rei' means universally or spiritually guided, 'Ki' means life force energy. The practitioner channels this "life-force energy" through the laying on of hands. According to one recipient of Reiki (who, like some Alpha participants, claimed his life had since changed significantly):

> "[The Reiki Master's] hands seem to get **hot**, and I **actually feel heat**, I could feel energy going through my body and out my toes".[7]

The touch of the Reiki Master's hands is one that:

> "...lovingly supports one's innate ability to heal and also balances the energy centers in the body. The Reiki energy and experience feeds the mental, emotional and physical aspects of an individual. **This results in a state of well-being and total relaxation**".[8] (In other words, peacefulness and relief do not mean an experience is necessarily from God.)

26:2 SPIRIT INVOCATION

In the sections following, we will see numerous testimonies where the Spirit was directly and personally "invited". Many people today practice this "invocation" of the Holy Spirit. This is the act of "inviting and welcoming Him to the gathering" or praying to Him in any way. A number of hymns include words of supplication, praise and/or worship to the Holy Spirit and this all seems very reasonable... He is, after all, part of the Godhead.

The only problem is that there is not a single example in Scripture of anyone 'inviting', or praying to, the Holy Spirit. There is a lone, Old Testament, case where God specifically commanded Ezekiel to PROPHESY (rather than pray) to the *wind*, but there are no instances whatsoever of any people speaking to the Holy Spirit whether in prayer or praise. Not one. Yet if it is so right and good we should expect at least a *few* passages to indicate that the early Church did this.

The question of where we should direct our prayers is patently crucial. Believers who are happy to base their view of such a central topic on just one verse invariably turn to 2 Cor. 13:14, which says:

---

[7] Donna M. Viggiano, *White Light Reiki*.
[8] *Ibid.*

"The grace of the Lord Jesus Christ, and the love of God, **and the communion of the Holy Ghost**, be with you all. Amen."

The word "communion" seems to suggest communication, and thus the possibility of dialogue. Surely, folks say, if we are to 'commune' with the Holy Spirit then that involves two-way conversation? Unfortunately, there are several problems with this conclusion:

- The Greek word translated "communion" here does *not* mean 'converse with'. Indeed, it is *totally* unrelated to the two Greek words translated "commune with" that *do* refer to discussion (as used, for example, in Luke 6:11 and Luke 22:4).

- The verse doesn't say that we are to have communion *with* the Spirit but that we need to receive the blessing that is "of" (i.e. comes *from*) the Holy Spirit. Just as the "grace" mentioned is "of" (i.e. from) Christ, and the "love" is "of" (i.e. given by) God, so this "communion" is a gift that comes *from* the Spirit. The phrase "be **with** you all" corroborates this, as does Php. 2:1 which translates the Greek as "fellowship **of** [i.e. not 'fellowship **with**']". Holy Scripture *never* uses "of" when talking of communing or fellowshipping *with* an entity.

- The Greek word translated "commune" means 'to experience something together' or 'to participate with others in utilizing something'. It is exactly the same word that is behind the phrase "Holy Communion", the corporate partaking of the bread and wine. The "communion" in both cases is *between believers*, i.e. all who are jointly receiving something (see 1 Cor. 10:16-17).

- As the end of the verse shows, the communion is not between God and man, but between fellow believers who walk in the Spirit. Far from teaching them to talk to the Holy Ghost, Paul is praying that the Church at Corinth be blessed with the unity that comes from sharing the same Spirit. Just as we are "one body" through the "one bread", so we are united *to each other* through the Spirit if we live in the Spirit.

- While we are certainly to Fellowship with God, scripture conspicuously omits the Person of the Holy Spirit when it says "**truly** our fellowship is with the **Father**, and with his **Son** Jesus Christ" (1 John 1:3).

Some readers may still think that we have a right to speak to the Holy Spirit on the basis of the text "try the spirits" (1 John 4:1). But, as is made clear from the rest of the verse and those immediately surrounding it, and also from the topic of the entire Epistle, it is the spirits of *men* that are in view. This is confirmed by v2 which refers to "**Every** spirit that ... is of God", whereas there is only *one* Holy Spirit. John is teaching that one of the indicators of whether a person is "of God" or not is whether such a person will consistently and happily confess the Deity of Christ when challenged. The reader is, as always, encouraged to check our statements; a perusal of 1 John, especially verses 2:19, 22-23, 26; 3:7-8, 10, 23-24; 4:1-8, 13-15 and 5:1, should dispel any doubts. See also Heb. 12:23.

Any reader who feels that the lack of biblical precedent is not a big deal needs to consider this: As others have written, petitions in all kingdoms are always addressed to the *throne* (Heb. 4:16) but unlike the Father and the Son, the Holy Spirit is never described as being a king or wearing a crown or being on a throne.

The three Persons of the Godhead have different ministries and must be seen differently (as Luke 12:10 illustrates). Christ instructed us to pray "Our **Father**" (Matt 6:9), and that the Holy Spirit "shall **not** speak of Himself; but whatsoever He shall hear, that shall He speak". It is not even the Spirit's decision whether or not to do a particular thing. The *Father* is the Person who directs the Spirit (John 14:16; 16:13-15). It is thus highly inappropriate for us to bypass our (perfectly accessible) Father and speak to the Spirit.

As we have stated, we must only relate to the spiritual realm in the ways God has ordained. He punishes those in Scripture who approach the Godhead in their own way. For example, His People suffered in 1 Chr. 13 because they "sought Him not after the **due** order". Likewise Saul in 1 Sam. 13:9-14. Note that, as in Saul's case, one punishment can be that the offending person is sent *another* spirit (1 Sam. 16:14-15, 2 Cor. 11:4), which means we must be very concerned about several of the following testimonies.[9]

26:3 WHITE LIGHTS Another occurrence among some Alpha guests is the 'white or bright light'. An article about the Course in London's *Times Weekend* reported on someone doing Alpha while in prison:

> "The man ... agreed to let two Christians pray with him .... 'I held my eyes tightly shut,' he wrote. 'After a couple of minutes a

---

[9] Num. 16:1-35 proves that we must not only approach God in the right *way*, but must also be on appropriate terms with Him when we do.

bright light came in from my right side, then disappeared, and I felt relaxed and at peace…'".[10]

God certainly wants people to know peace - provided it is a true peace (which comes from being reconciled to Him) rather than a false, if palliative, one. During one guest's attendance on Alpha, a woman preached at her church. The participant said:

"I didn't have a **clue** what she was on about but it **didn't matter**. At the end she invited people forward for prayer. All the leaders of the church went to the front and they were each powerfully touched by the Spirit. I was completely gob-smacked and suddenly I just knew, 'There's a God! He really exists! He's here!' [That is *not* the basis of salvation. Devils believe this too (James 2:19)!] I was trembling with fear but I knew I had to come out to the front for prayer too. Anne put her hand on me and said **'Come Holy Spirit'** and the most incredible thing happened. I felt as if someone took two torches and put them into my eyes. I saw this **incredible white light** and my whole body, from my head to my toes, was bathed with bright white light. **Liquid love** was pouring into me and I kept saying over and over again 'I've met Jesus. I've met Jesus.'…" [*Alpha News*].[11]

Compare this with the experience of a famous drunk. He cried out:

"If there is a God, let Him show Himself! I am ready to do anything, anything! … Suddenly the room lit up with a **great white light**. I was caught up into an ecstasy … All about me and through me there was a wonderful feeling of Presence, and I thought to myself, 'so this is the God of the preachers!'…".[12]

Although the resulting change in lifestyle was very desirable - "he stopped drinking alcohol" - nevertheless this man's god was not the God of the Bible. Consider the following points about his testimony:

"[H]e cried out to God as a … **victim, not** as a **sinner** … Thus he approached God from the … stance of a victim … and **commanded** God to show himself…

---

[10] *The Times Weekend*, 14:Dec:1996, pp1-2.

[11] *Alpha News*, Mar – Jun 1998, pp12-13.

[12] Quoted in Dave Hunt, *Occult Invasion*, p298.

"...there is **no mention** of faith in the substitutionary **sacrifice** of Jesus Christ and salvation from sin based upon Jesus' death and resurrection".[13]

26:4 MORE LIGHT   This 'white light' is often seen in 'Near-Death Experiences' (or NDEs). Betty Eadie, for example, was:

"[one of the] most popular yarn-tellers, who ... 'was literally **embraced by the Light**, Jesus'. Her book, *Embraced by the Light*, ... sold well in Christian bookstores ... Eadie passes herself off as a Christian, dedicating her book 'To the Light, my Lord and Saviour Jesus Christ, to whom I owe all that I have'. In fact, she is a Mormon whose 'Jesus Christ' is **not** the Jesus Christ of the Bible".[14]

As others have pointed out, "the idea of being embraced by the light comes neither from the Bible nor from 'Pentecostal parlance' but from the occult".[15] Another man, who apparently had two NDEs:

"...encountered a council of 13 beings of **light**, who ... gave him a mission to ... build centres where people could heal emotionally and spiritually [via a false gospel!]".[16]

The next example was found on a Reiki bulletin board recently: "I hold the healing journey walk in **pure white light** ... Love and healing **white light** to you now, and for the duration of the walk...".[17] While we read the following from one Western Mystic:

"The experience of the **clear white light** is a mystical vision seen with the mind's eye as vividly as one would see with the physical eyes ... [it] is the inner light flooding through the external mind ... Occasionally young aspirants burst into experience ... It is the dynamic vision of clairvoyantly seeing the head, and sometimes the body, filled with a **brilliant clear light** ...

This occultist goes on: "bursts of ... clear white light are only a **door opener to transcendental possibilities**".[18]

[13] Martin and Deidre Bobgan, *12 Steps to Another Gospel*.
[14] Dave Hunt, *Occult Invasion*, p378.
[15] Ibid, p351.
[16] *Ibid*, p379.
[17] //www.marianne.com/bb1/messages/1020.html posted by Dave to Dora, 12:Nov:96.
[18] 'Master' Subramuniya, *The Clear White Light*.

In his book *Living With Kundalini,* the 'Gopi Krishna' tells of his New Age "Kundalini awakening" (which we shall look at properly in a few moments). The similarities to the above Alpha testimonies are obvious:

> "...Suddenly ... I felt a stream of **liquid light** entering my brain through the spinal cord ... The illumination grew brighter and brighter...".[19]

> "When the Kundalini awakens, it is a dramatic transformational force, a **white**, quicksilver, **fluid** light ... Those who are very sensitive can actually feel and even see the light force rising in the body".[20]

> "A door seems to have been pushed open through which a **flood of light** flows ... a light of **incomparable radiance**...".[21]

Of course, on the road to Damascus, "there shone from heaven a great light" which Paul saw. But no-one on Alpha is describing the light as an external one, let alone one coming from heaven. Nor are they reporting the other elements of Paul's experience: Unlike Paul's colleagues, who all saw the light, the Alpha 'light' is only visible to one person. The light Paul saw was the result of Christ's glory as He revealed Himself from Heaven and audibly spoke to Paul. The Alpha 'light' appears to have no such point. Paul's experience was biblically unique, and resulted in an incredible about-turn and a fabulously anointed apostolic ministry. Alpha's 'light show' only seems to impress people with what the spirit realm can do inside a person's *body*.

26:5 TINGLING, SHAKING, ELECTRIC SHOCKS   In addition to excessive warmth and bright light, some Alpha guests experience 'tingling', 'shaking' and 'electric shocks'.

> "On the Saturday of the Holy Spirit retreat weekend ... It started like a **tingle** and then I felt waves of power starting to flow through me..." [*Alpha News*].[22]

---

[19] Quoted in Sirley Marques Bonham, *Kundalini Manifestations, the Lucid-Dreaming, and OBE Experiences.*
[20] *When Mercury Escapes.*
[21] *Kundalini Manifestations, Lucid Dreaming, OBEs.*
[22] *Alpha News*, Nov 1998 – Feb 1999, p15.

158

"It's not about what you **think** is it? It's about feelings really ... All the ... **shaking** on that Saturday ... It just came over me".[23]

"I was fascinated by the teaching on the Holy Spirit. I heard that the gifts were free from God, and that we should eagerly desire them. I particularly wanted healing because my mother was very ill. While they were praying for the gifts, my **left hand** started **tingling** ... It got more and more **painful**. It was **absolute agony** ... I didn't know what to do about it and it kept going all evening [Later, their Course leader told them 'how God sometimes gives a sense of tingling in the fingers when he is giving a gift of healing']" [Elsdon-Dew, Ed.].[24]

While Scripture refers to the tingling of *ears* (notably in connection with God's *judgment*) it is not possible to find incidents there of healing accompanied by a "tingling in the fingers" despite what the pastor above taught. Could this be an example of us making the Word of God to none effect by the traditions of men?

"During the afternoon we were singing a song '**Holy Spirit, we welcome you**', when I felt an **incredible tingling** in the back of my neck. I was filled with a feeling of excitement and well-being ... During the course I had been talking to people who were Christians and I had wanted them to prove their beliefs had meaning. And now suddenly I had had this **instant conversion**" [HTB's *UK Focus* magazine][25]

"On the Saturday Nicky Gumbel talked about the Holy Spirit. In the afternoon **he asked the Holy Spirit** to come. I was thinking to myself, "What's going on?" ... Then suddenly, as I stood there, I began to feel tingling in my left hand. It was **like** little **electric shocks** ... Then two team members laid hands on me ... Then suddenly I got **all hot** ... The next day ... **the Holy Spirit was asked** to come again. I was just standing there and it came quickly this time. First I had **all this tingling** in my left hand and up my arm. Then my leg started **shaking**. They laid hands on me again ... I was also **boiling** hot again..." [Elsdon-Dew, Ed.].[26]

When men heard the gospel preached in the *book of Acts*, they were "pricked in their hearts" and repented; they "believed and were baptized in water and in the Holy Spirit"; they "walked and leaped and praised God";

[23] David Richardson, Alpha – the Omega in Evangelism?, *Prophecy Today*, Vol 13, No. 5, p7.
[24] Elsdon-Dew, Ed., *The God Who Changes Lives*, Vol 2, pp114-115 & 120-121.
[25] *UK Focus*, Mar 1999, p2.
[26] Elsdon-Dew, Ed., *The God Who Changes Lives*, Vol 2, p149.

they "believed and turned unto the Lord"; they "believed being astonished at the doctrine of the Lord"; they were "glad and glorified the Word of the Lord"; they "believed and rejoiced". However, one will search the New Testament in vain to find any conversions accompanied by tingling, electric shocks, shaking, heat, and the various other things mentioned in these Alpha testimonies.

In contrast, those who are foolish enough to get involved in Eastern mysticism *do* experience such things. For example, this is a description of an experience had by "Bhagwan Shree" Rajneesh and his followers in 1953:

> "...a bolt of **electricity** passing through his body. Passing from one person to the next, moving around the circle, coming back to him. The group began **shaking** violently. It was as if they were all possessed, taken over by a powerful impersonal energy".[27]

Similarly, consider the satanic force that is Kundalini:

> "This serpent power, Kundalini, cannot be described fully ... When it awakens, it shoots through the body **like an electric shock**, and trembling and amazed, the person realises that a powerful event has taken place within him ... The whole body **trembles**".[28]

> "Our whole life is guided already. To follow this guide we only have to do what **feels right to us** ... The first phase of such a training to feel again must therefore be a deep body work breaking that harness. And the result of such a work **must** be **shaking**, trembling and autonomous body movements ... It is a therapeutic[!] reaction, an attempt on the part of the body to shake itself loose from the rigidities that limit its motility and inhibit the expression of feeling".[29]

It is worrying to notice that, in Scripture, uncontrollable shaking is associated *solely* with apostasy. Lack of power or control over a person's own body is termed 'para-luo', translated 'palsy' in the King James Bible. The word 'luo' means "to break (up), destroy, loose, loosen" and therefore encompasses both paralysis *and* spasms (i.e. uncontrollable jerking) – hence the old-fashioned saying "shaking like the palsy". Every single one of the thirteen references in Scripture shows that it is NOT a good sign:

---

[27] Quoted in Inner-City Christian Discernment Ministry, *Power Gurus.*
[28] *Kundalini Manifestations, Lucid Dreaming, OBEs.*
[29] *Zenhouse.com.*

"For unclean spirits, crying with loud voice, came out of many that were possessed with them: and many **taken** with **palsies**, and that were lame, were **healed**" (Acts 8:7). See also Matt. 4:24.

From the following Old Testament imprecation, we get the distinct impression that forced shaking is actually a *curse* from God, *not* a blessing:

"Let their eyes be darkened, that they see not; and **make** their loins continually to **shake**. Pour out Thine indignation upon them, and let Thy wrathful anger **take hold** of them" (Psa. 69:23-24).

Although Nicky has no problem whatever with Alpha attendees experiencing electric shocks,[30] it could also be observed that the only *electricity* mentioned anywhere in Scripture is in the form of *lightning* – not exactly something desirable to be struck by!

Similarly, talk of *unnatural* "pins and needles" seems to have more to do with being hit by darts or arrows than with receiving *helpful* things. In the Holy Bible, having lightning or arrows directed at one represents being *scattered* from God rather than reconciled to Him (as in 2 Sam. 22:15 and Psa. 18:14). Some people might feel justified in pointing out that being on the receiving end of darts is never a sign of blessing in Scripture, but the very opposite (as in 2 Sam. 18:14 or Eph. 6:16). They might even refer to the Psalmist's cry to God:

"Cast forth lightning, and scatter them: shoot out Thine arrows, and destroy them. Send Thine hand from above: rid me, and deliver me out of great waters, from the hand of **strange** [i.e. false] children" (Psa. 144:6-7).

---

[30] Talk 9.

CHAPTER **27**

*W*ORLD-CLASS EXPERIENCES

27:1 WHAT *IS* KUNDALINI?   We've now seen 'Kundalini' mentioned several times. So what is it? As we can see from the following description it is certainly not of *God*. Here is an introduction so that we can recognize its true source:

> "Kundalini is the **Hindu** word for the sacred, transformative energy that awakens consciousness. According to **esoteric** literature, this energy has been coiled at the base of the spine in a latent form since birth, awaiting the stimulus to unfold its potential".[1]

One American researcher reports that:

> "Kundalini **Energy** is typically described as a powerful energy source lying dormant in the form of a coiled **serpent** at the base of the human spine. When freed it reputedly has the capacity to effect great physical manifestations and healings".

Maybe this explains why snakes are sacred to Hindus whereas they are seen very differently by God. The Lord cursed them in the *first* book of the Bible (Gen. 3:14) and used them as a picture of Satan in the *last* (Rev.

---

[1] El Collie, *Kundalini and the Awakening of Spirit.*

12:9). Incidentally, yoga meditation also seeks to awaken the Kundalini "serpent".

27:2 LYING SIGNS As we noted earlier, the enemy is powerful and can mimic the gifts of God. Holy Scripture talks about "false visions", "false dreams", "false prophecies" and so on. That is not to say that such visions or dreams or prophecies are not necessarily going to come to pass, but that their source is falsely claimed to be from God.[2] But the enemy is more than capable of providing *true* words of knowledge, *true* visions and so on. He frequently uses these as a cover to bring in false doctrines about God:

> "If there arise among you a prophet, or a dreamer of dreams, and giveth thee a sign or a wonder, And the sign or the wonder **come to pass** ... [but the person also promotes a God other than that described in Scripture] ... Thou shalt **not** hearken unto the words of that prophet, or that dreamer of dreams: **for the LORD your God proveth** [i.e. is testing] **you**, to know whether ye love the LORD your God with **all** your heart and with **all** your soul. Ye shall walk after the LORD your God, and fear Him, and **keep His commandments**..." (Deut. 13:1-4).

That, then, is the situation for believers. Where Satan uses false visions, divinations etc on *un*believers it is to make them think they have found the true God. Satan will very happily give them miracles and *some* accurate information about God so that they are fooled into believing they know Him; just as long as they approach what they *think* is God, but isn't, then Satan has them seriously in his grasp. The only way out for either of these groups is to be given the pure Word of God so they can see where the flaws lie in the experiences they have had - and can then repent.

27:3 VISIONS AND VOICES We must be very careful when hearing of testimonies involving visions and voices. While there are certainly a few scriptural examples of visions, there are false ones too e.g. in Jer. 14:14, Jer. 23:16, and Ezek. 13:7. Apart from a handful of examples where God gave *dreams* to unbelievers for interpretation by mature men of God, *visions* from God are only ever given to obedient servants who are able to discern their

---

[2] Incidentally, if anyone *does* give a prophecy in the name of the Lord which fails to come to pass, then Scripture declares that person a false prophet - even if only *one* of their prophecies fails – see Deut. 18:20-22. (Under the Mosaic law, the People were commanded to put false prophets to death. Since Christ came we are commanded to reject them from our lives – see Matt. 7:15.)

source (e.g. Joseph, Daniel and Peter). Biblically, it seems all visions which actually *'picture'* God are only ever given to *extraordinarily* pure believers such as Isaiah, Stephen, Paul and John.

Regarding "heard" voices, Scripture contains quite a few examples, especially in the 'Old Testament', of God speaking audibly to men, i.e. from *outside their person into their physical ears*. Now that the Canon of the Bible is complete, God mainly speaks to us through the pages of His written Word. There are, of course, times when the Lord's Spirit will give believers *particular / specific* guidance through impressions (none of which will ever countermand Scripture). But these are received into our *spirits*; they are not the same thing at all as an audible voice *heard inside one's head,* such as are described by these New Agers:

> "an **inner voice**, indicating direction and elucidation ... This **inner** voice remains with him as ... an ever-ready guide to the unravelling of complexities in daily life...".[3]

> "As perception expands outside of consensus reality, people experience atypical visual phenomena, including visions of lights, ... Auditory input may include **hearing voices**...".[4]

These inner voices are *not* from God. Worryingly, an example of an Alpha participant 'hearing voices' was reported by the *Sunday Times*:

> "One business man confessed he had said his night time prayers for the first time in 20 years. They were answered. At 3.00am he had awoken with the words, 'Buy *The Economist* Magazine' ringing **in his head**. That morning he followed the mysterious advice and found that the journal contained an article about a career change he had been dithering over for a **long** time. **Surely** this was a sign from **God**".[5]

(As we saw in Part One, Satan can easily cause false miracles. His servants can even engineer coincidences which make us think the Lord is directing us. For example, they can use unbelievers to confirm things we have been wondering about, in order to make us think we've received a *sign from God*, rather than a *lying* sign. Since this man had been thinking about the career change for a "long" time, i.e. well before he began Alpha, the idea of a career change can readily have been from the enemy.)

---

[3] *The Clear White Light.*
[4] *Kundalini and the Awakening of Spirit.*
[5] *Sunday Times,* 14:Dec:1996.

The following appears to be another case of a voice *in the head*, since the lady makes no reference to where the voice came from. Had the voice been *audible* one would expect her to mention looking for the source. This is further testimony from an Alpha participant (who cropped up earlier) just prior to her having a 'white light' experience. (It is also interesting to compare the things she heard with the sort of things Christ said to people in the scriptures.)

> "All of a sudden, this incredible peace filled the front room. [My son's] photograph was on the side and I felt my eyes **drawn** to his face. **I heard a voice** say, 'Hold on tight Michaela. Look at Daniel's eyes – aren't his eyes, your eyes? Isn't he beautiful? Aren't **you** beautiful? Look at his face Michaela. He needs you.' There was a glow around Daniel's face and he seemed to be coming out of the picture..." [*Alpha News*].[6]

According to the Mystic referred to earlier:

> "[T]he inner voice **may** be falsely identified as an unseen master or god [for the Alpha participant, Jesus] talking into his right ear, but, when in the clarity of clairvoyantly seeing white light **and** at the same time clairaudibly hearing the inner sounds, he knows that it is his **super**consciousness, his **inner** self...".[7]

The "inner self" is also a false identification of the source of the voices. But the point is that, while this kind of experience has no parallel in Scripture, it certainly does in the occultism of the New Age movement.

Weeping

As well as visions and voices, the following Alpha testimony also involves weeping. Tears easily move us, but they still need careful testing since they are very common in New Age awakenings: "The nature of the cleansing process creates strange behaviour that might make the person **weep** and laugh within minutes".[8] The person crying ought to know *why* they are crying, or at the very least be able to stop crying if they so wish; otherwise they do not possess self-control and therefore the experience is not a blessing from God.

---

[6] *Alpha News*, Mar – Jun 1998, p13.

[7] *The Clear White Light.*

[8] *When Mercury Escapes.*

"The Saturday morning following the first Alpha talk, I woke up and I was crying ... I didn't know I was going to say it but I said, 'God, **why** am I crying?' Instantly, I felt **Jesus** was **at my side.** We were looking at a single bed and two figures, it was the ... hospital where my eldest son was born and the figure on the right of the bed was the nurse holding the baby, showing him to me. There were tears running down my face. I'd forgotten about that. Then Jesus **seemed** to **say** to me, 'You cried when your son was born and now you're crying *because you have been born again.'* Then I was back in my bed and he was gone" [*Alpha News*].[9]

There has to be a question-mark over this experience. Firstly, the crying was apparently uncontrollable (and the reason for it seems dubious, for if he was weeping with joy and relief - as at his son's birth - he would have been *aware* of those feelings). Secondly, the vision of *himself* in the past is much more like an out-of-body experience than anything in the Bible. Thirdly, the physical presence of a 'Jesus' is highly problematic as we shall see shortly. We have already discussed the serious difficulties associated with 'hearing voices' that claim to be from God. We will need to return to the matter of weeping a little later.

One young Alpha guest had suffered from paranoia, headaches and voices in his head for some time when, at a very low point in his life (*not* while on Alpha), he saw the image of a face on a door. Like Michaela, the lady quoted earlier, he says:

"I **knew** it was Jesus ... He **looked** so sad and a voice **inside** me said 'Enough is enough, Shane...'" [*Alpha News*].[10]

How did Shane distinguish this voice from the previous ones he had heard? Perhaps because the other voices were terrifying but this one was sad? He doesn't say. Nor does he explain how he knew it was Jesus before he had even attended his first Alpha talk.

Another participant had a vision of 'Jesus' standing in front of her, who said to her: "After all I have done for you all of your life, why do you reject me?" Then this 'Jesus' showed her all the times in her life he had been there for her:

"How can I describe it? I saw **intense, extraordinary** love ... I can say 'Yes, **I have met Jesus Christ personally**' ... I can

---

[9] *Alpha News*, Nov 1997 – Feb 1998, pp12-13.
[10] *Alpha News*, Jul – Oct 1998, p15.

never deny that fact of him **standing in front of me** and loving me in that way. After that vision I started going to Alpha every Wednesday..." [Elsdon-Dew, Ed.].[11]

But, like all the other visions referred to above, this 'Jesus' never once mentioned what He did for her on the cross. After that vision:

"...[E]very time the name Jesus was mentioned, I would just weep. I suppose that **was** my **conversion**" [Elsdon-Dew, Ed.].[12]

But how are those visions to be distinguished from the next two which are occultic? The 'Ascended Master', Djwhal Kuhl, appeared to New Ager Will Baron:

"...radiating an almost blinding **golden** light [Remember our "**gold** Catherine wheel" earlier] and a soothing **presence** that filled him with peace ... Will writes 'When I first saw him, my own initial thought was, He looks **just** like **Jesus Christ**...'".[13]

And, in a New Age meeting, one person reports that:

"I suddenly saw **Benjamin Creme's** face disappear, and in the frame of what had been his face was a completely different face which didn't look anything like him. It was a face that was a sort of **golden**-bronze colour, with ... very high cheek bones, and a longish face. And he also had a beard, this extraordinary being who was looking at me ... And I was **really moved**, to the very depths of my being, because what I actually experienced was a **tremendously powerful** and very pure **love**".[14]

One Christian teacher wisely notes: "Of course, in near death experiences Hindus see visions of their gods and Buddhists see the void. Is that because the brain is creating the vision from one's belief, or do demons paint a picture within the person's belief system? Visions are a poor basis for faith".[15]

27:4 MORE WEEPING Again, we must try to steel ourselves regarding tears. They naturally provoke emotion in us and can cause us to let down

---

[11] Elsdon-Dew, Ed., *The God Who Changes Lives*, Vol 2, pp111-2.

[12] Elsdon-Dew, Ed., *The God Who Changes Lives*, Vol 2, p113.

[13] Hunt, *Occult Invasion*, p391.

[14] Quoted in Nick Needham, *The Toronto Blessing – Part One*.

[15] Hunt, *Occult Invasion*, p379.

our guard and not rightly judge whether it is the *Holy* Spirit, or another, involved. Tears touch us, and this is only proper. But, as we have seen, pagan spiritualism can produce tears. The following refers to a New Age experience:

> "**Psychological Upheaval.** People find themselves beset by **inexplicable** emotional states as they move to clear out unresolved issues. The emotional roller coaster may swing from feelings of anxiety, guilt and depression, through to compassion, love and joy, with accompanying bouts of **uncontrollable weeping**".[16]

It would thus be extremely naïve to imagine that all spirit-inspired weeping must come from God. We need to be careful and weigh *everything* against God's Word. Does the person weeping know *why* they are crying? *Is* there a reason, or is it spontaneous and meaningless?

> "I began to go to church and to sing the worship songs. By this time I knew I was well **on the way** to becoming a Christian ... I went along to the **Holy Spirit day** mainly out of curiosity. When I received the Spirit, [still having not become a Christian] I **just wept** and then I felt so peaceful" [*Alpha News*].[17]

The following example, like others, refers to 'raising of the hands'. This is an act of submission, and surely assists the entity you are dealing with – whether or not it is God – in doing what they want to you. Similarly, putting one's hands out in a 'begging' position is a mark of acceptance and helps the spirit involved to give you whatever they want. It is thus crucial to make sure you know which spirit you are 'contacting'.

> "...while standing, I raised my hands and started praying that the Holy Spirit would come to me ...While continuing to pray, I felt tears well up in my eyes and roll down my face ... I experienced a **wave** of overwhelming love, deep down within me. This was **followed closely** by peace, joy and total happiness. I now felt that I was **alive** for the first time in my life" [*UK Focus*].[18]

Did this person not also feel "alive" after *conversion*?

> "...I wanted a positive **sign**. I prayed and prayed but nothing seemed to happen. Then on the **Holy Spirit day** we were talking

---

[16] Bonnie Greenwell, *Energies of Transformation, A Guide to the Kundalini Process*, quoted in Karin Hannigan, *Kundalini and the Awakening of Spirit*.
[17] *Alpha News*, Nov 1997 – Feb 1998, pp6-7.
[18] *UK Focus*, Jan 1999, p6.

in our discussion group and I **suddenly** started to **cry**. I **kept on** crying and the group prayed for me. And **then I stopped** crying and I knew **I believed from that moment**. I felt **intensely warm**. I had wanted to believe for so long and suddenly I did. [But believed what?]" [*Alpha News*].[19]

27:5 WHAT THEN?   Even if we accept that previously unchurched Alpha participants cannot be expected to distinguish between the sacred and profane, there is no excuse for the *Course leaders* – Christians, one would expect, for at least a reasonable time – to be blindly trusting of these highly questionable experiences. But they are. And the originators of the Course seem to delight in publishing ever more of these unbiblical 'conversion' testimonies in their newspapers and books. But what can we expect when they themselves promote such occult experiences? Nicky Gumbel himself speaks approvingly of receiving "electric shocks of love",[20] and encourages participants to *visualize* Jesus – for example when he says: "**Imagine him** [Jesus] ... **standing in front of you**".[21]

Where are we told in Holy Scripture that the early Church *ever* used visualization (whether or not of Jesus)? As was demonstrated in Part Four, visualization is a pagan activity.

Not one of the Alpha participants who had an experience of 'Jesus' (whether visual or audible), or of the 'white' or 'bright light', questioned whether it might conceivably have been something else. Yet we read, in 2 Corinthians 11, that unless we are questioning what happens in our churches then, if someone comes to our church and leads us: "[to] receive **another** spirit, which ye have not received ... ye might well bear with him ... For such are ... **deceitful** workers" (vv4,13-15).

We repeat, it is *vital* that we take care over what it is we are being exposed to, because there exist "**seducing** spirits" (1 Tim. 4:1). But we all know these scriptures, so why aren't Course leaders applying them to the bizarre experiences going on during their courses?

> "Since evil spirits **can counterfeit** God as Father, Son, or Holy Spirit, the believer needs also to know very clearly the **principles**

---

[19] *Alpha News*, Mar – Jun 1999, p6.
[20] Talk 9.
[21] Talk 3.

upon which God works, so as to detect between the Divine and the Satanic workings".[22]

27:6 KUNDALINI MANIFESTATIONS   We have already noted a few of the manifestations associated with Kundalini awakening. The following is a more complete list of manifestations of the risen Kundalini, drawn up by a New Ager. (The section following will expose even further just how demonic Kundalini is.)

"Many people know that the risen Kundalini flings open gates to all sorts of mystical, paranormal and magical vistas but few realise it can also dramatically impact the body… [It can cause:]

- **Energy** rushes or immense **electricity** circulating the body;
- Itching, **vibrating**, prickling, **tingling**, stinging or crawling sensations;
- Intense **heat** or cold;
- **Involuntary** bodily movements (occur more often during meditation, rest or sleep): jerking, tremors, **shaking**; feeling an inner **force** pushing one into postures or **moving one's body** in **unusual** ways. (May be misdiagnosed as epilepsy, restless legs syndrome (RLS), or PLMD);
- Numbness or **pain** in the limbs (particularly the **left** foot and **leg**);
- Emotional outbursts; **rapid mood shifts**; seemingly **unprovoked or excessive** episodes of **grief**, fear, rage, depression;
- **Spontaneous** vocalizations (including laughing and **weeping**) -- are as unintentional and uncontrollable as hiccoughs;
- Hearing an **inner sound** or sounds, classically described as a flute, drum, waterfall, birds singing, bees **buzzing** but which may also sound like roaring, whooshing, or thunderous noises or like ringing in the ears;
- Altered states of consciousness: heightened awareness; spontaneous **trance states**; mystical experiences (if the individual's prior belief system is too threatened by these, they can lead to bouts of psychosis or self-grandiosity);
- Heat, **strange** activity, and/or **blissful** sensations **in the head**, particularly in the crown area;

We have produced an article on our website (bayith.org) giving two examples each, from *official* HTB sources, of twenty-two of the above things

---

[22] Jessie Penn-Lewis, *War On The Saints*, p53.

taking place on *Alpha* Courses. But the above list does not stop there. It continues with the following additional results which could be mistaken for salvation by unsuspecting Alpha team members:

- Ecstasy, bliss and **intervals of tremendous joy, love, peace and compassion;**
- Psychic experiences: extrasensory perception; out-of-body experiences; **pastlife memories;** astral travel; direct awareness of auras and chakras; contact with spirit guides through **inner voices,** dreams or **visions;** healing powers;
- Increased creativity: **new interests** in self-expression and **spiritual communication** through music, art, poetry, etc;
- Intensified understanding and sensitivity: **insight** into one's own essence; **deeper understanding of spiritual truths;** exquisite awareness of one's environment (including "vibes" from others);
- Enlightenment experiences: direct **Knowing** of a more expansive reality; transcendent awareness".[23]

For anyone who has been wondering how Alpha can effect such dramatic, and seemingly good and spiritual, changes in participants, here is the answer: They experience the *New Age counterfeit* of true salvation. (For any reader who imagines speaking in 'tongues' is a way of distinguishing between true and false conversion, they need to be aware that false religions experience tongues – including Kundalini recipients.[24])

27:7 KUNDALINI TEACHING   Below are some of the deceptions that Kundalini's proponents teach. We list them not simply to show Kundalini's obvious satanic source, but for another reason which will become clear very shortly:

> "**Shakti** is also called Kundalini, which is the Sanskrit word meaning 'coiled-up' ... It frequently happens that an individual's Kundalini energy lies dormant throughout his, or her, entire life. The object of the **Tantric** practice of Kundalini **Yoga** is to awaken this cosmic energy and allow it to move along the spinal chord through the **chakras** to be united with **Shiva** ... In order for the Kundalini Shakti to be manifest, it must pass through the chakras that lie along the axis of the spine as consciousness

---

[23] El Collie, *Kundalini Signs and Symptoms.*
[24] See Roger Oakland, *New Wine or Old Deception?*, (The Word For Today, 1995), p58 for proof that kundalini can include "talking in tongues". This is actually included in our list under "spontaneous vocalizations".

potentials. The chakras are assumed to be situated not in the material body, but in the etheral body".[25]

Here are further lies routinely taught by Kundalini gurus but which help us to discern the real source of their power.

"In its dormant form it is the very essence of all life. Kundalini is also a **Goddess** of immense power, often called Kundalini Shakti. It is She who is the manifest universe, and when She wakens, She will sweep one up in Her tremendous passion to reunite with Her Lord, **Shiva** – the unmanifest – in order to **dance** again in his arms.

"...there is a familiar symbol of it in Western culture ... the symbol for medicine ... [T]he caduceus, the rod with two snakes coiled round it in spirals ... represents the central column akin to the spine in the physical body called **sushumna** ... The sushumna, our caduceus' rod, parallels the spinal column from the base of the body to the base of the skull. Just as the spinal column is a hollow structure that protects the spinal cord of the central nervous system, so the sushumna is a hollow structure that offers an ascending tube for the Kundalini, or **light force**...

"The hidden, or inner form of Kundalini is usually asleep in a small 'bulb' of energy ... [W]hen the inner Kundalini is awake it turns us inward to our **soul** and to our source – the **Divine** ... It is 'the beginning of the spiritual journey' that enables us to 'experience the inner, **spiritual** world'.

"As the inner Kundalini is awakened, it uncoils and ascends like a snake, so that is often why it is called '**serpent**-power'. This bulb of Kundalini can be awakened through **intense devotion** to God, **repetition of mantra** and various **yogic** practices, and, in my case, **shaktipat**, the Guru's **touch**".[26]

In the following chapter we will return to the Spirit *of Christ* and check some of the common notions held about Him and His ministry.

---

[25] David Burnett, *The Spirit of Hinduism*, pp209,211.
[26] Ruth Trimble, *When Mercury Escapes*.

CHAPTER 28

"𝒯HE SPIRIT OF TRUTH"

28:1 THE *HOLY* SPIRIT?   Unfortunately, the following quote shows that Alpha currently offers a rather unbiblical concept of the Holy Spirit:

> "Mr Gumbel led a session entitled 'How Can I Be Filled With The Spirit?' ... Mr Gumbel asked us to put our hands out. He prayed: 'Fill us with your Spirit', then described what he saw – 'The Spirit of God has come and is filling people all around this room. Some people are **shaking**. Some of you **feel** a great **weight** on your hands. Others, tears are rolling down your face and you are thinking '**Why** am I crying?' This is the Spirit of God, don't be embarrassed. **Don't resist** the Spirit. Some of you **feel** waves coming **over** you. **Waves and waves of liquid love...**'".[1]

The gifts of the Holy Spirit *are* still available today, but Nicky's description bears little relationship to that given in Scripture. Where in the Bible is anyone said to *physically* feel the Holy Spirit (whether or not as a "great weight" or "waves", and whether or not "on their hands")? The Holy Spirit is *spiritually*, not naturally, discerned (1 Cor. 2:14). There is some serious misteaching going on here between Who and What the Person of the Holy Spirit is and what He does. (We will explain this further below.)

---

[1] Quoted in *The Times Weekend*, 14:Dec:1996, pp1-2.

Where in the Bible do we find descriptions of 'waves and waves of liquid love' coming over the disciples? Nowhere. Yet 'waves' of love or power along with uncontrollable weeping, ecstatic laughing, unexplained feelings of joy, peace, or even anger, and shocks of 'electricity' are all commonplace in Alpha testimonies:

> "Others were being powerfully touched by the Spirit and I began to feel **angry**. Then **suddenly** a feeling of joy came over me and I began to laugh **uncontrollably**. At **that** point I knew I had become a **Christian**..." [*Alpha News*].[2]

28:2 THE PRESENCE OF GOD Giving support for Nicky's comments above, a lot of Alpha participants speak of physically sensing the presence of God in the room. Let us examine this in the light of Scripture to see what is happening. Let us start by verifying how the three Persons of the Godhead present themselves:

God the Father

Under the Old Covenant, God was said to "dwell" in the Tabernacle of Moses, and later in Solomon's Temple. Although these places were in geographic locations, this was a physical picture of God dwelling *in us*, His Temple (1 Cor. 3:16). God's *Name* dwelt in Israel (Deut. 12:11; 1 Ki. 8:29) but He Himself cannot be contained even by the whole of heaven, let alone in a house: "But **will** God indeed **dwell** on the earth? behold, the heaven and heaven of heavens cannot contain Thee" (1 Ki. 8:27, Acts 17:24).

When God's *glory* (i.e. still not His *Person*) was present in Israel the result was terrifying (Exod. 24:17; Lev. 9:23-24), but this is not what is being experienced on Alpha Courses. Finally, when Scripture talks of God "dwelling" in Jerusalem, it means that His *heart* is there. He may *bless* a meeting; He may even "turn His face toward" us and hear us, but none of this is the same as God the Father being *personally present*.

God the Son

When God the Son comes back to the earth it will be very evident to all (Matt. 24:26-27; Luke 17:22-24, 29-30, 21:27). Christ is currently seated at the right hand of the Father (Luke 22:69; Psa. 110:1). Scripture

---

[2] *Alpha News*, Jun – Oct 1997, p9.

tells us that the Lord Jesus Christ "after He had offered one sacrifice for sins forever, sat down on the **right hand of God**" (Heb. 10:12) where He will remain "until the times of restitution of all things" (Acts 3:21). So it is not the Son Himself who is being 'felt' on Alpha.

(Note: Christ's promise in Matthew 18:20 about being "in the midst of us" is often misunderstood. By looking at the preceding verse we will see what it really means in context, remembering that Christ Jesus is the "one **mediator between** God and men" (1 Tim. 2:5):

> "I say unto you, That if two of you shall agree on earth as touching any thing that they shall ask, it **shall** be done for them of My **Father** which is in heaven. **For** where two or three are gathered together in My Name, there am I in the midst of **them**" (Matt. 18:19-20).

Christ Jesus is not in *our* midst, but in the midst between us and the Father. God the Father answers our prayers when Christ *mediates for* us, not when He is in the *room* with us. The Greek word translated "midst" means that Christ stands "between" us and the Father; "occupying an inter**mediate** position". We simply receive a special degree of Christ's intercession when we make the effort to pray with others, just as happens when we make the effort to pray with fasting. Romans 8:34 explains the true position of Christ Jesus:

> "It is Christ that died, yea rather, that is risen again, who **is** even **at the right hand of God**, who **also** maketh **intercession** for us." See also Heb. 7:25.

Thus, when Nicky Gumbel says "Jesus is **here** ... he's right here now" he is being unnecessarily misleading.[3]

God the Holy Spirit

Alpha participants logically assume that the person they can feel in the room is the Person of the *Holy Spirit*. But there are some important (and interrelated) points that must be made here...

28:3 ***LOCAL* PRESENCE**   The Spirit dwells in *men*, not in geographical locations such as rooms (Rom. 8:9-11; John 14:17). He abides in the *spirits* of believers, not their physical surroundings. People may sense a God-given

---

[3] Talk 3.

peace in a room, but they cannot feel the Spirit's own "presence" in a room. He is *omnipresent*, not a local manifestation. It is for this very reason that the Psalmist writes: "Whither shall I go from Thy spirit? or whither shall I flee from Thy presence?" (Psa. 139:7-10). Thus, if we detect a presence from which we can physically alter our distance, it is certainly not the presence of *God*.

One watchman has made the following observations: As a young man, Benny Hinn reports having sensed the Spirit "present with me **in the room**".[4] On one of his videos, Hinn recalls the experience of having to go down to meals, leaving this powerful presence *behind in his bedroom*. He also relates how the Spirit *physically* walks *beside* us. But the Holy Spirit abides in the born-again *spirit* of man (1 Cor. 3:16; 1 John 2:27). He does not "walk beside" us, nor can He be "left behind" in our room when we go elsewhere to eat! The only presence that manifests locally in the way Hinn describes is a "familiar spirit" (i.e. what occultists call a "spirit-guide").[5]

Several of the Alpha testimonies quoted above make reference, in their full versions, to *localized* presences. Here is another such:

> "When I learnt that Jesus lives in us through his Spirit, I had to find out more. On our Holy Spirit Day, we watched the videos which I thought were really interesting. Then we all stood and ... I could sense a great presence **in the room**..." [*Alpha News*].[6]

Although the *Holy* Spirit does not come like this, demons certainly may do. One of Job's "miserable comforters", visited by a demon, reported detecting its nearby presence:

> "...a spirit **passed before** my **face**; the hair of my flesh stood up" (Job 4:13-15).

28:4 *PHYSICAL* PRESENCE   When we are in God's presence, it is in the spirit, and it is sensed *in our spirits*. Likewise if the Spirit is poured out on us, we discern it *spiritually*. This is an altogether different sensation from

---

[4] Benny Hinn, *Good Morning Holy Spirit*, p15.

[5] Nicky teaches that "Jesus said the Father will give you 'another' counselor. The word for 'another' means 'of the same kind'. In other words, the Holy Spirit is **just** like Jesus" [*Questions of Life*, p116]. Unfortunately, this implies that the Spirit does indeed walk beside us, just as Jesus did with His disciples.

[6] *Alpha News*, Nov 1997 – Feb 1998, p10.

that of many Alpha attendees who report feeling a *physical* presence. One participant who missed Talks 1 and 2 but who attended Talk 3 reported:

> "The next Sunday I went to both the morning and evening service [at HTB's sister church] ... As I opened the church door, I thought I was going to be knocked flat. I **felt** a **physical** presence I had never felt before in my life. I **had** to grab hold of both doors to stay upright ... I couldn't believe it. I **felt** the Spirit of God and it was incredible" [Elsdon-Dew, Ed.].[7]

Likewise,

> "I **felt** such a presence ... I felt I just **had** to get down...".[8]

People will understandably point to the time when Jesus "saw the Spirit of God descending **like** a dove, and lighting upon Him", or the time when "there appeared unto them [the disciples] cloven tongues **like** as of fire, and it sat upon each of them. And they were all filled with the Holy Ghost". Surely these experiences speak of *physical* manifestations of the Holy Spirit to *geographical* locations?...

The first point to make is that these manifestations are *likened* to physical things but are not actually described as physical in either case. The fact that they were visible to some people does not mean they were physical rather than spiritual (as Elisha demonstrated to his servant in 2 Ki. 6:17).

The second point is that, in both cases, the spirit fell *on the person* rather than "entering the room". Again, the point is made that God's spirit inhabits *us*, not our environs. Note also that the Bible does not say that the tongues of fire WAS the Holy Spirit. Also, there is no suggestion that the spirit was *felt physically* in either passage. Compare this with the following Alpha testimony:

> "I had always seen what people said was the Holy Spirit, but I had never experienced it. On the Saturday of the Holy Spirit retreat weekend, we watched a video about receiving the Holy Spirit. After it was over our pastor asked if there was anyone who would like to receive the Holy Spirit. Some people went up and he prayed over them and you could **feel something** start to **enter** the **room**, this amazing ... **presence**..." [*Alpha News*].[9]

---

[7] Elsdon-Dew, Ed., *The God Who Changes Lives*, Vol 2, p132.

[8] *The God Who Changes Lives*, Vol 2, p132.

[9] *Alpha News*, Nov 1998 – Feb 1999, p15.

Regrettably, Nicky again actively promotes this incorrect thinking - for example, through his publicized advice to the following participant:

"...I went along to the first Alpha ... I rang up Nicky Gumbel the next day ... I went along to Nicky's place ... after about an hour or so, he said to me, 'Well, do you feel like praying?' And I said, '**No, not really**.' But he said, 'OK, you don't have to pray but I am going to.' ... He prayed out loud for me ... And this **incredible** peace came on me [N.B. This happened *before* the person made a commitment to the Lord. If it had been the Holy Spirit, he would have felt conviction, not peace (John 16:8)]. It was just an overwhelming **presence** ... [A]fter a while [Nicky] said, '**I feel** a **very strong** presence of God. Have you **felt** it?' I said, 'Yes. I do as well'..." [Elsdon-Dew, Ed.].[10]

Nicky also quotes approvingly this 'healing' testimony:

"While they were praying for him, he was cast down to the ground as if **someone** had **hurled him violently** to the **earth**; groaning and sobbing, his whole body shaking so that he could not speak" [Talk 13].

We are obliged to point out that God does not "hurl" His obedient children about – but He does sometimes allow demons to throw around those in aspostasy (Acts 19:16; Matt 17:15; Luke 4:35). Nicky should have explained that if this was a God-given healing, rather than a similarly real but counterfeit one, then the man was being delivered of a devil in the process - and that it was the devil who was doing the hurling (on its way out). Otherwise Nicky's audiences may well suppose that this is what God sometimes does to those who serve Him.

28:5 *PERSONAL* PRESENCE   There is a very great difference between sensing *a* presence – i.e. the actual presence of a 'being' (whether visible or not) - and knowing that you are 'in touch with' someone. The "presence" of God and His personal company (or "Presence" with a capital "P") are two completely distinct things...

If someone telephones you, then you are 'in touch' with them. Their "presence" can be discerned in this way. That is very different from sensing the person actually being *present*. In the same way, whilst *we* can personally come into *God's* presence (by walking in the spirit), God's own

---

10 *The God Who Changes Lives*, Vol 2, pp223-4.

Presence does not "visit" our locality. Where a group of highly committed Christians is truly fearing God and humbly seeking Him, and when their meeting properly honours and glorifies Him, then God may bring a spiritual atmosphere among them. But this is still not His *personal* Presence. And still it is only spiritually discernable. *Our spirits* have come into the holy of holies, God has not come to our home (Psa. 51:11). Compare this with:

> "I **felt** as though **someone** had put their **hands** on my shoulders.
> I turned around to see if it was a lady I spent a lot of time talking
> to, but she was too far away..." [*UK Focus*].[11]

To repeat: God's 'presence' is not the presence of some (invisible) entity. The presence described in Alpha testimonies often implies some type of 'being'.

28:6 WHAT IS POURED OR GIVEN?   Readers may accept that it cannot be the Holy Spirit that is coming into *rooms*. But many will say that a person who is filled with the Spirit should expect to sense the Holy Spirit *inside them*. We have already seen that the Holy Spirit fills our spirit, not our soul or body, and that His presence is therefore only felt spiritually. (The *effects* of the Spirit's presence – e.g. a renewed mind – can obviously be discerned mentally or physically, but this is not the same as physically feeling the Person Himself.)...

But it is also worth asking how this 'works', for, when the Spirit is mentioned, many people expect to feel some sort of liquid or other type of force whereas researchers like Roger Oakland are convinced that the Holy Spirit is a Person and NOT an 'it'.[12] Why is it, for instance, that the Spirit is sometimes referred to as 'it' in the Bible? Here is our position:

If the tip of a man's finger had received a minuscule papercut and was beginning to heal, we would more readily say that '**it** [i.e. the **finger**] is healing' rather than 'HE is healing'. Thus, when referring to the Holy Spirit, the 'it' is not a force; it is simply an infinitesimal part of the Person. Hence: "For as yet **HE** was fallen upon none of them" (Acts 8:16). It is a 'HE' which falls on people. The Bible only calls the Holy Spirit 'it' in the sense of the infinitesimal part of the person of the Spirit into which our spirit has been immersed. Let's develop this point.

---

[11] *UK Focus*, Mar 1999, p2.
[12] Roger Oakland, *op. cit.*, pp60-62.

When the Bible talks about the "power" of God, it is not referring to some force but to the Person of the Holy Spirit (Luke 1:35). Perhaps the best way to describe the situation is this. The Holy Spirit is like a being (of infinite size) who, instead of comprising bones etc, is made up of intelligent, living water. (This is only an analogy!) When a person becomes a believer, their spirit becomes connected to this being, and when they are baptized in the Spirit they are immersed into this living water-person. It is in this sense that we are given "of" the Spirit of Christ (1 John 4:13).

Our spirit can be likened, in a way, to a sponge. Until we are saved, the sponge is dry and dead - separate from God. When we are saved, this 'watery-person' reaches out to the tiny, shrivelled sponge and attaches it to the outside of His water-body. We are then able to draw from the well of life. We can produce the fruit of the Spirit and we can hear God and receive from God in our spirit. We can serve God in many ways. But, if we walk sincerely enough with the Lord, and if we ask Him, He will immerse our sponge (i.e. our spirit) into Himself and it will be *filled* with the Holy Spirit. We can then receive certain special gifts. (Through sin, our spirit can be pulled away from being inside this water-person and, just like any sponge, our spirit will 'leak' and cease to be full of, or immersed in, the Holy Spirit.)

We believe this analogy reconciles all the relevant scriptures. If the reader is unhappy with the above, on the basis that God is definitely said to "**pour**" something, it should be remembered that this term is a Hebraism. In Jewish thought, when you make something *generously available* you may be said to be "pouring" it. Thus the Lord God will "pour" His wrath out on the damned (e.g. in Zeph. 3:8 and Rev. 14:10), and believers in distress are said to "pour" out their soul (e.g. in 1 Sam. 1:15 and Job 30:16).

We will need to say more on this matter in the next chapter. But the most crucial point here is that our *spirit* is submerged (i.e. baptized) to a lesser or greater extent, in the Spirit of God. Thus we should not expect to feel anything in our *bodies*. Evidence of an entity inside our body is actually evidence of possessing a demon - hence Biblical references to people being "possessed **with** [i.e. *not* **'by'**] a devil".

One clarifying note is necessary here. Even if our spirit is *full* of the Holy Spirit, this does not make us divine - just as the sponge remains a sponge, even when it is holding water. The sponge doesn't become water. Nothing of us becomes divine. God dwells in our spirit, but that does *not* make us God nor gods, just as the physical Temple in the Old Testament did not become God simply because God indwelt it in some sense.

How Can This Be?

Some readers may argue that the Spirit must be some sort of force or ethereal substance because they believe that the power of the Spirit can be transferred between humans by various methods. Below are four common arguments for the Holy Spirit being some sort of power which can be passed between humans, along with our answer to each:

1) *"Surely something flows between humans during 'laying on of hands'!"* It is true that we can receive things through the laying on of hands, but we receive it from *God* – not from the person praying for us. The word "through" in this context does not mean something travels through the hands but that we can be anointed as a result of obeying this ordinance. People receive things through the laying on of hands because they are obeying a biblical commandment and God respects it. The Bible never says that anything *passes through* the person's hands. It is a symbolic act like Holy Communion.

2) *"Surely something passed between Elisha's bones and the man who fell onto them in 2 Ki. 13:21!"* Again, nowhere do the scriptures say that the bones contained or transmitted any power. God was simply desirous to honour Elisha's ministry. Anyone who doubts this needs to remember that the Bible makes no mention of anyone else going to Elisha's grave for healing, yet some would have undoubtedly done so if the bones themselves transmitted power. Scripture actually says "He that toucheth the dead body of any man shall be **un**clean seven days" (Num. 19:11).

3) *"Surely some power was passed between Jesus and the woman with the issue of blood in the gospels?"* The clue for this is in the word used in these passages. The Bible does not say that "power" went out but that "virtue" went out. In other words, the power in question is the inherent power that the Lord Jesus has "by **virtue** of [his] nature".[13] Jesus is God. Since God's power healed this woman, Jesus perceived it. The Bible does not say that power passed through His garments and into the woman.

4) *"Surely the Bible talks about the 'power' of the Holy Spirit?"* Certainly the Holy Spirit has power, but when the Bible speaks of 'power' in the context of *humans* moving in the 'power of the Spirit' it is not referring to some magical force at our fingertips but simply refers to the ability to do God's will – e.g. the 'power to show grace under pressure'. Strong's

---

13 Strong's, 1411.

concordance makes clear that this power includes "**moral** power and **excellence** of soul" rather than some strange energy in our fingers.

28:7 A DEMANDING MATTER   Some Alpha attendees even *demand* physical 'evidence' of God before they will believe. (Could this be because the Gospel message being given is so watered down that God is not making Himself known through it?) Let us see some examples. The first individual thought the Course was "all conjecture" until he went on the weekend:

> "It was quite fun ... The arguments were logical and plausible but I still needed some **physical** evidence of the existence of God..." [*Alpha News*].[14]

> "...I just needed a final act of confirmation – something I could **feel** in the **physical sense**" [*Alpha News*].[15]

> "...I wanted a positive **sign**" [*Alpha News*].[16]

We have no warrant from Scripture to demand such things of the Lord. He has already shown His perfect love for us by dying in our place on the cross, and Scripture makes manifest the conditions for belief. Demands of the kind above are not included. In fact, they are *contrary* to the principle laid out in the Scriptures, which tell us that "faith cometh by **hearing**, and hearing **by the Word of God**" (Rom. 10:17). The Lord Jesus condemned the desire for any kind of 'sign' before people would believe on Him (Matt. 12:38-42). Yet consider this testimony:

> "After lunch we discussed a couple of things and had a prayer. I decided it was **worth a try**. I prayed for Jesus to **show himself**, to forgive my sins [was this person actually under conviction of his sins by the Holy Spirit at this point? Had he *repented*? Or did he just think it was 'worth a try' to ask Christ to give him some sign?] and **show me** his love [which the Lord Jesus did at Calvary]. I can't describe what happened. I just had my soul **ripped inside out**. An unbelievable **feeling**. Now I'm continuing to pray and every time I pray I get a **feeling** inside me" [*Alpha News*].[17]

---

[14] *Alpha News*, Jun – Oct 1997, p9.

[15] *Alpha News*, Nov 1997 – Feb 1998, pp6-7.

[16] *Alpha News*, Mar – Jun 1999, p6.

[17] *Alpha News*, Jun – Oct 1997, p9. The testimony also refers to feeling "overwhelmed by love", but as we have already seen, New Agers have also felt "overwhelmed by the love" due to their spiritual experiences. Such feelings cannot be trusted. (Nor can the 'forgiveness'

In her classic volume *War on the Saints,* Penn-Lewis makes some valuable comments regarding the 'physical' presence of God:

> "In seeking to obtain full control of the believer, the first great effort of evil spirits is directed toward getting the man to accept their suggestions, and workings, as the speaking, working, or leading **of God**. Their initial device is to counterfeit a 'Divine **Presence**', under cover of which they can mislead their victim as they will...

> "The condition on the part of the believer, which gives the deceiving spirits their opportunity, and the basis of this counterfeit, is the mistaken location of God; either (1) in them (consciously); (2) or around them (consciously) ... They use their imagination, and try to 'realise' His presence, and they desire to '**feel**' His presence in them, or upon them ... It may be said deliberately, that it is **never** safe in **any** case to *feel* God's presence with the physical senses...".[18]

(Note that several helpful books on the Holy Spirit are included in the Recommended Reading list at the end of this Part of our book.)

28:8 THE SPIRIT ON THE UNSAVED?

Another subject on which people are being tempted to ignore Scripture is regarding whether or not an *unbeliever* can receive the Spirit of God:

> "Even the Spirit of truth; Whom **the world cannot receive**, because it seeth Him not, **neither** knoweth Him" (John 14:17).

> "But the natural man **receiveth not** the things of the Spirit of God ... **[N]either can** he **know them**, because they are **spiritually** discerned" (1 Cor. 2:14).

> "And **because** ye are **sons**, God hath sent forth the Spirit of his Son into your hearts..." (Gal. 4:6).

The Spirit may certainly *convict* an unbeliever, but other than that He will not bless one or indwell one (John 16:8). It is an impossibility, since they are spiritually *dead* to God (Gen. 2:17; Luke 9:60). Sadly, Nicky says

---

toward others that some people may profess as a result of their blissful state.)
[18] Jessie Penn-Lewis, *War On The Saints*, pp124&112.

that non-Christians *can* "feel things in their **spirit**",[19] thus denying this. There is no precedent in Scripture for anyone receiving the Spirit who was not *already* a true believer. There are examples of God's *enemies* having, or being sent, *evil* spirits however (Judg. 9:23; 1 Sam. 16:14; 2 Chr. 18:18-22).

(There are times in the Bible where those who are opposed to God are forced by Him to *prophesy*. But (a) this is not a *good* sign, for it only ever happens to those who are going *against* God's ways, and (b) it is far from clear that these events are produced by the *Holy* Spirit. Regardless, the following instances of unbelievers sensing or receiving a spirit are not even of prophecy and so are certainly from another spirit.)

> "[O]n the weekend away, the Holy Spirit came and I felt moved ... I **wanted to become** a Christian [but hadn't!]. It was an emotional **and physical** sensation ... It is difficult to describe the experience ... You cannot buy the **buzz**..." [*Alpha News*].[20]

> "One night I finally bottled up the courage to say a prayer out loud. I just said, 'I **don't** really know you, but I would **like** to be able to **get to know** you **if** you are there.' [That is *not* a prayer of commitment.] When I said that prayer I felt a **really funny feeling** within me. It was exciting to say it. It gave me a **buzz** – like **Ecstasy**..." [Elsdon-Dew, Ed.].[21]

> "I came along to HTB... I felt this incredible sort of peace come over me ... I was still quite anti-HTB but I decided I was going to do the Alpha course to give it a chance. ... I heard about the ... **existence** of Jesus ... and I thought, '... I don't believe it'".[22]

For further examples of a spirit falling on unsaved guests, see the testimonies quoted in section 14:2 plus the one at the end of 15:7. See also some of the testimonies in section 26:1. The first testimony in 28:4 was from a non-Christian journalist.

(Of course, Alpha hints that these manifestations are directly related to the point of conversion; i.e. they are the "assurance of salvation" which the Bible promises the Holy Spirit will bring. Thus *Alpha News* is overrun with testimonies in which the guest assumes that their strange experience *was* their conversion. See sections 25:5, 26:5, 27:3-4 and 28:7 for examples

---

[19] *Questions of Life*, p150. They can certainly feel things in their *conscience*, but this is not what Nicky says.
[20] *Alpha News*, Jul – Oct 1999.
[21] Elsdon-Dew, Ed., *The God Who Changes Lives*, Vol 2, p38.
[22] Elsdon-Dew, Ed., *op. cit.*, Vol. 2, pp222-223.

in this volume. The whole of John 14 gives details of the calibre of person who is *truly* given the Spirit).

To justify the idea that novices can receive the baptism in the Holy Spirit, Nicky Gumbel refers to the experience of Cornelius - as described in Acts 10. But, by not explaining that Cornelius was already a very faithful, God-fearing man who was thoroughly obedient to the Scriptures, Nicky causes hearers to think that being filled with the Spirit is something which people can experience *before* they show any real commitment to God.

Love?

Another explanation posited by Nicky is that the manifestations are simply 'God expressing his love to a new convert'. But there are several major problems with this theory beyond the fact that these manifestations are often experienced by *unsaved* Alpha guests. (They need *conviction of sins*, not ecstatic experiences!)

- Jesus came to set us free, yet there are numerous reports of Course participants *not* being free to avoid *or* stop the manifestations. As we once asked HTB, "Surely someone in a relationship based on love would not force their will on the object of their love - and would permit the other party the freedom to stop some advance if they wanted to?"

- Some of the manifestations seem to have little to do with feelings of *love*. People at HTB have been "thrown, literally, across the room".[23] This doesn't seem terribly loving! People have also received "painful" physical sensations such that they described them as "absolute agony" [Video Talk 2][24] And participants have been literally half *choked*: "I ... couldn't breathe properly. I was coughing ... I think I was there 45 minutes later, still coughing ... It came to a point where ... I couldn't take it anymore" [*Alpha News*].[25]

The Enemy

How can we possibly expect participants to question which spirit they are encountering? They are among Christians who seem to know what they are doing, so the newcomers naturally think they are meeting with the Spirit of Christ. After all, the Course doesn't talk about Satan and his work until AFTER the Holy Spirit weekend – too late to allow biblical testing.

---

[23] Nicky Gumbel, quoted in Elizabeth McDonald, *Alpha: New Life or New Lifestyle?* (SMP, 1996), p4.
[24] This is part of a testimony given by Gumbel in Talk 2.
[25] *Alpha News*, Jul – Oct 2002, p33.

We ask again: How can participants possibly discern which spirit they are encountering given that the Course leaves the subject of Satan and "How to resist evil" until *after* the 'Holy Spirit' talks! Even when he does broach the subject, Nicky doesn't do a sound job:

• He claims that we "don't know" Satan's origins.[26] By omitting the details in Ezekiel 28:12-20 (a passage telling us things about the enemy that should make us very alert) Nicky ends up gaining a free hand to dispense the Alpha spirit without fear of challenge.

• He also avoids describing Satan's final destination (see Rev. 20:10 for it). If he were to reveal the truth, perhaps his horrified hearers would put more effort into avoiding the enemy's clutches.

• Because of the events in the Garden of Eden, Nicky characterizes Satan as somebody who "concentrates on the prohibition".[27] This suggests that those who alert people to God's prohibitions are satanic, whereas concentration on the prohibitions is *not* Satan's usual tactic (see the Wilderness temptations for example). Indeed, it is *God* who says "thou shalt not" over 200 times in Scripture - including ten times when laying down the Ten Commandments (Exod. 20:1-17).

---

[26] Talk 11, Edn. 2.1
[27] Talk 11.

CHAPTER **29**

*M*AJOR OUTPOURINGS RELATED TO ALPHA

29:1 ALPHA, TORONTO, PENSACOLA   An inadequate grasp of the gospel is one reason for guests' acceptance of these 'spiritual' experiences as coming from God. Another reason is almost certainly the close relationship that exists between the Alpha Course and the Toronto Blessing (TB) which also displayed these (and other even more remarkable) manifestations. This relationship is evident in the original edition of the Alpha videos - recorded in the first part of 1994. In one of these, Nicky relates to Alpha participants how the Toronto Blessing came to HTB - and then encourages participants to receive it likewise.[1]

However, in the *2nd* edition video set (recorded in the autumn of 1997), there are *no* overt references to the Toronto Blessing. Although the spirit behind Alpha has obviously not changed, Nicky apparently realised that many churches felt Toronto did not line up with God's Word and that they had thus distanced themselves from that movement (and from anything associated with it - including Alpha). Given the way that the Toronto spirit has now spread worldwide, not least via Alpha, there was no longer any

---

[1] Talk 9.

need to make specific reference to "Toronto". Such an alteration would thus help Alpha to be more widely accepted.

Most, if not all, of the manifestations seen in Alpha conversions were also experienced by folks involved with the TB. The more extreme behaviour seen in Toronto - such as drunken staggering, barking, roaring, acting like animals, 'birthing the baby', and 'holy vomiting' - seem to have been rare among Alpha's converts. Instead these things were experienced by people who were *already* professing believers. This difference in spiritual position may explain the different patterns of manifestation.

(Incidentally, most, if not all, of the 'TB' manifestations are also present at churches which have received the spirit via Brownsville Assemblies of God church in Pensacola, Florida. It is worth noting that the Pensacola outpouring was brought there by Steve Hill shortly after he had received the Toronto 'anointing' from **HTB's** 'vicar', Sandy Millar. It is thus the same spirit as that from Toronto, and we shall therefore refer to both outpourings under the one title. Some readers may feel that it is 'old hat' to discuss either, but there are extremely good reasons for doing so which will become obvious shortly.)

29:2   THE 'BLESSING' COMPARED WITH SCRIPTURE   The Toronto / Pensacola phenomenon ('T/P') has had unprecedented success in spreading itself throughout much of the professing church. It has achieved this because its supporters have seen the "fruit" of the T/P spirit and have wanted to experience and share it. The overriding justification for accepting T/P has been the "fruit" rather than the scriptural position on it because, after early (and not always honest) attempts to find biblical support, it became clear that the manifestations occurring were surprisingly extra-biblical. We will return to the subject of "fruit" in a moment.

Bereft of any unambiguous scriptural precedent, many folks turned instead to Church history – to Jonathan Edwards and the other revivalists of the 18th century – for justification of these manifestations. But in order to elicit support from Edwards these people had to edit out substantial chunks of completely contrary material. We rarely see the following, for example, being quoted by T/P apologists:

> "My design … is to show what are the true, certain, and dist-
> inguishing evidences of a work of the Spirit of God, by which we
> may safely proceed in judging of any operation we find in our-
> selves, or see in others … [W]e are to take the ***Scriptures***

[emphasis in original] as our guide in such cases. **This is the great and standing rule which God has given to his church, in order to guide them ... and it is an infallible and sufficient** rule.

"There are undoubtedly sufficient marks given to guide the church of God in this great affair of judging of spirits, **without which it would lie open to woeful delusion** ... Doubtless that Spirit who [produced] the Scriptures knew how to give us good rules, by which to distinguish his operations from all that is falsely pretended to be from him" [Jonathan Edwards].[2]

"... **tears, trembling**, groans, loud outcries, agonies of body, or the **failing of bodily strength** ... We **cannot** conclude that persons are under the influence of the true Spirit because we see such effects upon their bodies, **because** this is **not** given as a mark of the **true Spirit**" [Edwards].[3]

Although the Great Awakening was certainly often characterized by shrieking, tears, fainting and great joy, there was an enormous difference between that and what has been seen in 'T/P' meetings:

"[T]he phenomena in Edward's day did **not** occur through the laying on of someone's hands, **or** from repetitive chorus singing and chanting, but from the **preaching** of the **Word of God** [as per Acts 10:34-44] ... The shrieking and tears were the result of the **conviction of sin and terror at the possibility of going to Hell**. The rejoicing followed the assurance that **sins were forgiven** and that the person concerned was accepted by God. The faintings came about in both instances".[4]

Jonathan Edwards made clear that the joy which comes from the true Holy Spirit does "**not** corrupt and debase the mind".[5] This cannot be said of the uncontrollable laughter and beast-like behaviour from T/P.

George Whitefield likewise discouraged those in the Awakening who were "tempting God to require such signs" as it would lead them "to pretend to be guided by the Spirit without the written word". He insisted that *all* experiences be tested against "the unerring rule of God's most holy

---

[2] Banner of Truth Trust, *Jonathan Edwards on Revival: The Distinguishing Marks of a Work of The Spirit of God*, p87.

[3] *Ibid*, p91.

[4] Stanley Judd, *No Laughing Matter*, p12.

[5] *A Treatise Concerning Religious Affections*, p95.

word" and if found to be without Scriptural support discarded as "diabolical and delusive".[6]

Much is made within various Alpha resources of the fact that Charles Finney allowed T/P-style manifestations in his meetings.[7] Much less is made of what followed. A fellow worker who revisited Finney's 'harvest fields' reportedly "groaned in spirit to see the sad, frigid, carnal" state into which the churches had quickly fallen.[8] Still less is made of the shocking statement Finney himself made towards the end of his life about his followers. He said "the great body of them are a **disgrace**".[9]

And John Wesley relates the following in his journal:

> "Friday 9th May 1740: I was a little surprised at some who were buffeted of **Satan** in an unusual manner, by such a spirit of **laughter** as they could **in no wise resist** …".[10]

29:3 FRUIT ACID TEST   Unfortunately, the identical-looking "fruit" (e.g. the healings and deliverances *as well as* the manifestations) of the T/P spirit can be found in many *other* religions, so this is obviously not a wise test to use. At this point many will quote the verse: "Wherefore by their fruits ye shall know them" (Matt 7:20) but it has been rightly pointed out that this test refers to *people*, not to a 'move of the Spirit'. Testing of the latter must be based on whether the doctrine behind the move, and the nature *of* the move, agrees with the Spirit-inspired Word. And besides, it might also be noted that the fruit from T/P in many churches has actually been a *reduction* in Bible teaching, a *reduced* commitment to biblical prayer and an increase in worldliness and compromise.

Those "fruit" that (outwardly) *do* appear to be good, are things that can easily be counterfeited by the enemy. And where T/P recipients claim a "greater love for Jesus", they must be referring to "another" Jesus, because a greater love for the Lord Jesus Christ of Nazareth will always be followed by a greater love for, *and obedience to*, His whole Word (John 14:15&23). Frankly, this greater love for, and obedience to, the Bible seems to have been noticeable by its *absence* from T/P-associated churches.

---

[6] Quoted in Eric E. Wright, *Strange Fire?* pp116-117.
[7] See, for instance, Gumbel, *Telling Others*, p47.
[8] Benjamin Warfield, *Perfectionism*, Vol.2.
[9] Joseph Foot, *Literary and Theological Review*, Mar 1883.
[10] Quoted in Judd, *No Laughing Matter*, p13.

The Western Church has made the mistake of focusing on the fruits instead of on the *roots* of T/P. Vineyard's leaders openly admit that the *roots* lie unashamedly in the 'Faith' movement (whose own roots lie firmly in 'Christian Science' and the occult). But let us *irrefutably* demonstrate this claim about the 'Faith' movement being the source of T/P.[11]

1) Kenneth Hagin Snr. founded the 'Faith' Movement and its 'Rhema Bible Centers'.

2) The South African 'Rhema Church' is part of Kenneth Hagin Snr.'s 'Faith' Movement.

3) Rodney Howard-Browne (RHB) is from the South African 'Rhema Church' and is thus from a branch of Hagin's 'Faith' Movement.

4) In his book *The Touch of God*, RHB describes experiencing the 'T/P' phenomena as long ago as 1979: "My whole body was on fire … I began to laugh uncontrollably and then I began to weep … I was so intoxicated on the wine of the Holy Ghost that I was literally beside myself".

5) Two years *after* this, RHB helped pioneer a 'Rhema' (i.e. Hagin) Church in Johannesburg (so he was clearly acceptable to Rhema).

6) In 1987 RHB visited, and then moved to, America. He began his 'revival' ministry in Orlando, Florida (the home base, at that time, of Benny Hinn).

7) In April 1989, RHB presided over a full-blown 'T/P' meeting. Folk felt a "sensation like a heavy blanket" coming over them. "People began falling out of their seats; some were laughing and others were crying. The noise got so loud that RHB **had to interrupt his sermon**."

8) In Spring 1993, Browne held a four week meeting in Florida. As *Charisma* magazine reported: "No matter what Howard-Browne did or said, hundreds who attended the daily sessions always ended up on the sanctuary floor in **helpless** laughter".

9) Kenneth Copeland heads "Kenneth Copeland Ministries" which is part of Hagin's 'Faith' Movement.

10) RHB was a repeated guest of Kenneth Copeland Ministries.

11) In August 1993, Copeland "anointed" RHB to expand the 'revival'. The video, taken at the home of Kenneth Copeland Ministries (in Fortworth, Texas), also shows both men laughing hysterically and falling over.

12) Also in August of that year, Vineyard's Randy Clark received the 'Blessing' from RHB at Kenneth Hagin's Rhema Bible Church in Tulsa, Oklahoma. "It was as though he [Clark] was pinned to the

---

[11] We are indebted to Ed Tarkowski and others for their help in compiling this evidence.

floor ... 'two bodies down from me there was someone oinking' ... Randy ... start[ed] laughing, and he couldn't stop. After he finally got up he got more and more drunk in the Spirit." At a later meeting, Clark was prayed for by RHB on four separate occasions.

13) John Arnott, the pastor of Toronto Airport Vineyard Church, was very close to Benny Hinn for many years. Note that Hinn did not 'repent' of his 'Faith' teachings until AFTER the Toronto spirit had already arrived on the scene. Arnott was also prayed for by RHB in June 1993. Subsequently, Arnott invited Clark to minister at the Toronto Church. Clark did so on Jan 20 1994. The rest, as they say...

The 'Faith' movement is a group whose errors were recognized by most of the Church quite a few years ago. Nevertheless, it has managed to inject its false teachings into many Fellowships. (Much of this has been achieved through the bridgehead provided by the Vineyard movement). 'Faith' teachers have been so successful in this that they are now considered part of the "mainstream" by the bulk of the Church. (For a substantial look at the dangerous deceptions of the 'Faith' movement, see Part Four of this book.)

Below is just a very quick reminder of some of the teachings with which the 'Faith' Movement has 'blessed' us. Note that there are scripture references listed here which do not appear in our treatment in Part Four - and vice versa.

Hagin:
- "Christ's physical death on the cross was **not** enough to save us".[12] (But see Col. 1:14&20-22; Php. 2:5-9; Gal. 6:14; 1 Cor. 2:2; 1:23; Lev. 17:11; Heb. 9:12&22; Heb 10:10&19-20; 1 Pet. 1:18-19; 1 John 1:7, 3:16; Eph. 2:13; Rev. 1:5; 19:13.)
- "Man was created on terms of **equality** with God, and he could stand in God's presence without **any** consciousness of **inferiority**".[13] (But see 1 Cor. 15:45-47; Gen. 2:15-17; 3:19; Isa. 40:25; 45:5-6&21; 46:9; Isa. 64:8; Psa. 71:19; and Job chaps 38-42:6.)
- "The believer is called Christ ... That's who we are; **we're Christ**".[14] (But see Rom. 7:18; John 1:14; Gal. 2:20, 1

---

[12] *How Jesus Obtained His Name,* quoted in CROSS + WORD, *Word-of-Faith Sayings.*
[13] *C in C,* pp11,108
[14] *Ibid,* p108.

Cor. 8:6; John 20:28; 1:19-20; 8:23; Col. 1:16-17; Rev. 1:8; 5:1-5, 9&12-14, plus the whole of Ephesians!)

- Hagin has quoted Jesus as saying: "It would be a **waste** of their time to pray for **Me** to give them the victory. They have to **write their own ticket**".[15] (But see Matt. 6:9-13; Luke 21:36; 2 Thess. 1:11-12; 1 Thess 5:17; John 5:13-15; Matt. 7:7-8; 26:36; 1 Cor. 15:57-58, 1 Chr. 29:11-12; 16:34-35; Psa. 7:1; 31:13-17; 2 Sam. 22:3-7; Psa. 33:18-22; 37:39-40 etc.)

- "Spiritual death also means having **Satan's nature** ... Jesus tasted death – **spiritual death** – for every man".[16] (But see Eph. 5:2; 1 John 3:4-5; Heb. 4:15; Luke 23:46-47)

- "Jesus is the first person ever to be **born again**".[17] (But see Heb. 13:8; Luke 23:36; John 3:3-10; 1 Pet 3:18-19; Heb. 5:5-6, Php. 2:6-11; Rev. 1:8.) Since the Lord was already sinless, why did He need to be born again??

- "No believer should **ever** be sick ... **Satan** is the author of sickness ... It is God's will that we be healed...".[18] (But see Gal. 4:13; 1 Tim. 5:23; 2 Tim. 4:20; 2 Cor. 12:7, Lam. 3:38; Job 2:1-10; John 11:1-4.)

Copeland:
- "Faith is a **power** force. It is a **tangible** force. It is a **conductive** force".[19] (But see Matt. 28:18; John 16:8-9; 14:1&12; 15:5; 12:44-46; 11:25-26; Acts 26:18; John 7:38; 6:40&47.)

- "Jesus' death on the cross was **not enough** to save us".[20] (But see earlier references associated with Hagin's almost identical statement.)

- "Satan **conquered** Jesus on the Cross".[21] (But see John 9:17-18; Col. 1:13-14; 2:14-15; Gen. 3:15; Luke 23:46; John 17:1-5; 19:30.)

- "God is ... a being that stands somewhere **around 6'2", 6'3"** that weighs somewhere in the neighbourhood of a

---

[15] *Ibid*, p75.
[16] Hagin, *The Name of Jesus*, p31.
[17] *Ibid*, p29.
[18] *C in C*, pp248,258
[19] *Ibid*, pp65,379 fn5
[20] *What Happened From the Cross to the Throne*.
[21] *C in C*, p33.

couple of hundred pounds".[22] (But see Jer. 23:23-24; John 4:24; Deut. 3:24; 7:21; 10:17; Psa. 89:8.)

- "Technically, if God ever broke the Covenant [with Abraham] He would have to **destroy Himself**".[23] (But see Dan. 4:34-35; Gen. 17:7-10, 13&19; Num. 23:19; Eccl. 3:14; Isa. 43:13; Rom. 11:29; Heb. 7:1-3; Rev. 5:14; 21:3-7; 22:3-6.)

- "God's reason for creating Adam was His **desire to reproduce** Himself ... [Adam] was not *almost* like God. He was **not** subordinate to God even".[24] (But see John 1:18; Rev. 4:11; Rom. 9:20-21; Eccl. 12:13; Gen. 2:7&15-17; Psa. 66:4-5; Neh. 9:6; Rom. 1:25. See also some of the earlier references, including Hagin ones.)

- "**Adam** was **God** manifested in the flesh".[25] (But see John 3:18; Gen. 3:8; 1 Tim. 3:16; 1 Cor. 15:21-22; Gen. 3:19&22-23; Rom. 5:12-14; Psa. 113:5; Jer. 10:6-7. See also earlier references.)

- "Jesus existed **only** as an **image** in the heart of God, until such time as the prophets of the Old Testament could positively **confess Jesus into existence**".[26] (But see Mic. 5:2; Dan. 3:25; Rev. 1:1-2&8; 3:14; 2 Tim. 1:8-10; John 8:58; John 1:1; 6:62.)

- "He [Jesus] was **literally** ... **reborn** before the devil's eyes".[27] (But see earlier references.)

- "The biggest **failure** ... in the whole Bible is **God**".[28] (But see Gen. 3:14-21; John 3:14-21; Matt. 28:1-9&18-20; Gen. chaps 6-9; Jude 1:5-6; Exod. chaps 3-15:21; Isa. chaps 45-55 & 65-66; Zeph. chaps 1-2; Zech. 14; all 150 Psalms, and the entirety of the book of Revelation for the utter blasphemy of that statement.)

---

[22] *Ibid*, pp121,356.

[23] *Ibid*, p126.

[24] *Ibid*, pp108,379 fn13.

[25] *Following the Faith of Abraham*.

[26] *The Power of the Tongue*, quoted in CROSS + WORD, *Word-of-Faith Sayings*.

[27] *C in C*, p383 fns 51-53.

[28] *Ibid*, pp125,380 fn25.

Hinn:

- "Jesus ... became **one in nature** with ... Satan".[29] (But see 1 Cor. 6:15; 2 Cor. 6:14-15; 5:21; Heb. 13:8; John 14:6 cf. John 8:44; 2 Pet. 2:1.)
- "The Lord giveth and **never** taketh away".[30] (But see Job 1:21-22; Hab. 3:17-18; 2 Sam. 7:15; Exod. 32:32-33; Rev. 3:5; 22:19.)
- "Adam ... used to **fly**. Adam not only flew, he flew to **space** ... [W]ith one thought he would be on the **moon**".[31] (But see Deut. 33:26; 2 Tim. 2:23; 1 Tim. 6:20; Psa. 71:19; 86:8-10.)
- "I've **seen** the presence of God ... I've felt the presence of God ... I've **smelled** the presence of God ... **Whenever** I talk to Him, I **see Him**. I can tell you what He wears, I can tell you what color He has on. **I've** seen that **so many** times".[32] (From the age of eleven, while being trained by monks, Hinn was having visions of 'God' and says Jesus walked into his bedroom while he was asleep and it caused him to have an incredible "electric" sensation.[33]) But see John 1:18; 1 John 4:12; 2 Cor. 11:2-4; Lam. 2:14; Ezek. 13:3; Rom. 1:21-22; 2 Cor. 12:2-6. And contrast Hinn's 'visions' of 'God' with those of some of the great men of the Bible: Exod. 3:2-6; Ezek. 1:1-28; Dan. 10:5-9; Acts 9:3-6; Rev. 1:10-17a.
- "**No** sickness should come your way".[34] (But see earlier references.)
- "**God** has given us ... many sources of healing. Look at **Lourdes**. People have been healed going to Lourdes **and Fatima**".[35] (But see Jas. 5:14-15; Exod. 15:26; Psa. 103:3; Matt. 24:24-26; Luke 17:23.)
- "The Lord said to me to build a healing centre ... with **healing statues** of biblical healing saints from the Old Testament".[36] (But see Deut. 16:22; Lev. 26:1&30; Num.

---

[29] *Ibid*, pp155-156.
[30] *Ibid*, p98.
[31] *Ibid*, p119.
[32] Honolulu, 28:Feb:1997.
[33] *Good Morning Holy Spirit*, p15.
[34] *C in C*, p242.
[35] *Larry King Live*, 23:Apr:1998.
[36] *This is Your Day*, Trinity Broadcasting Network, 23:Aug:1999.

33:52; Psa. 115:4-8; Ezek. 16:17; 2 Ki. 23:24; Ezek. 13:6-8; Matt. 7:22-24.)

- When Hinn encountered "the Spirit" in 1973, his whole body *vibrated*. He later asked this mysterious power, that *forced* him onto his knees, "Can I meet you?" He was then hit by "a jolt like **electricity**" and his body began to vibrate again.[37] (But see our comments elsewhere in Part Five on these things.)
- "I am a 'little **messiah**', ... [Y]ou are a little god".[38] (But see Luke 21:8 and earlier references.)
- "Man, **I feel revelation knowledge** already coming on me here ... **Holy Spirit, take over** in the name of Jesus ... God the Father ... the Son ... the Holy Ghost ... **Each one of them** is a triune being **by Himself** ... [T]here's **nine** of them".[39] (When challenged, Hinn laughed these words off, but see 2 Tim. 2:15-16; Jer. 14:14; 23:28&32; Matt. 24:11; Jas. 1:26.)
- "I place a curse on every man and every woman that will stretch his hand against this anointing. I **curse** that man who **dares to speak a word** against this ministry".[40] (But see Rom. 12:14; Matt. 5:44; 1 Thess. 3:12; 1 John 3:7-8; Luke 21:15; Titus 1:9; Gal. 5:22-23.)

Do we *really* suppose, despite Scripture's pronouncements about those who teach heresy, that God would legitimize (and even *honour*) the Word-of-Faith movement by making it the fountain of a global blessing? That is not the God of the Bible. Do men really have a mandate to proclaim that T/P is unquestionably 'of God' and that anyone who is cautious about 'throwing themselves into its river' is grieving the Holy Spirit? (Note that Copeland, Hagin and Hinn are all linked to HTB in various ways.[41])

---

[37] Benny Hinn, *Good Morning Holy Spirit*, p12.

[38] *C in C*, p110.

[39] *Ibid*, p123.

[40] Denver Crusade, Sep 1999

[41] Hinn is linked to HTB through, for instance, Andrew White and Rodney Howard-Browne, both of whom have worked with HTB leaders. Copeland and Hagin are linked because, for instance, they, like Hinn, all influenced Wimber who was a huge influence on HTB. See our second 'Powers' article, and the documentation behind its accompanying chart, for further links between these men and HTB. Both of these can be found in the 'Better Than Rubies' section of our website (bayith.org).

29:4 GREATER WORKS   The Lord promised that His disciples would do even "greater works" than He had done during His incarnation. Some people argue that these "works" include the (seemingly pointless) behaviour coming from the T/P spirit. Christ's words were:

> "Verily, verily, I say unto you, He that believeth on Me, the works that I do shall he do also; and **greater** works than these shall he do; because I go unto My Father" (John 14:12).

Once again, a single passage is made to mean so much. But does it? For a start, Christ also prophesied of such a person that "the works **that I do** shall **he** do also". However, the T/P proponents are *not* doing the same works that Christ did, otherwise we would have seen real revival. On the rare occasion that a testimony from 'T/P' remotely compares with those in the Gospels, it is always something the enemy can have counterfeited.

The next point is that the T/P manifestations can hardly be said to be "greater" works than, for example, the healing of a man born blind or the raising to life of someone who had been dead for four days. Indeed, it is hard to justify the epithet "work" at all. In what sense is staggering around a room a "work"? Lying flat on the ground for hours seems to be as far from the concept of "work" as can be imagined. And how is pogoing on the spot blessing the Kingdom of God in a "greater" way than Christ did? Indeed, how is it blessing the Kingdom *at all*?

While the disciples are never recorded as having done the "works" that T/P is producing, they did do awesome, *genuine* exploits - including various things which Christ did not (because they weren't appropriate before the cross). For some examples see Acts 5:5-16; 8:26-40; and 19:11-12. (Of course, it is Christ who makes all such works possible). Note that these acts were all of a similar *character* to those which Christ had done. This cannot be said of the manifestations from T/P.

Finally, the word "greater" can also mean "larger" (as it did a few verses later when Christ referred to His Father as being "greater" than He - v28). For instance, *more* people were led to believe on Christ after His death than before it.

29:5 OTHER ARGUMENTS   A popular response to any suggestion that T/P might not only be wrong but might actually be dangerous, is to turn to "Gamaliel's argument" as set out in Acts 5:35-39. This is where the leaders of Israel were threatening the apostles for preaching that Christ Jesus was the

Messiah and that He had been resurrected. Supporters of T/P claim that we shouldn't worry about T/P's adherents but should instead "let them alone, for if this counsel or this work be of men, it will come to nought". But is it reasonable to compare these two situations?...

Certain folks believe it was Gamaliel who went on to have the disciples beaten, but the Bible does not say this. In fact, we *do* actually think Gamaliel's advice was wise and God-inspired. But it was the *nature of the circumstances* that made his advice so good and right. The special situation was this: a group was preaching that a man who had died was the promised Messiah of Israel. If this man was not the Messiah, then **(a)** he wouldn't have been resurrected, nor have fulfilled all of the Messianic prophecies, **(b)** he wouldn't have subsequently been seen by people and been able to give the "infallible proofs" to which Acts 1:3 refers, and **(c)** this group would therefore be found to be liars and would be rejected. They would be forced to 'scatter'. This had already happened to followers of other 'messiahs' who ultimately proved to be mortal (vv36-37).

If, as was the case, the Man in question *was* the promised Messiah however, then the Sanhedrin would be battling against God in opposing the disciples, and this scenario would *never arise again*, because the Messiah will never die again. Gamaliel's principle therefore did apply to this special situation.

History proves that it is a nonsense to apply Gamaliel's argument to *other* movements amongst the People of God. Imagine telling Moses that he shouldn't oppose Korah (see Num. 16:1-35), or that Elijah should "let alone" the false prophets in Israel (in 1 Ki. 18:17-40). Imagine instructing Christ Himself that he should "refrain from" denouncing the Pharisees, or telling Paul that he should allow the sheep to go (unhindered) in whatever direction they wanted. Sadly, this very argument was employed by people close to HTB in order to discourage criticism of T/P.[42]

29:6 "DECENTLY AND IN ORDER"?   Another mark of the Holy Spirit is that He is not going to lead us to do something we would not reasonably expect ourselves to do if we were ever to be in the physical presence of the Lord Himself. In the Bible, believers shook in His presence (but with real fear); they threw themselves to the ground (in deliberate worship); they cried out (in clear prayer and praise). Their behaviour was reverential, sober and self-effacing. But would any of us *bark* in the presence of royalty? Would

---

[42] E.g. Michael Green [see Boulton, Ed., *op. cit.*, p16].

one stagger drunkenly in front of a King? Would we hop or slither or pogo or roar before the Lord God Almighty? We are called to bring honour on our Lord, and to make Him the focus of attention, yet these manifestations often draw attention *away* from God and towards us and do not seem terribly honouring at all (see 1 Cor. 6:20).

"But what about Acts 2?... the disciples were acting drunken!" is a frequent retort. This is such a common "proof text" for such an important matter, that it bears careful examination. Consider the following points:

- Crucially, it was the *mockers* who claimed that the disciples were drunk: "Others **mocking** said, These men are full of new wine" (Acts 2:13). One of the main tools of mockery is *exaggeration*. There is nothing to suggest that anyone else thought the disciples were drunken - despite the fact that it would have been an almost inescapable conclusion for *all* those present if the disciples had *truly* acted like drunks.

- Previously a frightened little huddle, the disciples were now *boldly* and *publicly* proclaiming "the wonderful works of God". No wonder those who heard them "marvelled". Alcohol invariably makes people act more fearlessly - hence the phrase "Dutch courage". It is no surprise that other people, determined to reject the Divine message from the disciples, put their boldness down to excess drink.

- Formerly a group of uneducated people from a very "backward" region of Israel, the disciples were now speaking clearly in the languages of the others present. What a bizarre sight, and what a cacophony, that must have seemed like to some. (Such an unusual experience may even have caused the disciples themselves to be somewhat amazed and to have appeared a little awe-struck.)

- There is not a *single* verse, in the whole of that chapter, which speaks of the disciples staggering or slurring their words or rolling their eyes or falling over or doing any of the other drunk-like activities which T/P has produced. Indeed, Peter and the eleven were all *standing* and Peter was apparently perfectly able to give a *clear*, *biblical* speech - something all too rare in modern meetings.

- If the disciples were staggering, or otherwise truly giving the appearance of drunkenness, then how do we reconcile this with the clear command to "Abstain from **all appearance** of evil" (1 Thess. 5:22) and to "Let your **moderation** be **known** unto all men" (Php. 4:5)?

- Why is there no reference whatsoever to drunken behaviour in any of the *other* biblical descriptions of the early Church - including those times of substantial outpouring of the Holy Spirit?

The other scripture frequently used to defend this whole area is "Be not drunk with wine, **wherein is excess**; but be filled with the Spirit" (Eph. 5:18). But let's also take a proper look at this too:

- Drunkenness and being filled with the Holy Spirit are comparable insofar as they both frequently lead to joy (and boldness too, as we have already seen). That does not mean we are supposed to take the analogy further.

- In fact Paul is *contrasting* the two. One of them, drunkenness, "leads to excess",[43] but the Spirit of God should *not* - yet we frequently see excess as a result of T/P's "drinking meetings".

- In the very same Chapter, Paul commands us to act "as becometh saints". He not only condemns "foolish talking" and "jesting" but also condemns the very *mention* of such activity. Yet jesting is often *exactly* the "fruit" to which this T/P "drunkenness" leads.

- The verses immediately preceding verse 18 are very telling:

  "For ye were sometimes darkness, but now are ye light in the Lord: **walk** as children of **light**: (For the **fruit** of the **Spirit** is in all **goodness** and **righteousness** and **truth**;) Proving [i.e. determining carefully] what is acceptable **unto the Lord** ... **Awake** thou that sleepest ... See then that ye walk **circumspectly**, not as **fools**, but as wise, Redeeming the time, because the days are evil. Wherefore be ye not unwise, but understanding what the will of the Lord is" (Eph. 5:8-17).

- If we are meant to be made 'drunk in the Spirit', why are there *so* many scriptures which command us to be *sober*-minded? For example:

  "[T]he end of all things is at hand: be ye therefore **sober**, and watch unto prayer" (1 Pet. 4:7).

---

[43] Nicky deletes this from his quotation of this verse. See edition 1 videos as cited in Elizabeth McDonald, *Alpha: New Life or New Lifestyle?* (SMP, 1996).

"They that sleep sleep in the night; and they that be drunken are drunken in the night. But let us, who are of the day, be **sober**" (1 Thess. 5:7-8). See also v6 and 1 Pet. 2:11-12.

"Wherefore gird up the loins of your mind, be **sober**, and hope to the end" (1 Pet. 1:13). See also 1 Pet. 5:8.

The exhortation to be 'sober' in these passages implies more than simply "not getting drunk". It is requiring the believer to be self-controlled; to be of prudent behaviour and of a sound mind. The command to be sober is especially serious when we consider the pitiful spiritual condition of the world. We should be *grieving* rather than giggling, sorrowful rather than sozzled. Even beyond calling for 'soberness', the Scriptures go so far as to say:

"It is better to go to the house of **mourning**, than to go to the house of **feasting** ... **Sorrow** is better than **laughter**: for by the sadness of the countenance the heart is made better. The heart of the **wise** is in the house of **mourning**; but the heart of **fools** is in the house of **mirth**" (Eccl. 7:2-4).

"Blessed are they that **mourn**: for they shall be comforted" (Matt. 5:4).

"Be **afflicted**, and **mourn**, and **weep**; let your **laughter** be turned to **mourning** and your **joy** to **heaviness**. Humble yourselves in the sight of the Lord, and He shall lift you up" (Jas. 4:9-10).

Interestingly, drunkenness induced "without wine" is, in Scripture, always a mark of *apostasy* - notably where people reject the nation of Israel, God's ancient People (see chapter 24 for more about Israel):

"[T]hey are **drunken**, but **not with wine**; they **stagger**, but **not** with strong drink. For the LORD hath... closed [their] eyes" (Isa. 29:9,10).

And to those who dishonour His People:

"Therefore hear now this, thou **afflicted**, and **drunken**, but **not with wine**" (Isa. 51:21). See also Jer. 48:26 plus Jer. 51:39 and 51:57.

29:7 A TICK OR A CROSS?   Another example of behaviour which does nothing to glorify God is the involuntary jerks, or ticks, exhibited by many

T/P supporters. Such activity not only takes attention away from the Lord, but also dishonours God. Nor is it appropriate behaviour before a Monarch. People suffering lack of bodily control in Scripture were not hailed as being blessed by God but actually the opposite:

> "And they brought unto Him all sick people that were taken with divers diseases and **torments**, and those which were possessed with **devils**, and those which were lunatick, and those that had the **palsy** [palsy refers to lack of bodily control]; and He **healed** them" (Matt. 4:24). See also Matt. 17:15.

What about the inability to speak, which sometimes gets reported? What should we say about this? Throughout Scripture dumbness is certainly not a blessing (see, for instance, Matt. 9:32-33; Matt. 12:22; Mark 9:17).

The nations of the world derided T/P manifestations. While God's People can certainly expect persecution and tribulation at the hands of the world, being a *reproach* is NOT a good sign according to the Bible. Where the Lord's People go into *apostasy*, He promises that:

> "Ye provoke Me unto wrath ... that ye might be a curse and a **reproach** among all the nations of the earth" (Jer. 44:8.) See also Jer. 29:18; Ezek. 22:4-5; and 23:32.

> "I will make thee waste, and a **reproach** among the **nations** that are round about thee ... So it shall be a reproach and a **taunt**, an instruction and an astonishment unto the **nations** that are round about thee, when I shall execute judgments in thee in anger ... I the LORD have spoken it" (Ezek. 5:14-15).

> "Thou **makest** us a strife unto our neighbours: and our enemies **laugh** among themselves. **Turn us** again, O God of hosts, and cause Thy face to shine; and we shall be saved" (Psa. 80:6-7). See also Psa. 44:9-14.

29:8 PASS 'IT' ON   The reason for the incredible pace at which 'T/P' has spanned the globe is that, once a person has received this 'anointing', they are able to *pass it straight on* to others. These other people are themselves instantly blessed with the power in their bodies to pass it around further, and so on. The trouble is that this 'infectiousness' is actually an indication of the transference of *uncleanness*, not of God's spirit (see Hag. 2:11-14; Lev. 7:19-21; and Num. 19:11-22 – especially verse 22). Nowhere in Scripture is there an anointing which a person can receive and suddenly be able to pass on to others.

At this juncture some readers may well raise the matter of "laying on of hands". While this is obviously a biblical practice, it does not make the recipient godly. The recipient must already be living a godly life if they are to be blessed through this act. But if the person laying hands on us is not 'right with God' then *filthiness* can be transferred, hence Paul's warning to Timothy to: "Lay hands suddenly on **no man, neither be partaker of other men's sins**" (1 Tim. 5:22).

The T/P spirit is transferred primarily through physical contact or very close proximity. Under the Old Testament Law, the scapegoat had the *uncleanness* of Israel transferred to it by the laying on of hands (Lev. 16:22-22), and there were numerous instructions about what people (especially priests) could and couldn't touch (e.g. see Num. 6:6-9; Lev. 11:23ff). Such is the importance of right understanding of this matter - to avoid receiving spiritual uncleanness - that apparently the doctrine is absolutely *foundational* (Heb. 6:1-2). Sadly, Alpha does not consider proper teaching of this matter similarly vital and basic. (As phrases like "**catch** the fire" demonstrate, the T/P spirit is "catching" and therefore cannot involve the *Holy* Spirit.)

For more about 'Toronto', see the next chapter. See also a new book we have written which goes into all the other arguments used to defend T/P. It is called *Consuming Fire: 'Holy Laughter' Disentangled Through a Decade's Reflection* and full stockist information is available from the 'Better Than Rubies' section of our website (bayith.org).

CHAPTER **30**

$\mathscr{T}$HE NEW AWAKENING

30:1 WHY WERE THEY DRY?   Another reason for T/P's phenomenal uptake has been the spiritual "dryness" reported by many of those involved. But, rather than jump on an aircraft to Toronto or Pensacola, would it not have been better for such people to get down on their knees where they were and earnestly seek God over the *cause* of their dryness? Through Christ we can reach God wherever we are. The requirements are simply that we fear Him and are humble and contrite of heart, not that we disappear halfway across the world. The solution to spiritual thirst in Scripture is to "come unto **Me**, and drink", not "go unto Rodney Howard-Browne and get drunk". Rivers of living water shall flow out of the belly of him who "believes on" **the Lord Jesus Christ**, not him who relies on Benny Hinn.

According to the Lord, "whosoever drinketh of the water that **I** shall give him shall **never** thirst; but the water that I shall give him shall be in him a well of water springing up into everlasting life" (John 4:14). It is a judgment on *apostasy* if God makes someone's "springs dry" (Jer. 51:36). So if people are suffering spiritual dryness they must accept that they have been departing from the truth, and that they need to repent before God, not seek some short-cut to the blessings which only actually result from a holy life. We have seen that God gives His Holy Spirit to those who obey His commandments, not to those who jump on a plane and seek an easy blessing rather than examining their walk with Him.

> "But they that **wait upon the LORD** shall renew their strength; they shall mount up with wings as eagles; they shall run, and **not be weary**; and they shall walk, and **not faint**" (Isa. 40:31).

Many T/P supporters believe that the manifestations do not appear in Scripture. In their minds, God chose not to include them for some reason. After all, the Bible was written so long ago(!). It is argued, for instance, that if the concept of 'Sunday School' isn't in Scripture then why should the T/P manifestations be (as if the two are remotely comparable!).

What few people seem to realise is that the manifestations *are* ALL present in God's eternal Word - although not as signs of blessing. Rather, they are there as marks of God's judgment on a Babylonian / Chaldean (i.e. apostate) or Egyptian / Edomite (i.e. worldly) people. Earlier in this book we looked at: shaking, electricity, 'pins and needles', 'drunkenness', and ticks. Scripture shows that each one is a sign of disobedience and apostasy. Some other behaviour is checked below. Anyone reading these examples with an open mind will conclude that they *cannot* be there by coincidence! If T/P manifestations are blessings from God in obedient believers then why does Scripture only give examples relating to *apostates*?

Roaring like lions

Although Christ Jesus is called the "lion of the tribe of Judah", this is because of His strength and boldness, not because He *roars like a lion*. By contrast, the enemy is likened to "a **roaring** lion" (1 Pet. 5:8, also Psa. 22:12-13; and Prov. 28:15). The apostate church likewise:

> "Woe to her that is filthy and polluted, ... She **obeyed not** the voice; she **received not correction**; she trusted **not** in the LORD; she drew **not** near to **her** God. Her princes within her are **roaring lions**; ... Her prophets are light and treacherous persons: her priests have **polluted** the sanctuary, they have **done violence** to the **law**" (Zeph. 3:1-4). See also Ezek. 22:25-28!

> "Therefore is the anger of the LORD kindled against **His people**, and He hath stretched forth His hand against them, and hath smitten them ... Their **roaring** shall be **like a lion**, they shall **roar** like young **lions**: yea, **they shall roar**" (Isa. 5:25-30).

"And **Babylon** shall become heaps, a dwellingplace for dragons [i.e. demons] an astonishment, and an hissing ... They shall **roar** together like **lions**: they shall **yell** as lions' whelps" (Jer. 51:37-38).

Behaving like dogs

Dogs, wolves and jackals are looked down upon in Scripture. See, for example, Deut. 23:18 and Matt. 7:15. Note that wolves are mentioned in the first two references above as well, i.e. in Zeph. 3:3 and Ezek. 22:26-27. "**Beware** of dogs, **beware** of evil workers..." (Php. 3:2). See also Jer. 15:3 and Psa. 22:16&20. Those who are not the true People of God *and* those who are foolish are both likened to dogs (see Matt. 15:26; 7:6.) Yet barking like a dog is a common feature of T/P meetings.

"O my God: defend me ... Deliver me from the **workers of iniquity**, ... be not merciful to any wicked **transgressors**. Selah. They return at evening: they make a **noise like a dog**" (Psa. 59:1-6).

"For the sin of their mouth ... let them even be taken in their **pride**: and for cursing and **lying** which they speak ... let them return; and let them make a **noise like a dog**" (Psa. 59:12-15)

"Blessed are they **that do His commandments**, that they may ... enter in through the gates ... For **without** are **dogs**" (Rev. 22:14-15). See also Matt. 10:16; Luke 10:3; and Acts 20:29.)

Other Beast-like Behaviour

In Scripture, wild beasts are very often used as a picture of demonic activity, yet T/P meetings have seen people acting like snakes, frogs, bulls and a variety of other animals - and apparently without them having any say in the matter. The solitary occasion in Scripture where God *made* someone act like an animal was in *judgment*, not blessing (see Dan. 4:33). Desperate supporters claim that the animal behaviour is "prophetic" but are still unable to produce the necessary precedents in the early Church. Indeed, being "as a beast" before the Lord is a sign of foolishness and ignorance (Psa. 73:22), whereas God has "given us the spirit ... of a **sound** mind" (2 Tim. 1:7).

Needless to say, snake-like behaviour (such as slithering, hissing and tongue-flicking - all of which can be seen, for example, on videos of Kenneth Hagin meetings) reveals the spirit of the *serpent*, not the Spirit of God!

> "And **Babylon** ... shall be as when God overthrew Sodom and Gomorrah ... [W]ild **beasts** of the desert shall lie there; and their houses shall be full of doleful **creatures**; ... And the wild **beasts** of the islands shall **cry** in their desolate houses, and dragons in their pleasant palaces: and her time is near to come, and her days shall not be prolonged" (Isa. 13:19-22). See also Ezek. 8:8-10.

> "And an highway shall be there, and a way, and it shall be called The way of **holiness**; the unclean shall **not** pass over it ... **No lion** shall be there, nor **any** ravenous **beast** shall go up thereon, it shall not be found there; but the **redeemed** shall walk there" (Isa. 35:8-9). See also Ezek. 5:17.

Burning Sensations

This is a common feature in both T/P *and* Alpha meetings. In fact, as we have noted, a popular term used by pro-T/P people for receiving the 'Blessing' was to "catch the **fire**". Yet the Bible shows that fire in this sort of context is always a mark of judgment rather than blessing. So instead of *catching* the fire, people should be *fleeing* it. As these verses confirm, it is the fire of judgment on churches which have forsaken God's true ways:

> "The **Chaldeans** ... Behold, they shall be as stubble; the **fire** shall **burn** them; they shall not deliver themselves from the power of the **flame**" (Isa. 47:1,14). See also Hos. 7:1-14.

> "For I have set my face against this city for **evil**, and not for good, saith the LORD: it shall be given into the hand of the king of **Babylon**, and he shall **burn** it with fire" (Jer. 21:10). See also Jer. 21:11-14; 34:2; 38:23; and 51:30.

> "**Babylon** ... shall be utterly **burned** with fire: for strong is the Lord God who **judgeth** her" (Rev. 18:2,8). See also Lev. 10:1-2 and Ezek. 24:2-12!

Falling Backwards

This is often termed as being "slain in the Spirit" – an unbiblical phrase only truly applicable to Ananias and Sapphira! In Scripture, saints only ever fall for good, understandable reasons (e.g. through fear of God), not because some unseen force knocks them over. Nicky's 'Holy Spirit', in contrast, caused a man to "**find** himself flat on the floor" for no apparent reason.[1] Note also that only those who are *opposing* God go *backwards*.[2]

> "As soon then as He had said unto them, I am *He*, they [the servants of the **Pharisees**] went **backward, and fell** to the ground" (John 18:6).

> "Ah **sinful** nation, ... children that are **corrupters**: they have forsaken the LORD, they have provoked the Holy One of Israel unto anger, they are **gone away backward**" (Isa. 1:4).

> "He [God] said, **This** is the rest wherewith ye may cause the weary to rest; and **this** is the refreshing: yet they **would not hear**. But the word of the LORD was unto them [**nonsense**] ... that they might go, and fall **backward**, and be broken, and snared, and taken" (Isa. 28:12-13). (*God's* "refreshing" is not the same as T/P's: the Word of the Lord was considered *nonsense*, and laughed at, in T/P churches.) See also Psa. 70:2-3.

> "They hearkened not, nor inclined their ear, but walked in the counsels and in the imagination of their evil heart, and **went backward, and not** forward" (Jer. 7:24).[3]

Carpet Time

Another description for this phenomenon is involuntary sleep or being forced to the ground. Scripture exhorts: "Therefore let us **not** sleep, as do others; but let us watch and be **sober**" (1 Thess. 5:6).

> "**Woe** ... [T]here shall be heaviness ... And thou shalt be **brought down**, and shalt speak out of the **ground**, and thy speech shall be **low out of the dust**, and thy voice shall be, as of one that hath a familiar spirit, out of the **ground**, and thy speech shall whisper out of the **dust** ... For the LORD hath poured out upon you the spirit of **deep sleep**, and hath closed your eyes: the prophets and your rulers, the seers hath he covered" (Isa. 29:1-10).

> "And I will make drunk her princes, and her wise men, ... and they shall **sleep** a perpetual **sleep**, and not wake ... The broad

---

[1] Talk 9.

[2] As a steward of a 'Toronto' church, Dusty often witnessed people falling backwards onto people already on the floor. This is reminiscent of the effects of God's judgment in Jer. 46:14-16.

[3] God "brings down" those who are haughty. See 2 Sam. 22:28b and also v48.

walls of **Babylon** shall be utterly broken, and her high gates shall be burned with fire; and the people shall labour in vain, and the folk in the fire, and **they shall be weary**" (Jer. 51:57-58). (Note also the references to burning and enforced drunkenness.) See also Jer. 51:35-39, which includes references to dryness, heat and enforced drunkenness as well.

"All ye beasts of the field, come to devour, yea, all ye beasts in the forest. His watchmen are blind: they are all ignorant, they are all dumb dogs, ... **sleeping, lying down**, loving to slumber. Yea, they are greedy dogs which can never have enough, and they are shepherds that cannot understand" (Isa. 56:9-11). (Note also the references to devouring beasts and to dogs.)

Inappropriate laughter

There have been reports of T/P adherents laughing scornfully while being read the Word of God - or at hearing about the men of God mentioned in it. In Scripture, such behaviour is ascribed to the *un*godly (see Job 12:4-5 or Job 16:19-20 or Matt. 9:23-24). It was ungodly people who laughed "to scorn" both Job and Christ. And it was ungodly people who mocked Elisha and Nehemiah. It is with exceeding frequency that the laughing (and deep bowing) at T/P-style meetings is described as "mocking" or "derisive", but we must beware – for "God is **not** mocked". (In truth, we are supposed to *mourn* the fallen state of the nations, and *grieve* over the souls being lost for eternity, not laugh inanely.)

"**Thy word** hath quickened me. The **proud** have had me **greatly in derision**: yet have **I** not **declined** from Thy law" (Psa. 119:50-51). See also Jude 1:17-19.

"Blessed is the man that walketh not in the counsel of the **ungodly**, nor standeth in the way of sinners, nor sitteth in the seat of the **scornful**. But his delight is in **the law of the LORD**; and in His law doth he meditate day and night" (Psa. 1:1-2). See also Jer. 20:5-9.

"But they **mocked** the messengers of God, and despised His words, and misused His prophets, until the wrath of the LORD arose against His people, till there was no remedy." (2 Chr. 36:16-17). See also Prov. 3:34; 24:9; and 1:22-30.

When the Lord God calls us to "think soberly", to "be sober, grave, temperate", to be "vigilant" and "holy", to live "soberly, righteously, godly" and so on, there can be relatively little call for laughter – especially of the long-lasting and uncontrollable T/P variety (See Eccl. 7:3-6; 2:2 and Jas. 4:8-10.)

The following manifestations seem rare but are still seen in some T/P meetings:

Disrobing

Is this a feature of the early Church, or a disgraceful thing to do in a worship meeting (bearing in mind that nudity is increasing in popularity in our Godless Western world)?[4]

> "Come down, and sit in the **dust**, O virgin daughter of **Babylon**, sit on the ground: ... O daughter of the **Chaldeans**: ... make bare the leg, uncover the thigh, ... Thy **nakedness** shall be uncovered, yea, thy shame shall be seen: ... Sit thou silent, and get thee into darkness" (Isa. 47:1-5). (Note the reference to silence; dumbness is another feature of some T/P churches.)

> "Behold, I am against thee, saith the LORD of hosts; and I will discover thy skirts upon thy face, and I will show the nations thy **nakedness**, and the kingdoms thy shame" (Nah. 3:5). See also Ezek. 23:29-30 and Rev. 3:17-18.

> "O daughter of **Edom**, ... thou shalt be drunken, **and** shalt make thyself **naked**" (Lam. 4:21). (Note the reference to drunkenness. And compare with John 21:7 where Peter puts *on* clothes when coming into the presence of the Lord. See also Luke 8:35; Exod. 28:42 c.f. 1 Tim. 2:9; 2 Sam. 10:4-5; and Isa. 20:4.)

"Holy" Vomiting

The following passages surely speak for themselves:

> "Make ye him drunken: for he **magnified himself** against the LORD: ... [He] shall wallow in his **vomit**" (Jer. 48:26). (Note also the *enforced* drunkenness.)

---

[4] In 2002, after attending an Alpha Course, Geri Halliwell published a book entitled *Just for the Record* which thanked "Pippa and Nicky" in the back. (Pippa is the name of Nicky Gumbel's wife.) Alpha and the Gumbels obviously made a great impression. The content of Halliwell's book? Several dozen photographs of Geri in various states of undress, including topless shots and even a complete nude of her. (The book also promoted yoga!) Additionally, HTB's own bookshop sells two postcards featuring drawings of naked women.

"Thus saith the LORD of hosts, the God of Israel; Drink ye, and be drunken, and **spue**, and fall, and rise no more..." (Jer. 25:27). (Note the reference to drunkenness, falling and 'carpet time'.)

"Thou art filled with **shame** for glory: ... shameful **spewing** shall be on thy glory" (Hab. 2:16). See also Isa. 19:14 and Prov. 26:11 (noting the reference to dogs).

30:2 A WORD ON LEVITATION   A more attention-grabbing act than levitation is hard to conceive of. It may not be a mark of judgment, but it is not a good sign either. Being "lifted up" *physically* above others is also to be "lifted up" (or exalted) in their sight; hence popes and Babylonian kings - and their religious statues - have frequently been carried (or driven) high off the ground.

While God lifts our *spirits*, it is very wrong to be "lifted up" (in *any* sense) in a worship meeting, when it is *God* who should have all the honour and notice. It is alarming to note that yogis, witches, Jesuits and the like have been levitating for centuries. Unlike Elijah (who was lifted by God all the way to Himself), levitators use Babylonian forces to make them ascend. According to passages like Jer. 51:53 and Isa. 14:4,13-14, Babylon loves to lift herself up in one sense or another:

"Thus saith the LORD; Behold, I will raise up against **Babylon**, and against them that dwell in the midst of them that **rise up** against me, a destroying wind ... and against him that **lifteth himself up**" (Jer. 51:1&3).

To repeat: allowing oneself to be "lifted up", whether in the air or in the heart, is to exalt (rather than humble) oneself. The Lord will bring such people low (perhaps to add to their 'carpet time'?)...

"Enter into the rock, and hide thee in the **dust**, for fear of the LORD, and for the glory of His majesty. The **lofty looks** of man shall be humbled, and the **haughtiness** of men shall be **bowed down**, and the LORD **alone** shall be exalted in that day. For the day of the LORD of hosts shall be upon every one that is **proud and lofty**, and upon every one that is **lifted up**; and he shall be brought low: And upon all the cedars of Lebanon, that are **high and lifted up**, and upon all the oaks of Bashan, And upon all the high mountains, and upon all the hills that are **lifted up**, ... And the loftiness of man shall be bowed **down**, and the haughtiness of men shall be **made low**: and **the LORD alone** shall be **exalted** in that day" (Isa. 2:10-17). See also Ezek. 31:10-11 and 2 Chr. 25:19.

Note also that, just as the "fowls **of the air**" are usually a reference to the enemies of God's People (e.g. Deut. 28:26; 1Ki. 14:11; & Mark 4:4), so Satan is said to be the "prince of the **power of the air**" (Eph. 2:2). It is he and his "powers of the **heavens**" (Matt. 24:29; Eph. 6:12) who are the ones responsible for this physical lifting up into the air. The only time the Church will be levitated *by God* is at the 'Rapture' when Christ returns (1 Thess. 4:16-17). Yet Kenneth Hagin boasted of levitation in his meetings.[5] One woman, during one of a series of Hagin meetings in St. Louis (USA), levitated from an *altar* and "stood in mid-air dancing".[6] Where do we see *any* in the early Church doing that? Likewise, Rodney Howard-Browne has proudly claimed that levitation occurs in his meetings.[7]

30:3 THE BOTTOM LINE   Some may try to use the excuse that all the similarities between God's judgment and the Toronto 'Blessing' are just coincidences. But it CANNOT be an accident that *every* manifestation seen in Toronto – and Pensacola – is to be found in just two adjacent chapters of the Bible, both of which are indictments of apostasy. These chapters, i.e. Jer. 50 and 51, contain everything from burning and 'birthing' to barking and 'barfing'. See, for example, Jer. 51:35-39, 51-58; & 50:43-44. Even the "wind" that has been reported in some meetings gets mentioned (see 51:1-2, 16).

There is a huge amount more we could say to prove the real spirit behind T/P. In the final analysis, T/P can be shown, from *every* angle, to be a *false* move. (The Recommended Reading at the end of this Part includes unanswerable books exposing the truth about the T/P spirit.) But pride, plus a lack of fear of God and lack of faith in (and hence knowledge of) His Word, has resulted in people going their own way. People are refusing to soften their hearts and prayerfully study their Bibles - and so to see the truth. In desperation, some "leaders" have tried to claim that Satan and God have similar spirits that cause similar bodily responses in people...

> "The primary Charismatic argument is simply this *'we have the genuine, and the occult is the counterfeit.'* ... [However,] the manifestations from Rodney Howard-Browne / Toronto / Pensacola have **no contextual biblical support**. There is **no**

---

[5] McConnell, *The Promise of Health and Wealth*, p74.
[6] Hagin, *Why Do People Fall Under the Power?*, p10.
[7] See Hanegraaff, *Counterfeit Revival*, p25

genuine biblical example of these manifestations, thus there **is nothing to counterfeit**".[8]

Beyond this, we have now seen that these things are only biblical insofar as they point to judgment. Can you tell the difference between the following New Age testimonies and the type frequently attributed to God in T/P meetings?

> "I **understood nothing** about the various experiences ... **[or]** the **radiant light** that had come to me on the first day. ... Sometimes I would **jump and hop** like a frog [but see Exo. 8:1-13; Rev. 16:13], and sometimes my limbs would **shake** violently ... Sometimes my body would **writhe and twist** like a snake's while a **hissing** sound would come from inside me...".[9]

> "...People **vibrated** in his energy field as **he threw out waves of power** into the audience...".[10]

> "For the next three days my **body** was **pulsating** with the energy that surged through it. I laughed **ecstatically**".[11]

As we have seen, God does not *force* His true children to do things. Yet both New Age and T/P manifestations are uncontrollable. Furthermore, the New Age and T/P experiences affect the soul and/or body - whereas God resides in the *spirits* of His faithful children. He indicates *apostasy* by using the enemy to force certain effects on the body or soul. For example:

- God makes us *spiritually* "wise as serpents", but the apostate counterfeit is just to make us physically slither like serpents.
- God gives us *spiritual* warmth in our spirits, but rebellious children only manage physical warmth.
- God gives us *spiritual* light (wisdom and understanding), but Satan gives soulish, physical light.
- God blesses us with *spiritual* joy, but Satan's equivalent is carnal and produces pointless laughter.
- God makes us *spiritually* bold as lions, but Satan's pathetic version has people just physically roar like them.

---

[8] Inner-City Christian Discernment Ministry, *Counterfeit: Is it Live or Memorex?*.

[9] Inner-City Christian Discernment Ministry, *Power Gurus*.

[10] *Ibid*.

[11] *Ibid*.

People accepted T/P when their leaders told them to "move out of their comfort zones".[12] It is entirely right to help people out of their *carnal* "comfort zones", but teachers should have pointed out that discomfort in one's *spirit* is a sign of *danger*. God *brings* comfort to our spirits! The Holy Spirit is even called the Comforter (John 15:26 & 16:7), and both God and His Word bring comfort to our hearts (2 Cor. 1:3-4; Rom. 15:4). Any activity on our part which causes *spiritual* discomfort is patently deadly. Unfortunately, many have shut out the warnings emanating from their spirits and have now lost sensitivity to the lack of peace that T/P initially caused them.

30:4 ALPHA   Despite the outward "toning down" of Alpha's relationship with T/P, we have seen that Alpha's false teaching on the Holy Spirit is still very much in evidence and that Alpha conversion experiences are occultic rather than scriptural. Another point to consider regarding the relationship between Alpha and T/P is prayer. Alpha participants still unsaved by the time of the Holy Spirit weekend are encouraged to pray for the outpouring of the Spirit upon them. Since they have been presented with an inaccurate image of God, they are not actually praying to Him but elsewhere…

Perversely, *saved* members of 'T/P' churches have been told by their leaders *not* to pray while the Spirit is poured out. But whom do we cut out of the proceedings when we stop praying? The Bible says we are to "pray **without ceasing**" (1 Thess. 5:17), that we "ought **always to pray**, and not to faint" (Luke 18:1), and to "**pray always**" (Luke 21:36; see also Eph. 6:18). It is the selfsame spirit present in both Alpha and T/P, and in both cases it was permitted entry into folk by causing them to omit the true God.

If, as one participant claims, it is possible to find "**whatever** [one is] searching for" on Alpha, then it cannot be the Holy Spirit in evidence as He will only lead us to *the truth* (John 16:13-14). We urge the reader to search for nothing but this. To wander from the truth into false ways is to reject God and effectively to commit idolatry…

The idols of old had mouths and eyes and ears but could not speak or see or hear. Scripture says that anyone who deviates from the truth into idolatry will be "**like** them" (Psa. 135:15-18). In other words, worshipping anything other than the one true God of the Bible is spiritual adultery and is *so* serious that the Lord promises He will make those who trust in such false

---

[12] This is a phrase used by John Arnott in an HTB book [*The Collection*, p206].

ways *incapable* of perceiving the truth - by stopping their ears, eyes and minds working properly:

> "And He said, Go, and tell this people, Hear ye indeed, but **understand not**; and see ye indeed, but **perceive not**. Make the heart of this people fat, and **make their ears heavy**, and **shut their eyes**; lest they see with their eyes, and hear with their ears, and understand with their heart, and convert, and be healed" (Isa. 6:9-10). See also Ezek. 12:2; Matt. 13:10-16; Mark 4:9-12; Acts 28:22-27.

As we have seen, the Lord has even supplied ambiguous scriptures to enable those to whom He has sent "strong delusion" (2 Thess. 2:10-12) to think that they have biblical support for their erroneous ways. We need to understand that it can actually be *THE LORD GOD* who blinds.

People who are so judged will subsequently have to fight very hard against their error if they are ever to be able to see the truth. They will have to be *very* determined to overcome this blindness and must really *long* to know the truth – even if it means having to admit publicly that they have been wrong. But there can even come a point when they are *permanently* given over to their error (see 2 Cor. 4:4; 2 Thess. 2:10-12; Exo. 7:3-4&13 etc). We must never let ourselves or our brothers reach that stage. *Please* can we encourage those in oversight to take note of this?

30:5 TORONTO COMPARED WITH KUNDALINI YOGA   It has been well documented by others that the supernatural phenomena seen in the 'Toronto Blessing' – and, by extension, Alpha - are very similar to those experienced by practitioners of Kundalini yoga. For example, by Banner Ministries;[13] or *Alarm Call For Concerned Christians*;[14] or Anntti Huima.[15] At least one *Kundalini* website agrees:

> "There is a natural, biological energy center in us, which is usually sleeping … When this center becomes alive a growth-process starts and unmistakable symptoms are observable in the body and in the psyche (for example shaking, trembling and feeling heat etc) … [I]n the last years these Kundalini awakenings happen more often than ever before … [I]n the 1970s … occurred a marked increase in the number of people undergoing intense psychospiritual experiences … But the 1970s fall short

---

[13] 'Strange Bedfellows!' in *CROSS + WORD, First News Update 1999.*
[14] Spring 1998, pp1-3.
[15] *Comparing Kundalini Yoga and TB / Pensacola.*

when compared to the ten thousands of people who came into contact with the Kundalini energy since 1994 in the **so-called Toronto Blessing…**".[16]

This power is even dispensed using the same methods, including the tap (or pat) on the forehead - known in Kundalini as the "shaktipat" - and by hands hovering over the body. Consider also how unmistakably identical the following descriptions are to what Alpha and T/P have given us:

"The process of Kundalini awakening can vary greatly from person to person. Some have **intense physical symptoms**, while others experience mainly **emotional** or **psychological** symptoms … As this energy becomes active, it is usually sensed as a **vibrational** or **energetic** force in the body, together with a strong **sense of spirit** … Regardless of the specifics of each individual's experience, the Kundalini awakening heralds a **great period of change** in a person's life".[17]

"When [the Kundalini] becomes active, it is usually felt as a high vibrational, electromagnetic energy or **powerful force** in the body, and/or a strong sense of the inner **presence** of the Spirit".[18]

It would be a *very* grave mistake to think, just because some of the more extreme manifestations of T/P have subsided, that the 'Blessing' was merely the latest fad that has now run its course. Kundalini teachers reveal that:

"**After one or two years,** the symptoms **gradually disappear,** because the body is then adjusted to the higher level of bioenergy and **calms down**".[19] (We would estimate that T/P lasted between one or two years at practically every church it hit, so the above is a *highly* significant statement that the Church surely needs to consider most carefully.)

According to another writer, the Kundalini symptoms listed earlier can be divided into seven categories of manifestations. Here we quote just some of those that are common also to the experiences of T/P supporters and to Alpha participants. (Note that we've already quoted part of the article,

---

[16] *Zenhouse.com.*
[17] Karin Hannigan, *Kundalini and the Awakening of Spirit.*
[18] El Collie, *Shared Transformation Kundalini Signs and Symptoms.*
[19] *Ibid.*

specifically the information on "Psychological Upheaval", so that paragraph won't be repeated here.)

> "As deeply held armouring and blockages to the smooth flow of energy are released, the person may re-access **memories and emotions associated with past trauma and injury.**
>
> "People experience atypical visual phenomena, including **visions** of **lights**, symbols, **entities**, or review of **past life experiences**. Auditory input may include hearing **voices**, music, **inner sounds** or mantras. Even the olfactory system may be stimulated with perception of scents...
>
> "With the opening up of psychic abilities, a person may experience precognition, ... awareness of auras, and **healing abilities**.
>
> "A person may shift into altered states of consciousness where they directly perceive the unity underlying the world of separation and experience a **deep peace** and **serenity** with a profound knowing of wisdom".[20]

Not long before the spirit behind T/P emerged, the 'pope' made a chilling prediction:

> "In 1981 **the Pope** spoke of the special place Rome accords to **Eastern** religions. 'Ways must be discovered,' he said 'to make the dialogue with all religions become a reality everywhere, but **especially** in **Asia**, the cradle of ancient cultures and religions.' Just nine years later [i.e. just 4 years before Toronto's arrival] he **predicted** that a **new injection** of life for the Church in **the next few years** would come from the **East...**".[21]

More amazing still is the realization that Kundalini 'awakenings' are being claimed by New Agers as initiation into the next stage in man's alleged evolution:

> "Usually the awakening of Kundalini was a process which only occurred after years of spiritual practice and meditation ... These increased reports of spontaneous Kundalini awakening at this time of planetary upheaval may be indicative of a larger purpose at work, the beginning of the **planetary wake up call** ... Anyone who is on a spiritual path, or engaging in practices which change body energies ... may find they begin to resonate with the

---

[20] Bonnie Greenwell, quoted in Karin Hannigan, *Kundalini and the Awakening of Spirit.*
[21] Michael de Semlyen, *All Roads Lead to Rome*, p95.

changing energies ... and begin their own Kundalini awakening process".[22]

"Kundalini is the ... sacred transformative element that awakens consciousness ... This process is also called **shamanic** awakening, ascension, awakening the light body or the energy body, rebirth, or simply transformation ... Judging by the current condition of the world, had my own Kundalini not risen, I would have doubted the New Age proclamations that we are in the midst of **a collective developmental leap in human consciousness.** But from what has transpired in my own life, on top of the testimony from countless others going through similar experiences, I have a growing spark of hope that **as a species, we are truly evolving**".[23]

But evolving into what?

"The awakening of Kundalini is a ... major step towards realisation of the **divine** ... to attain **Godhood**...".[24]

In Part One of our book, we noted that 'pope' John Paul II allowed himself to accept the mark of Shiva from a Hindu priestess. Let us consider the following, from an ex-New Ager, in light of that:

"I discovered the god Shiva was also called Bhudapati, 'Prince of **demons**', a Biblical description for Beelzebub or **Satan**. Shiva originated the system of Yoga with its 'Kundalini' (psychic energy) and system of 'chakras' (energy points apparently in the spiritual body), to try to bring his disciples into union with Brahman – or **to realise their godhood**, the **lie of Satan** in the garden of Eden (see Genesis 3:5)".[25]

30:6 BORN AGAIN?   The New Age may seem a long way from the Alpha Course, but is it? As we have seen, the source of the Alpha / Toronto spirit (i.e. the Word-of-Faith movement) teaches that "You don't have a God in you, you **are** one". Alpha participants may not consciously be seeking to become divine but they are undergoing the same encounters as New Agers do. As a result of their experiences, many of them become more "aware of

---

[22] Karin Hannigan, *Kundalini And The Awakening Of Spirit.*
[23] Ruth Trimble, *When Mercury Escapes.*
[24] El Collie, *Shared Transformation: Kundalini Signs And Symptoms.*
[25] Paul James-Griffiths, Out of the Twilight Zone, *Dawn of the New Age: 5 New Agers Relate Their Search for the Truth,* p10.

who they are, and better adjusted to their environment",[26] just as New Agers do. Compare the Alpha testimonies we have seen so far with the following New Age commentary:

> "It is as if the new energy invites a **spring cleaning** throughout the entire system, with **unresolved** physical or emotional conditions coming up for **resolution** and release. The **life transforming changes** which accompany a Kundalini awakening cover the **entire** physiological, emotional, mental and spiritual spectrum ... Spiritual emergence often includes expanded perceptual abilities, increased energy, creative expression and a **dedication to being of service for the greater good**".[27]

> "...[T]his cleansing, divine, light snakes its way up through the subtle nerve threads of the body and expels the darkness of the past, unknotting any traumas that are caught in the memory of the body, so that a person ceases to be limited by past life, present life traumas or old thought forms ... **It is an opportunity to become new or reborn** ...".[28]

> "[T]he Kundalini process involves a **redefinition and reintegration of self** ... of greatest benefit is a supportive framework which can allow people to make sense of the intricate connection between spirit and the movement of physical energy in the body [*isn't this 'supportive framework' exactly what the Alpha Course – and T/P – provides?*] ... The enormous changes associated with a spiritual awakening may demand psychological and social adjustments ... [*which Alpha interprets as being the new life coming from being 'born again'*]".[29]

30:7 GOD OR TAO? The fact that Alpha leaders are calling on the "Holy Spirit", rather than the "Kundalini serpent", is no guarantee that it is the Holy Spirit who responds. Hear what New Age writers have to say in that regard:

> "Traditionally the terms *Kundalini, divine energy, energy of nature, God, Tao* and **many more** have been used (like bioenergy). But the **name** you may give to it is **irrelevant**...".[30]

---

[26] *Institute For Consciousness Research: What Is Kundalini?*
[27] *Kundalini And The Awakening Of Spirit.*
[28] *When Mercury Escapes.*
[29] *Kundalini And The Awakening Of Spirit.*
[30] *Zenhouse.com.*

"Yoga is a system for realising your connection to God, which only comes with realisation of the Holy-Spirit, Higher-Self or Paramatma (the name depends **only on the cultural or religious context** you grew up within)".[31]

"Some speak of God, **Christ**, Goddess, **the Holy One** [N.B. The phrase "the Holy One" *on its own* is used frequently by the New Age, but rarely in the Bible], **Spirit**, or simply a magnificent Whole in which we all partake ... Individuals who are having experiences of an obvious spiritual nature are usually more able to integrate and benefit from the process, **regardless of how they may label it**".[32]

It is not surprising that the enemy should go "all the way" and try to convince us (through false 'brothers', and without any scriptural proof of course) that Christians *are supposed to* awaken this coiled serpent:

"...I also experienced a process called *Christian* Kundalini ... Kundalini is a vital force at the base of the spine ... Our **vital force will answer to the term Holy Spirit and then it is Christian**, or any other term that means spirit of God and then it is God's time to introduce Himself".[33]

The writer of the above is a New Ager, not a *true* Christian. And his Kundalini snake is just as hateful as the other snakes in Scripture. "The wicked ... go astray as soon as they be born, speaking lies. Their poison is like the poison of a serpent" (Psa. 58:3-4). Eve may have been deceived by a serpent but we should not!

30:8 THE FOCUS HAS CHANGED   Where once the Church was utterly devoted to the Lord Jesus Christ (as required by the Father and as aided by the Holy Spirit), there has been a marked shift in attention away from our Saviour...

"The need for a One World 'Spirit' or 'Holy Spirit' is vital to the forming of a World Religion. ... [T]he **'Holy Spirit'** can fit each and every faith, in a sense. It could mean the great white spirit of the Australian aboriginals, or the Red Indian pantheistic creation spirit, or the Green Man spirit of the environmentalists – the sky is the limit.

---

[31] *Introduction To Spirit.WWW.*
[32] El Collie, *Kundalini Signs and Symptoms.*
[33] Michael Foster, *Recovery By Discovery.*

> "When Alpha stresses the 'Holy Spirit' and down-plays Jesus
> Christ they are being very politically correct in a way, although
> the deceived leaders in different countries may not realise this".[34]

Ironically, if Alpha focused properly on exalting Christ above all,
then the real Holy Spirit would be very active. Alpha concentrates on 'the
Spirit', when the real Holy Spirit actually wants us to concentrate on Christ.
Alpha looks to the Spirit, rather than the Person who sent Him (John 14:16).
Nicky even labels the *Spirit* (rather than Christ) "the **most** wonderful and
exciting subject",[35] and HTB has admitted that the Course does not 'work'
without the retreat where the 'Holy Spirit' is the focus.

Alpha claims to desire that people be led by the Spirit of Christ, yet
HTB demands that the Course be run "as is" – thus discouraging Course
leaders from being led by that Spirit. Unpalatable as it is, the very spirit that
Alpha seeks to hear is gagged by the rigid restrictions laid down, and instead
Satan's counterfeit is given free rein. A further danger is that this false spirit
could subtly lead Christians involved in the Course into accepting pagans as
being saved because they share the same spirit (a spirit which tells them
both to see the final Antichrist as their leader).

30:9 SATAN'S PLAN   To help us put all the pieces together, we include
the following helpful quote from Don Clasen:

> "Just as God has a plan for His Church, so Satan has a plan for us
> too, and he knows he cannot do all the damage he wants to the
> human race just by attacking man's *conceptual* knowledge of
> God. He also wants to manipulate us into counterfeit spiritual
> *experiences* that will lead the unsuspecting into delusion and
> ultimately, eternal damnation with him.
>
> "While it is true that Christianity is an *experiential* relationship
> with a Living being – ('The Spirit itself *bears witness* with our
> spirit, that we are the children of God' Romans 8:16 etc.) – it is
> nonetheless a relationship based upon *objective truth* (that is, the
> Word of God). It is *not* basically the *seeking of an experience,* as
> in the Eastern mystical religions, because God is a Person and
> not an impersonal 'Force' to 'tap into'. And because it's a
> *relationship* with a *Person,* that is why Christianity is so morally
> and ethically orientated. In Christianity, spirituality is not

---

[34] W.B. Howard, The Alpha Course: Friend Or Foe?, *Despatch Magazine*, p40.
[35] Talk 8.

essentially spiritual *experiences,* but the development of character and integrity.

"And that is why it's so hated, because while spiritual experiences puff up our pride, knowledge of sin deflates it ... [If someone's] Christianity veers off into being a mere experience-based religion, that is the day it will cease to exist. It will become just another form of cultic Gnosticism ... Most Christians ... would be incredulous to think that a purported Christian movement could ever end up in the New Age without even knowing it. But ... that is exactly the direction these groups are heading in as they are perhaps the primary movers and shakers pushing the Body of Christ into the fulfilment of Mystery Babylon".[36]

30:10 NEW AGE CHRIST   With little understanding of the objective facts of the gospel, and an apparent lack of real conviction of sin by the Holy Spirit, the experiences of Alpha guests are not biblical evidence of their having been born again. The very things claimed by Alpha as proof of conversion to Christianity, although not to be found in Scripture, *are* frequently seen during Kundalini awakening or initiation into the New Age. So, are Alpha Course participants actually undergoing (albeit unknowingly) New Age initiation? Kundalini Yogis think so. As does New Age guru Benjamin Crème:

"Benjamin Crème was recently asked what he thought of the TB ['Toronto Blessing' as dispensed on Alpha]. His response was that he thought the TB was a **good** thing: it is, according to him, the method being used by his spiritual Masters to soften up Christian Fundamentalists to accept the New Age Christ when he appears".[37]

30:11 CONCLUSION   In closing, consider this Alpha testimony:

"Things reached a climax at the away weekend in Pontins. By now, thanks to a lot of background reading and reflection, I was certain where I stood – but at least my **atheism** was an informed

---

[36] Don Clasen, *Last Days Leaven - Part IV: The Destroyed Foundations – The Spirit,* First published in The Kingdom Gospel Messenger, Vol 8, No 4, Aug 1996. Reproduced in CROSS + WORD.
[37] Nick Needham, *The Toronto Blessing – Part One.* See also Ed Tarkowski, *Laughing Phenomena: Its History and Possible Effects on the Church.*

choice, rather than a woolly 'feeling'. Others in the group, however, were ripe to be 'taken' by the Holy Spirit…"

"That evening, he [Nicky] **asked for the Holy Spirit to visit** the congregation. All around the room, grown men and women began to shake and weep … One member of my group … fell into a trance-like state, his mouth open and his head back as Tom prayed for him. 'I felt like I was a balloon being inflated, that I was **absorbing** a supernatural experience. There was a swirling in my mouth and I **felt** myself **engulfed** by the Holy Spirit' he told us next morning. 'I was ready. It was time to open myself up to God'".[38]

… and compare it with part of the testimony we saw earlier from a former New Ager:

"My eyes lowered. Tears fell to the ground as I was overcome by a sense of **shame** before God. I remember praying, gently confessing that I was a **wretched** sinner. I believed that Christ died **in my place** on the **cross** – for my sins. I was overwhelmed by His unwarranted love for me through this act. There were **no bright lights** or **tingling sensations**, only **remorse** mingled with **gratefulness**, a sense of peace **in reconciliation** and assurance of security for eternity. I had confidence in a joy and safety I'd never known before".[39]

---

[38] Report by Julia Llewellyn-Smith, *The Express*, 16:Nov:1998, reproduced in *UK Focus*, Dec 1998, pp4-5 and in *Alpha News*, Mar – Jun 1999, pp10-11.
[39] Caryl Matriciana, Outer Beauty, Inner Despair, *Dawn of the New Age: 5 New Agers Relate Their Search For The Truth*, pp48-49.

RECOMMENDED READING

Discernment

Dave Hunt, The Seduction of Christianity: Spiritual Discernment in the Last Days, (Harvest House, 1985)
"The Bible clearly states that a great Apostasy must occur before Christ's Second Coming. Today Christians are being deceived by a new worldview more subtle and more seductive than anything the world has ever experienced." This book is a very important treatment of the Faith movement and the spirit behind it, as well as other false ways that have slipped into Western Church life.

Dave Hunt, Occult Invasion: The Subtle Seduction of the World and Church, (Harvest House, 1998)
This book seeks to "give you the skills you need to recognise the subtle incursions of the occult and provides tools you can use to halt its destructive advance."

Jessie Penn-Lewis with Evan Roberts, War on the Saints (Unabridged Edition), ('Diasozo Trust', 68 Elm Road, Erith, Kent, DA8 2NW, UK, 9th ed., 1987)
"This book is an enduring classic of the Christian's conflict with the hidden works of darkness. Since it was first published in 1912 there have been many testimonies to deliverance and help received through its pages."

Campbell McAlpine, The Practice of Biblical Meditation (Marshall Pickering, 3 Beggarwood Lane, Basingstoke, Hants., RG23 7LP, UK, 1981)
This book is the finest we have ever seen on the subject. It is written with compassion and gentleness and is a beautiful aid to learning how to meditate on God's Word.

Janet Lumb, Guidance, Finding God's Plan for Our Lives, (Scripture Union, 130 City Road, London, EC1B 2NJ, 1985)
A small but very helpful book on how to hear what God wants to communicate to believers.

227

The Holy Spirit

Jessie Penn-Lewis, The Work of the Holy Spirit, (CLC, 51 The Dean, Alresford, Hants., SO24 9BJ, UK)
"In this short book, Jessie Penn-Lewis outlines the ministry of the Holy Spirit to us as Comforter, Teacher, and Witness to Christ. The outcome of the life in the Spirit is examined, and the purpose of God in sending the Holy Spirit is explored." An excellent little book.

A.W. Tozer, How to be Filled With the Holy Spirit, (OM Publishing, P.O. Box 300, Carlisle, Cumbria, CA3 OQS, UK)
A collection of Tozer sermons on the subject. A small but important booklet.

A.W. Tozer, Paths to Power, (OM Publishing, P.O. Box 300, Carlisle, Cumbria, CA3 OQS, UK)
A tiny gem of a book, which deals both with certain errors alongside the truths of the outpouring of the Holy Spirit.

Edmund Heddle, The Biblical Basis of Spiritual Gifts, (PWM Trust, The Park, Moggerhanger, Bedford, MK44 3RW, UK, 1989)
A very clear treatment of the entire subject.

The Toronto Blessing
(Please note that all of the following books were written by people who, like us, believe that the gifts of the Holy Spirit are still available today.)

Dusty Peterson, Consuming Fire: 'Holy Laughter' Disentangled Through a Decade's Reflection (stockist details are available from the 'Rubies' section of www.bayith.org)
Written to be a gracious, clear and unarguable introduction to the various different issues surrounding this topic. Due for release in 2006.

Clifford Hill, ed., Blessing the Church? (Eagle, St. Nicholas House, 14 The Mount, Guildford, Surrey GU2 5HN, UK, 1995)
"Writing from within the Charismatic movement the four contributors review its history and direction and sound a warning concerning many recent phenomena and the Toronto Blessing in particular."

Bill Randles, Weighed and Found Wanting: The Toronto Experience Examined in the Light of the Bible, (SMP, 24 Geldart Street, Cambridge, CB1 2LX, UK, 1995)
A fine and extremely readable early analysis of the Toronto Blessing. Very highly recommended.

Ed Tarkowski, Laughing Phenomena: Its History and Possible Effects on the Church, (P.O. Box 233, McKean, PA 16426, USA, 1995)
A comprehensive treatment of the history of the Toronto Blessing. Demonstrates, through clear comparisons between the New Age religion and the teachings of those at the root of Toronto, how both movements are on the same course.

Larry Thomas, No Laughing Matter, (Double Crown Publishing, P.O. Box 563, Excelsior Springs, MO 64024-0563, USA, 1995)
An uncompromising, biblical, and very insightful book on the background and nature of the "laughing revival" and the spiritual forces present in today's church. The style is probably too confrontational for most people, but the work does contain a lot of truth and some superb quotes.

Dr. Eddy Cheong, Deceiving the Elect, (Sanctuary Productions, P.O. Box 441, 75760 Malacca, West Malaysia, 1995)
A very helpful treatment of the Toronto Blessing.

The Word-Faith Movement

VIDEO
The Signs & Wonders Movement Exposed, vols 1-3. Available from various bookshops and publishers including NPN.

The New Age Movement

Dave Hunt and T.A. McMahon, The New Spirituality, (Harvest House Publishers)
An amazing and very readable study of the rise of the New Age Movement in Western countries and the Eastern mysticism that lies at its heart. Highly recommended.

Various Contributors, Dawn of the New Age: 5 New Agers Relate Their Search for the Truth, (Penfold Book and Bible House, P.O. Box 26, Telford Rd Industrial Estate, Bicester, Oxfordshire, OX6 8PB, UK, 1998)
"This unique and powerful book contains five fascinating true-life stories of New Agers whose desire for truth lead them down amazing pathways. From Britain, India and America come gripping tales of adventure, in search of ... reality."

Helpful Websites
Good articles concerning the Toronto Blessing and the 'Third Wave' movement, Word of Faith, and the New Age Movement, plus many useful links to other sites can be found on the following pages, although we cannot endorse every page of each:

The Second Coming of Our Lord and Saviour Jesus Christ -
//www.velocity.net/~edju

Let Us Reason -
//www.letusreason.org

Lighthouse Trails Research Project –
//www,lighthousetrailsresearch.com

Deception in the Church -
//www.deceptioninthechurch.com

APPENDIX

Alpha is an amazing bridge. According to one advertisement in a secular newspaper:

> "Lots of people have little interest in ordinary 'Churchy' religion. Some find it boring or irrelevant to their lives ... There seems to be a gap between the Church and many ordinary people. Alpha tries to **bridge that gap**".[1]

The Course has been well received by the secular press in general, and HTB has been quick to repeat their comments:

> "In an article headlined 'Alpha Plus', the influential *Economist* magazine has described Alpha as being 'a powerful medicine' for the church. 'It is clear that Alpha is already changing British church life ... Alpha is certainly a powerful medicine for a sickly old church'" [*The Economist*].[2]

> "In the past, Christianity's only advert has been a building with a cross on the top. Now Alpha employs modern marketing, ... designed to appeal to consumers of all ages" [*Channel 4*].[3]

> "Nicky Gumbel's Alpha Course [is] the saviour of Christianity" [*Evening Standard*].[4]

---

[1] Rev. Eric Foggitt, *The Good News*, Advertisement, *Aberdeen Evening Express*, Summer 1998.

[2] *The Economist*, quoted in *Alpha News*, Mar – Jun 1999, p11.

[3] *Tempting Faith*, C4 TV documentary, quoted in *Alpha News Online*, Mar – Jul 2000.

"Alpha makes Christianity relevant to modern life" [*Express*].[5]

"British Christianity has stumbled across the big idea that has eluded it ... What distinguishes Alpha from other initiatives is the easy-going, relaxed feel of the proceedings..." [*The Times*].[6]

"'Alpha to the rescue' ... The Alpha Course is coming to the rescue of the Christian Church in Europe and throughout the world" [*Time*].[7]

But what does the world know?

"The world ... **hateth** [Me], because I testify of it, that the works thereof are evil" (John 7:7).

"But the **natural** man receiveth **not** the things of the Spirit of God: for they are **foolishness** unto him" (1 Cor. 2:14). See also John 14:17 and 1 Cor. 1:27-28!

"Blessed is the man that walketh **not** in the counsel of **the ungodly**, nor ... of **sinners**" (Psa. 1:1a).

"**Woe** unto you, when all men shall speak well of you! For so did their fathers to the **false** prophets" (Luke 6:26).

A:1 WALKING LIKE AN EGYPTIAN?   The act of turning to the world, of making use of *its* ways and methods rather than seeking the Lord God and following *His* ways, is described in Scripture as "going down to Egypt". This was something the Israelites were often tempted to do instead of simply trusting the very God who had brought them *out* of the bondage of Egypt:

"**Woe** to the rebellious children, saith the Lord, that take counsel, but not of Me ... That walk to go down into **Egypt**, and have not asked at My mouth; ... to trust in the shadow of Egypt! Therefore shall the ... trust in the shadow of Egypt [be] your confusion ... **Woe** to them that **go down to Egypt** for help; ... but they look not unto the Holy One of Israel, neither seek the Lord!" (Isa. 30:1a-2, 31:1). See also Deut. 17:16 and Judg. 2:1-3.

---

4 *Evening Standard Magazine*, 19:May:00.

5 *The Express*, as quoted in HTB's booklet *An Introduction to the Alpha Course*, p2.

6 *Times* Newspaper, Feb 1998, quoted in *Alpha News*, Jul – Oct 1998, p3.

7 *Time* Magazine, quoted in *Alpha News Online*, Mar – Jul 2000.

Yet HTB seems perfectly happy to "go down to Egypt" to ensure that Alpha is 'acceptable' to the world and successful *on the world's terms*. The Team Training videos, for example, were re-filmed because "the earlier video had been filmed in a small seminar room which made it difficult for the camera team to give it the **professional 'feel'** of the Alpha Course talks themselves".[8] And, after Nicky Gumbel had revamped the Course itself, HTB staff observed that "The **image** makeover ... seems to have been the **all-important** thing ... Nicky bought standard lamps [for a more attractive lighting effect] ... [W]e have ... plenty of flowers [now]"...[9]

Under the title "Oh, What a Party", *Alpha News* reported the launch of the British 'Millennium Alpha Initiative' in September 1999. The launch party in London included performances from a "regular Covent Garden entertainer ... who juggled with knives and lay on a bed of nails", while clowns provided entertainment for the launch party in Nottingham. And the 'Alpha Millennium Survival Kit' containing party hat, party popper, blower, balloon, Alka Seltzer, corkscrew and an invitation to Alpha, were distributed at various "regional roadshows" in Britain, as well as being sent to all the nation's MPs.[10]

But Paul did not consider the Gospel he preached to be any less effective because it wasn't 'professionally' presented (see 2 Cor. 10:10). Neither did he see any need for entertainment or an "image makeover". He simply gloried in the *cross of Christ alone*. The disciples did not feel the need to present commendations or "positive comments" from unbelievers to endear them to the multitudes. Indeed that would have been impossible, since the common reaction to their message was persecution; just as the Lord Jesus warned it would be for *anyone* bringing the true gospel of salvation to an unbelieving world (e.g. Acts 4:1-31 and Matt. 10:16-25). As for handing out worldly fripperies to gain a hearing, actually by encouraging worldliness and triviality, where do we see God ever using such a technique anywhere in Scripture?

There *is* a 'gap' between the Church and the world. The Church is the redeemed of Christ, while the world is not:

"If ye were of the world, the world would love his own: but because ye are **not** of the world... therefore the world **hateth**

---

[8] *Alpha News,* Nov 1998 – Feb 1999, p9.
[9] *Evening Standard* Magazine, 19:5:00.
[10] *Alpha News,* Nov 1999 – Feb 2000, pp3-5.

you" (John 15:19). "...In the world ye **shall** have **tribulation**..." (John 16:33).

"I have given them Thy Word; and the world hath **hated** them, because they are **not** of the world, even as I am not of the world" (John 17:14).

A:2 BE YE POPULAR?   The comments below, from an American article on another popular enterprise in the modern church, are surely applicable to the Alpha Course too:

> "Another factor contributing to the decline of discernment in the contemporary church ... is a preoccupation with **image and influence**. Many Christians have the misconception that to win the world for Christ we must first win the world's favor. If we can get the world to **like** us, they will embrace our Savior ... The express design of this user-friendly philosophy is to make unconverted sinners feel comfortable with the Christian message. People won't come to hear the Gospel proclaimed? ... Give them something they want. Put on a show. **Entertain them**. Avoid sensitive subjects like sin and damnation. Accommodate their worldly desires and felt needs. Slip in the Gospel in small, diluted doses.
>
> "The whole point is to make the church a place where non-Christians can enjoy themselves. The strategy is to tantalize non-Christians rather than confront their unbelief. That is altogether incompatible with sound doctrine. It is compromise with the world. James called it spiritual adultery (James 4:4) ... In practical terms, the movement to accommodate the world has diminished Christians' confidence in divinely revealed truth. If we can't trust the **preaching of God's Word** to convert the lost and build the church, how can we trust the Bible at all – even as a guide for daily living?".[11]

And perhaps the vast Alpha 'business operation' would do well to ponder the following gem from A.W.Tozer:

> "We who preach the gospel must not think of ourselves as **public relations agents** sent to establish goodwill between Christ and the world. We must not imagine ourselves commissioned to make Christ **acceptable** to big business, the press, or the world

---

[11] John MacArthur, *Reckless Faith*, p52-54, quoted in 'The Emperor's Closet, March For Jesus: Commitment Or Compromise?', *The Christian Conscience*, May 1995.

234

of sports, or modern education. We are not diplomats but **prophets**, and our message is not a compromise but **an ultimatum**".[12]

HTB might also be advised to consider the following observations (sent to us via an email forum):

"We all know [that] numbers and popularity in themselves prove **nothing**. However, the average Christian mind in this modern age is very impressed with numbers and popularity. Especially when it is all dressed up like the Alpha package is.

"Our problem is that Alpha is packaged for a Christian world that does not want to work too hard for its religion. A world that is conditioned with neat packaging. A world that is conditioned by all things instant – like tea or coffee. A world that teaches [that] doctrinal rigour is divisive [and thus wrong]. A world that is happy with religious shallowness ... A world that will lead all the unwary into the World Church: all things to all men, and sloppy lovey-doviness, that will eventually be so far removed from Biblical Christianity as to be unrecognisable...

"It has to be admitted, the producers of Alpha have done a remarkable job. It is being swallowed wholesale by thousands. Its Ecumenism is total ... So what kind of 'believers' are we talking about when we talk about the fruit of Alpha?".[13]

Consider these words from Nicky's own lips: "The Devil's tactic is to take us on a path that leads to destruction ... [H]e doesn't tell us that at the beginning".[14] How true this is of the enemy. Unfortunately it is true of Alpha too...

1. In Part One we saw that Alpha is trying to relate to other religions in *man's* way rather than God's.

2. In Part Two we demonstrated that Alpha deals with Rome in *man's* way, not God's.

3. In Part Three we showed that Alpha tries to evangelise in *man's* way rather than God's way:

---

[12] A.W.Tozer, *The Old Cross And The New.*
[13] Rev. Ian Cook, email on file, 26:Sep:1998.
[14] Talk 11.

Romans 1:16 shows that the true, God-anointed, way of bringing people to salvation is not slick videos or easy chats or shallowness: "*For I am* **not ashamed** *of the* **gospel of Christ**: *for* **it** *is the* **power of God unto salvation** *to every one that believeth; to the Jew first, and also to the Greek.*" *We have already demonstrated that it is not so common for men to be truly saved; that few find the "narrow way" (Matt. 7:13-14). Alpha, however, seems to be turning the narrow way into a broad one by preaching "another Jesus ... another spirit ... another gospel..." (2 Cor. 11:4) and teaching "[an]other doctrine" (1 Tim. 1:3).*

4.   In Part Four we saw how Alpha handles the matters of unity and purity in *man's* way rather than God's way in the Bible.

5.   Part Five revealed how Alpha encourages us to approach the spiritual realm in *man's* way rather than the God-ordained way.

But Scripture tells us:

"There **is** a way which **seemeth right** unto a man, but the end thereof are the ways of **death**" (Prov. 14:12). See also Isa. 55:8-9.

Could it be that Alpha is so successful in today's culture precisely because it *doesn't* come out of Egypt but stays right in it?

"Know ye not that the friendship of the world is enmity with [i.e. hatred towards] God? Whosoever therefore will be a friend of the **world** is the **enemy** of God" (Jas. 4:4); "Be **not** conformed to this world" (Rom. 12:2a).

"Do I seek to please men? for if I yet pleased men, I should **not** be the servant of Christ" (Gal. 1:10).

"Except the **LORD** build the house, they labour **in vain** that build it" (Psa. 127:1); "He spake a parable unto them, Can the blind lead the blind? ... Shall they not both fall into the ditch?" (Luke 6:39).

Alpha is indeed a bridge. But the traffic on that bridge is all going to the wrong destination. The island of God's pure, separate, ways now has a man-made scaffold connection to the enemy's mainland. And we are all being encouraged to meet in the middle, unaware of the flimsy, useless, structure we are relying on. As Philip Foster rightly observes, Alpha is "a bridge too far".

A:3 HAVE WE APPROACHED HTB?   Many readers will be very keen to know if we have challenged Nicky over the material in this book. After all, Matthew 18 says "if thy brother shall trespass against thee" one must go to him privately first. We should all be cognizant of the following points:

1. As we saw in section 18:6, the Matthew 18 passage refers to *private hurts*, where one brother has "**trespassed** against" another. It does not refer to *public teaching of falsehoods*. Since Nicky has taught publicly, his teachings can be dealt with publicly.

2. From the copious evidence we have supplied, it should be obvious to all that Nicky Gumbel knows what he is doing. Sending him this study would therefore be pointless, especially in view of his publicised attitude to criticism, although we have indeed sent him a pre-publication copy.

3. Nicky Gumbel knows what the Bible says. He has no excuse for what he is teaching. Besides, he has already been challenged by others - on many occasions. Must *everyone* troop into his office before they can warn the flock about his material?

4. In fact, we *did* give our primary criticisms about Alpha to HTB several years ago. Subsequently, new versions of the Alpha Course videos were produced, to "take account of a wide range of comments and suggestions from theologians and others".[15] However, these new videos were just as deceptive and erroneous as before! They simply replaced the quotations we had highlighted and continued to propagate the same falsehoods as previously. Our main points were ignored.

   We gave HTB staff our first ever copy of our 'Overview' volume of this *Unofficial Guide*. We also sent HTB the first copy we received from the printers of the main 'World' volume. We also know that HTB possess a copy of the current (sixth) edition of our 'Overview'. We have received no comment whatsoever on the content of any of these, and Alpha's deceptions remain.

5. Since then, many other pieces have been written about Alpha, and HTB itself states that it is careful to read all that is published on the subject. No repentance has been forthcoming and no recall of material has been sent out to our knowledge.

---

[15] *Alpha News*, Jul – Oct 1997, p1.

We would love to believe that the Alpha organisation might go back to the Scriptures and thus recognise the ways of the saints in the early church who turned the world upside down. The paths that the Lord mapped out of old are the only ones that will bring rest to us and to the souls of the unsaved around us. But the signs are not at all good.

> "Thus saith the LORD, Stand ye in the ways, and see, and **ask** for the **old** paths, where is the **good** way, and walk therein, and ye shall find rest for your souls. But they said, We will **not** walk therein" (Jer. 6:16). "[God's] counsels of old are faithfulness and truth" (Isa. 25:1)

> "I think ... the Course is now about **as perfect as it can be**" [Sandy Millar, *Introductory Talk*, 2nd Edn. Alpha videos].

A:4 WHAT IF I'VE ALREADY DONE THE COURSE?   Now that we have seen the truth about Alpha, what are people to do if they realise they have been adversely affected by their experience of attending it? It would be a major omission if this book failed to offer advice for those so damaged. As always, the answers are given us in God's wonderful and eternal Word...

- The first step needs to be to cry out to God for His mercy and guidance. But, as we have seen, that prayer must be directed to the *true* God, the one supreme and Holy God, the Lord God of Israel. In order to ensure you are indeed directing your prayers aright, we recommend reading the Book of Psalms; for here God is described very clearly.

- If you have never been on your face before God in deep repentance over the past direction of your life and over every area of sin that you can think of; if you have never sincerely cried out for His unmerited mercy and forgiveness and begged for His salvation from your sinful nature and the destiny it will bring then you obviously need to do this.

Spend time asking the Lord to reveal your sins and convict you of them so that you see can them in the same way He does. (Read passages like Mark 7:20-23 too.) Then go through your past ways, renouncing and turning away from each one. Believe that Christ is Who He claimed to be and that, by physically dying in our place, He paid the penalty for our sins. Ask God to wash you in His Son's pure, cleansing, blood that you might be totally clean and able to stand before Him on the Day of Judgment. (See the gospel summary at the beginning of Part Three for more. See also onr or two of the books we recommend on repentance, salvation, and discipleship at the end of that Part.)

- If you have been exposed to the Alpha spirit (or any other occult spirit – e.g. from drug mis-use or other activities with a spiritual dimension like martial arts, 'homeopathic' healing techniques, Freemasonry and other false religions, fortune telling or other mystical / pagan practices, etc) then you need to ask God for deliverance from any curses you may have brought upon yourself. (If you don't currently believe that Christians can have any curses operating in their lives, despite the experiences of men of God like David and Paul, then please see the relevant articles in the 'Rubies' section of our website.)

  If you repent of your involvement, and then fast and pray, it is entirely possible for most people be released without anyone else needing to be involved. If this doesn't suffice, ask the Lord to supply godly people to pray with you for deliverance. But beware, for many such ministries today are seriously compromised and pose even more danger. The most important thing is to keep repenting, renouncing your involvement, day by day until you sense God's forgiveness in your spirit. (If you don't know what it is like to sense something in your spirit then you need to check that you were ever saved. Sensing something in your spirit can be likened to having a clear – or troubled – conscience, or having total assurance about something even when outward evidence points in a different direction.)

- Pray too for sound fellowship. Don't go just anywhere; seek the Lord as to where *He* wants you to go. And, if you don't feel led by God to go anywhere, simply wait patiently on Him and fellowship with God-fearing people on an ad hoc basis until He shows the way.

- Consider purchasing the follow-up to the book you are holding – i.e. '7 Deadly Dangers with the Alpha Course'. (If you cannot obtain this for any reason, the next best follow-up would be appendices B & C of the 'Overview' volume of this *Unofficial Guide*, because these comprise nearly fifty pages of advanced material for people who have been well able to cope with the volume you are now reading.)

- Last, but DEFINITELY not least, "study ... the Word of truth". We would recommend reading a few pages of the Hebrew Scriptures (i.e. the 'Old Testament'), a portion of the Greek (i.e. the 'New Testament') and a Psalm or a Chapter of Proverbs each day. This will ensure that you get to read the marvellous whole. (We would urge you to read our articles on the subject of Bible versions, available from our website, before using a version other than the KJV.)

If you want a ready-made structure for your reading, then *Lamplight*, by Christian Voice is a one-year reading plan of this type. (It is available from Roy Silver, P.O. Box 62, Royston, SG8 7UL, UK. Tel: +44 1763 241726. Fax: +44 1763 231980. The charge is very small indeed, but please contact Roy to check on the *current* price.) Alternatively, you can follow the guidance at the end of Part One of our book before starting to read the Scriptures and you will find the Lord is most willing to give you understanding...

Some Christians find daily reading notes, such as *Daily Bread*, helpful. But it is important not to come to depend on them, for they are a poor substitute for the pure Word of God itself. The pre-set Bible verses can distract us from the portions of Scripture the Holy Spirit would have us read and meditate upon. More especially, the accompanying comments of men do likewise – and can discourage us from seeking God for ourselves. It is better to read through the whole of the Bible, asking God the Father to speak to us through the portion we are reading. Bible commentaries can also aid our Bible studies, but again, we should not allow ourselves to rely on them, rather than the Spirit who leads us into all truth, for our understanding of the Word of God.

A:5 FINALLY, A PURE BRIDE   Thank you for persevering through these many pages. We hope you have been strengthened and helped. Let us complete this journey on a very special note. The following is a radiant and inspiring testimony about a group of believers who lived circa 150AD. It was written by a careful observer who was clearly deeply moved by the way they lived their lives. Note the total rejection of the world's influence. The account is very uplifting and contrasts immeasurably with many of today's (supposedly Spirit-led) churches...

A LETTER TO THE EMPEROR ANTONIUS PIUS

"As for the Christians, they trace their line from the Lord Jesus Christ. He is confessed to be the Son of the most high God, who came down from heaven, by the Holy Ghost, (for the salvation of mankind) and was born of a (pure) virgin, (without seed of man, and without defilement) and took flesh, and in a daughter of man there dwelt the Son of God. This is taught from that Gospel which a little while ago was spoken among them as being preached; wherein if ye will also read, ye will comprehend the power that is upon it.

"This Jesus, then, was born of the tribe of the Hebrews; and he had twelve disciples, in order that a certain dispensation of his might be fulfilled. He was pierced by the Jews and he died and was buried; and they say that after three days he rose and ascended to heaven; and then these twelve disciples went forth into all the kingdoms of the world, telling of his greatness with all humility and sobriety; whence they who still serve the righteousness of his preaching are called Christians, who are well known.

"Now the Christians, O king, by going about and **seeking** have found **the truth** and as we have comprehended from their writings they are nearer to the truth and to **exact knowledge** than the rest of the peoples. For they acknowledge God the Creator and Maker of all things, ... from whom are all things: (in the only-begotten Son, and in the Holy Ghost), and **other** God than him they worship **none**. They have the **commandments of the Lord Jesus Christ** himself **engraven on their hearts**, and **these they observe**, looking for the resurrection of the dead and the life of the world to come.

"They commit neither adultery nor fornication; nor do they bear false witness, they do not deny a deposit, nor covet other men's goods: they honour father and mother, and love their neighbours: they give **right judgment**; and they do not worship idols... They do not unto other that which they would not have done unto themselves. They comfort such as wrong them, and make friends of them: they labour to do good to their enemies: (they are meek and gentle). And their wives, O king, are pure as virgins, and their daughters modest: and their men refrain themselves from all unlawful intercourse and all uncleanness, in the hope of the recompense that is to come in another world.

"But as for their servants, or handmaids, or their children if any of them have any, they persuade them to become Christians for the love that they have towards them; and when they have become so, they call them without distinction brethren: they do **not** worship strange gods: and they walk in all **humility** and kindness, and **falsehood is not found among them**, and they **love** one another. They despise not the widow, and grieve not the orphan. He that hath, distributeth liberally to him that hath not. If they see a stranger, they bring him under their roof, and rejoice over him, as it were their own brother: for they call themselves brethren, not after the flesh, but after the spirit and in God: but when one of their poor passes away from the world, and any of them sees him, then he provides for his burial according to his ability; and if they hear that any of their number is imprisoned or oppressed for the name of their Messiah, all of them provide for his needs, and if it is possible that he may be delivered, they deliver him.

"And if there is among them a man that is poor and needy, and they have not an abundance of necessaries, they **fast** two or three days that they may supply the needy with their necessary food. For Christ's sake they are ready to lay down their lives: **they keep his commandments faithfully**, living righteous and holy lives: as the Lord commanded them, giving him thanks every morning and every hour, for meat and drink and every blessing. And if any righteous person of their number passes away from the world they rejoice and give thanks to God, and they follow his body, as if he were moving from one place to another: and when a child is born to any one of them, they praise God and if again it chance to die in its infancy they praise God mightily, as for one who has passed through the world without sins. And if again they see that one of their number has died in his iniquity or in his sins, over this one they weep bitterly and sigh, as over one who is about to go to punishment; such is the ordinance of the law of the Christians, O king, and such their conduct.

"As men who know God, they ask from him petitions which are **proper** for him to give and for them to receive: and thus they accomplish the course of their lives. And **because** they acknowledge the goodnesses of God towards them, lo! On account of them **there flows forth** the beauty that is in the world. And truly they are of the number of those that **have found the truth by going about and seeking it**, and as far as we have comprehended, we have understood that **they only** are near to the knowledge of the truth.

"But the good deeds which they do, they do not proclaim in the ears of the multitude, and they take care that no one shall perceive them, and hide their gift, as he who has found a treasure and hides it ... And they labour to become righteous as those that expect to see their Messiah and receive from him the promises made to them with great glory. But their sayings and their ordinances, O king, and the glory of their service, and the expectation of their recompense of reward, according to the doing of each one of them, which they expect in another world, thou art able to know from their writings. It sufficeth for us that we have briefly made known to your majesty concerning the conversation and **the truth** of the Christians. For truly great and wonderful is their teaching to him that is **willing to examine and understand it**. And truly this people is a new people, and there is something divine mingled with it ... [N]ot of myself have I brought these things forward nor as their advocate have I said them..."

Aristeides, Apology, XV, XVI
Christian Theology and Ethics, c150

$\mathscr{P}$UBLISHER'S NOTE

St Matthew Publishing hopes the reader has found this book informative and of benefit. This 'CHURCH' volume of *Alpha – the Unofficial Guide* has explored, in the context of Alpha, the Bible's view of the Church. The appendix has brought us neatly back to the main subject of the companion 'WORLD' volume, viz. the Bible's view of the *World*.

There is no overlap between the two volumes, except the standard of research and the number of thought-provoking observations. Gracefully written, the insightful 'WORLD' volume focuses on very different issues from those raised so far (including: other religions, Rome and the core of the gospel). Readers are sure to appreciate the top-quality material and the clear way in which each topic has been presented.

Many of those important questions to which Christians frequently yearn to know the biblical answer are tackled, and each is dealt with in a logical and irrefutable way. We at St Matthew Publishing believe with all our hearts that the committed believer will not for one moment regret reading it but will want instead to share this powerful handbook with their friends. (Ordering details appear overleaf.)

$\mathscr{H}$ow to Obtain Copies
of the WORLD Volume

For details of how to order the sister 'World' volume or further copies of this 'Church' volume, the first port of call is the 'Better Than Rubies' section of the authors' website (www.bayith.org), or:

St Matthew Publishing –
> 24 Geldart St, Cambridge, CB1 2LX, **UK**
> Tel: +44 1223 504871, *Fax: +44 1223 512304*
> Email: PF.SMP@dial.pipex.com

or

Christian Witness Ministries –
> P.O. Box 353, Loch Sport, Vic 3851, **Australia**
> Tel: +61 3 5146 0280, *Fax: +61 3 5146 0270*
> Email: Maureen@Christian-witness.org

Below are some other ministries which should be able to help in this regard, but a much more extensive list of outlets worldwide is given on our website.

Americas	Europe	Africa	Australasia
Christ The Way 43120 Eastwood Square, Kitchener, ON, Canada Tel: +1 519 576 2600 christtheway.ca	**St Matthew Publishing** 24 Geldart Street, Cambridge, CB1 2LX, UK Tel: +44 1223 504871 stmatthewpublishing.co.uk	**Discernment Ministries** P.O. Box 2336, Krugersdorp 1740, SA diakonia@icon.co.za discernment-ministries.com	**CWM** P.O. Box 353, Loch Sport, Victoria 3851, Australia Tel: +61 3 5146 0280 christian-witness.org
UnderstandThe Times P.O. Box 27239, Santa Ana, CA 92799, USA Tel: +1 800 689 1888 understandthetimes.org	**B. McCall Barbour** 28 George IV Bridge, Edinburgh, EH1 1ES, UK Tel/*Fax*: +44 131 225 4816	**Elijah Ministries** P.O. Box 55468, Northlands 2116, Jo'burg, South Africa Tel: +27 11 788 5733	**Margaret Godwin** P.O. Box 112, Trafalgar, Victoria 3824, Australia Tel/*Fax*: +61 3 5633 2300 marg@moriel.org

$\mathscr{C}$ROSS-REFERENCE

Certain fundamental areas come up more than once in this book. The following mini-index is supplied in order to assist navigation where such topics cannot easily be tracked down via chapter titles and section headings. Each section of the book that contains help on the listed topic is identified. (Italicized entries refer to sections in the sister 'CHURCH' volume. See preceding pages for more details.)

Key:

'RR-4'	- the 'Recommended Reading' section at the end of Part 4.
'(x2)'	- the topic is referred to twice in the given section.
'A:3'	- the third section of the Appendix that appears at the end of the CHURCH volume.
'See also'	- means 'the following sections are not as relevant as the earlier ones in the list'

Alpha Quotes (Quotations from Course teaching materials. Note that Nicky sometimes modifies video talks *within* editions.)

Talk 1 "Christianity: Boring, Untrue and Irrelevant?" – TBC; See also our WORLD volume.

Talk 2 "Who is Jesus?" – TBC; See also our WORLD volume.

Talk 3 "Why Did Jesus Die?" – ; See also our WORLD volume.

Talk 4 "How Can I Be Sure of My Faith?" – TBC; See also our WORLD volume.

Talk 5 "Why and How Should I Read the Bible?" – TBC; See also our WORLD volume.

Talk 6 "Why and How Do I Pray?" – TBC; See also our WORLD volume.

Talk 7 "How Does God Guide Us?" – TBC; See also our WORLD volume.

Talk 8 "Who is the Holy Spirit?" – TBC; See also our WORLD volume.

Talk 9 "What Does the Holy Spirit Do?" – TBC; See also our WORLD volume.

Talk 10 "How Can I Be Filled With the Spirit?" – TBC; See also our WORLD volume.

Talk 11 "How Can I Resist Evil?" – TBC; See also our WORLD volume.

Talk 12 "Why and How Should We Tell Others?" – TBC; See also our WORLD volume.

Talk 13 "Does God Heal Today?" – TBC; See also our WORLD volume.

Talk 14 "What About the Church?" – TBC, See also our WORLD volume.

Talk 15 "How Can I Make the Most of the Rest of My Life?" – TBC; See also our WORLD volume.

Questions of Life – TBC; See also our WORLD volume *and* the **Talk number** related to chapter of interest in *Questions of Life*.

Searching Issues – TBC; See also our WORLD volume.

Telling Others – TBC; See also our WORLD volume.

30 Days – TBC; See also our WORLD volume.

Why Jesus? – TBC; See also our WORLD volume.

(***Numerous*** other HTB publications are referenced in this *Unofficial Guide*, but the above are the most commonly cited ones.)

Babylon (Also known as Chaldea. An enemy of the truth and of God's People in the Bible.) *2:4-10, 3:1, 3:3, 4:0, 5:4, 6:6, 7:4, 7:9, 7:12, 8:5-7, 9:2-4, 11:0-1, 11:5-8, 12:1, 12:7-9*, 30:1-2, 30:9, *RR-2*, RR-4. See *also 5:2, 5:6, 7:1, 9:5, 10:2*, 17:6, 19:6, 24:5.

Believer's Security (Verses and comments on salvation and the requirement for security.) *2:6, 8:1, 9:1, 9:5*, 18:3, 24:2, 24:4-5, 25:2, *RR-3*, RR-4. See also *1:5, 9:6, 13:3*, 18:4, 18:9, 19:3.

Bible Versions (Information on different Bibles, including Alpha's version, and how they compare.) *2:5, 4:0, 9:3, 10:2-6, 11:8*, 17:6, 18:6, 20:3, 23:3, *RR-1, RR-2*, RR-4. See also *12:5-6, 16:2*, 17:1, 17:6, 26:5.

Character of God (What God has revealed about Himself, plus Alpha's coverage of this.) *7:8, 13:2, 15:4-5*, 19:2-5, 19:7, 20:1, 23:1, 24:6, 25:4-6, 28:2, 29:3, *RR-3*. See also A:4.

Church (Information on the operation, or ordinances, of a Fellowship.) *12:4*, 17:2-3, 17:6, 18:1-8, 18:10, 20:2, 21:1-3, 22:1-3, 23:1-7, 24:2-8, 25:3-4, 25:8, 26:2, A:2, A:5. See also *7:12, 8:2, 11:9*, 20:6, 24:1, 28:5.

Criticism (Guidance about correction, judgmentalism, etc.) *2:7, 3:3, 10:1, 12:1, 12:6*, 17:1, 17:3, 18:1-10, 22:1-3, A:3. See also *2:9, 6:6, 10:5, 12:10*, 20:3, 21:1-3, 23:1-5, 25:2.

Deity of Christ (Bible verses proving Christ's Godhood. See also entries under 'Trinity'.) *1:1, 1:3-4, 2:2, 2:4, 3:5, 6:2-4, 6:6, 7:3-4, 7:7-9, 8:1, 9:1, 10:3, 13:2, 15:1, 16:1*, 19:4, 20:3, 21:4, 23:1, 26:2, 28:2, 29:3-5. See also *8:2, 10:4*, 28:6.

End Times   (What we will – and won't – see in the last days.   Also known as 'Eschatology'.) *16:2*, 22:1, 22:3, 24:2-8, 25:1-2, 28:6, *RR-2, RR-3*, RR-4. See also *13:2*.

Fear of God   (Treatments of the crucial subject of what it means to be 'God-fearing'.) *14:4, 15:4*, 19:2-3, 19:7, 20:1-2, 22:1, 23:6, 27:2.   See *also 2:1, 5:4, 8:6, 12:4, 13:2, 14:2, 15:7*, 19:5, 21:1, 21:3, 23:2, 23:7, 25:4, 28:5, 29:6, 30:1-3.

Gospel   (What salvation – or 'justification' – involves.) *3:1, 5:5, 9:1-2, 13:2, 14:2-4, 15:1-7, 16:2*, 17:5-6, 21:4, 23:6, 24:2, 25:5, 26:5, 28:7, 30:11, A:4, *RR-3*.   See also *8:4, 9:4-5, 10:3, 11:1, 14:5*, 17:2, 17:4, 18:2-3, 18:5-6, 19:6, 23:1.

New Age Movement   (Information on this dangerous religion and its roots.) *2:6, 2:8, 3:2, 3:4, 4:0, 10:3, 11:8, 16:2*, 20:4, 25:5-6, 26:4, 27:3-4, 28:7, 29:3, 30:3, 30:5-11, RR-5. See also *2:3, 16:2*, 24:8.

Trinity   (References to the triune Godhead and to Satan's counterfeit version.) *1:3, 2:6, 4:0, 6:6, 10:3, 13:2, 16:1*, 20:3, 20:5-6, 23:1, 23:6, 24:2, 25:4, 26:2, 27:5, 28:2, 28:6, 29:3, *RR-1*, RR-4. See also *7:8, 15:2*.

Truth   (The significance that God's Word attaches to truth and error.) *1:1-5:8, 8:3, 8:6-7, 12:1, 16:2*, 17:1-2, 17:4-6, 18:4-9, 22:1-3, 23:1-7, 24:2, 24:4, 25:2-3, 25:8, 26:2, 27:2, 30:4. See also *10:8, 12:5*.

Word of God   (The approach that Alpha and Bible figures take to the holy scriptures.) *1:1-4, 5:7-8, 6:6, 10:1, 10:6, 10:8, 12:6, 16:2*, 17:1-5, 18:3-4, 19:2, 20:2-3, 21:3, 22:1-3, 23:1-7, 24:2, 24:9, 25:8, 29:3, 30:1.   See also *4:0, 5:6, 8:1, 10:5*, 19:1.